Barra Brava

A backpacker's guide to Latin America and its football clubs

For more info and photos please visit:
www.barrabravabook.com

@TheBlueBarra

For Nige – English by birth, brummie by the grace of God!

Introduction

Barra bravas are generally perceived to be Latin America's equivalent of hooligans or ultras. In some countries they were friendly, genuine fans who passionately supported their team. In others the barra were a feared mafia who controlled the football clubs they followed and influenced national politics. I spent 18 months travelling from the United States to Brazil, attending 67 football matches covering the most important leagues, clubs and stadiums.

Firstly I'd like to clarify that I'm not a hooligan, nor have I ever been involved in such activity. I am someone who is passionate about football, music and drinking beer. Whilst at university I went home and away watching my team and mingled with some of the rougher edges of our fan base. At the time I had a Zulu Army flag printed (the nickname of Birmingham City's hooligans) which accompanied me to a variety of games, but have to confess I've never thrown a punch in anger. Violence doesn't appeal to me, and at a less than commanding five foot eight, I'm not particularly intimidating.

Prior to 2009 I worked for an internet bank and lived with my long-term girlfriend in a terraced house. The most interesting thing I'd done was spending a year roaming and working in Australia and New Zealand during my early 20's. Even that was relatively par for the course in the grand scheme of adventuring.

Approaching my 30th birthday I was heading for marriage, children and a settled life. When my employer put me at risk of redundancy, including a promise of a generous five figure severance package, my world was turned upside-down. I had the opportunity to consolidate my finances or throw caution to the wind and have one last hurrah before conceding to domesticity. Choosing the bolder, less responsible option, I split with my partner and put my house up for sale. Through an unfortunate set of circumstances there was no redundancy or pay-out, but at that stage I'd committed myself to the idiotic plan. So I saved as much money as possible and booked a one-way flight to Chicago.

Prologue

Blues v Bolton – (EPL) - 1 v 2
Saturday 26th September 2009 – 15:00
St. Andrews, Birmingham, England

When you plan to leave home for a significant period of time I believe it's important to spend some time with your friends and family before you go. In the weeks leading up my departure I went for drinks and dinners with the people closest to me, as I intended to be away from England for more than a year. This was a perfect excuse for me and my father to visit St. Andrews. My love of Birmingham City comes from the man I call Nige, a brummie by birth who instilled in me the passion for his hometown club from an early age. Having grown-up in southeast Kent (where my parents still lived) I'd become used to travelling a substantial distance to watch my side play, although at the time I was living down the road in Coventry.

On the morning of my last Blues game for almost two years I only had a 20 minute train journey to endure. Mr Freeman senior had to go for three hours, negotiating two connections. He'd evidently started on the beers when he set off (09:30 - not an unusual occurrence) as he wasn't at the meeting point we'd arranged. By the time I'd got to New Street station he was already three sheets to the wind, wandering around a dual carriageway somewhere near St. Andrews, slurring into his phone something along the lines of: 'where the bloody hell are you?'

I waited patiently in The Rainbow, which over the years had evolved from a Digbeth dive to a cool indie pub boasting a decent line-up of live music. Eventually he staggered into the bar with less than an hour to kick-off, armed with a thoroughly unconvincing story about taking a wrong turn when leaving the railway station. We had just enough time for a swift few in The Clements Arms, where Phyliss, the resident great-grandmother and barmaid, was in a jovial mood collecting glasses and flirting with the lads. She'd always been the life of Saturday's pre-match drinks, and thinking it could possibly be the final occasion I'd see her, I took the chance to get a priceless photo of the three of us holding my flag.

It was a pleasant autumnal afternoon for football; the sun cast shadows across the pitch, while there was a slight chill in the air. Following relegation in 2008, Blues had bounced back to the Premier

League at the first time of asking under the guidance of former Scotland manager, Alex McLeish. Visiting that day were a hardworking Bolton side managed by the gritty Gary Megson. My excitement about the trip was soon tempered by my beloved football team. Israeli defender Tamir Cohen exposed some slack defending to head Bolton into the lead.

From my favourite vantage point in Block 19 of the Kop Corner, I witnessed Blues dominate possession without really hurting their opposition. With less than ten minutes remaining it looked like we were never going to breakthrough, until legendary OAP Kevin Phillips won possession and fired a low shot into the corner of the net. Our joy was short lived, two minutes to be precise, as Bolton scored a winner. When Matt Taylor's free kick rebounded off a post, South Korean Chung-Yong Lee (WHO?) reacted quickest to fire past on-loan keeper Joe Hart.

Walking down the Coventry Road with that familiar feeling of disappointment, we reflected on a toothless performance whilst agreeing it was going to be a long, hard season. Little did we know that this was our last home defeat for over a year and Blues would go on a run of form which saw us finish in our highest position for over 50 years.

I alighted at Coventry station, leaving my dad to try and make it back to Kent without falling over or asleep. Before returning to my shared accommodation I sat on Hearsall Common to watch the sunset. It was a wonderful clear, pale orange sky, punctuated by a few low clouds dotted on the horizon. With such a big adventure ahead of me I was trying not be daunted by the prospect of it all. I knew it was going to be eventful, but without any concrete plans I just wasn't sure what on earth I'd end up doing.

Contents:

39 – Uruguay v Ecuador U-20, Arequipa, Peru
40 – Chile v Argentina U-20, Arequipa, Peru
41 – Brazil v Colombia U-20, Arequipa, Peru
42 – Blooming, Santa Cruz, Bolivia
43 – Nacional Asunción, Asunción, Paraguay
44 – Olimpia, Asunción, Paraguay
45 – Cerro Porteño, Asunción, Paraguay

Buenos Aires, Argentina

46 – Argentinos Juniors, La Paternal
47 – Argentinos Juniors, La Paternal
48 – Lanús, Lanús
49 – Argentinos Juniors, La Paternal
50 – Huracán, Parque Patricios
51 – Vélez Sársfield, Liniers
52 – All Boys, Floresta
53 – Atlanta, Villa Crespo
54 – River Plate, Belgrano
55 – San Lorenzo, Flores
56 – Estudiantes, La Plata
57 – Independiente, Avellaneda
58 – Argentinos Juniors, La Paternal
59 – Quilmes, Quilmes
60 – Arsenal, Sarandí
61 – Racing Club, Avellaneda
62 – Boca Juniors, La Boca
63 – Argentinos Juniors, La Paternal

64 – Colón, Santa Fe, Argentina
65 – Internacional, Porto Alegre, Brazil
66 – Portugusea, São Paulo, Brazil
67 – Santos, Santos, Brazil

Season 1

UNITED STATES OF AMERICA

Population – 312 million
Size – 9.6 million km^2
Time Zone – GMT $^-$5 to $^-$9
FIFA World Ranking – #14 (2009)
Best World Cup Finish – 4th (1930)
Biggest Teams – New York Red Bulls, LA Galaxy, Seattle Sounders

You might have heard of:
Ronald Regan, George Bush, Brad Friedel, Tim Howard, Jonathon Spector, Clint Dempsey, Landon Donovan, Hunter S Thompson

Essential Spanish:
Fútbol - Soccer
Estadounidense, Gringo, Gringa – All mean a person from the USA

Please Note: The US Dollar is used throughout this book, with an exchange rate of around £1 = $1.50 or $1 = £0.66

Game 1

Chicago Fire v Chivas USA – (MLS) - 1 v 0
Thursday 22nd October 2009 – 20:00
Toyota Park, Chicago

I was perched on a red plastic seat bouncing up and down to the beat of a nearby drum. My left hand was clutching a $7 beer in a paper cup and my right hand was clinging to a girl from Arkansas. A man of Polish origin was stood on a little platform ten rows in front of me barking instructions at the crowd through a megaphone, directing the singing and clapping. It was pouring with rain and I was wearing a child's size, yellow Mickey Mouse poncho.

On day three of the trip, as part of my limited preparations, I'd arranged to attend a Major League Soccer (MLS) game. I flew from Heathrow to Chicago to spend some time with a girl from the US, whom I'd met on an island in South East Asia during a tester trip earlier that year. She'd never been to a soccer match and I wanted to show her what it was all about. We set out early intending to find a bar near the arena with a bit of atmosphere for a few cheeky ones. It had been grey and raining all day, the bus from the train station broke down, and arriving in a taxi I was frustrated to discover there was nowhere around Toyota Park to drink. As it turned out a lot of Chicago Fire supporters drank in designated, centrally-located bars and caught a special bus to the venue before kick-off.

According to certain domestic television ratings from that period, soccer wasn't one the country's biggest ten sports. Apparently it lagged behind WWE (actors in swimming costumes pretend fighting) NASCAR (celebrating the fact participants can steer a car left better than their opponents) and women's basketball. Immigrants, mainly of Eastern European and Latin descent, were the largest supporter groups in USA's domestic league. Factions between these sets of followers meant that in most MLS stadiums there were at least two distinct sectors of home aficionados who had their own chants, banners and rituals. We'd found our way into the Harlem End amid the passionate locals in Section 8 and were surrounded by members of the Fire Ultras 98, a group who originated from Poland and Ukraine. At the opposite end Latinos were singing their own songs, right next to a handful of Chivas faithful who'd braved a 5,600 kilometre return journey from Los Angeles to Illinois.

A lack of bars outside had been disappointing, a $20 entrance fee was tempered by a free flag, and forgetting a rain jacket (not just for the game, but the whole trip) was solved by finding the aforementioned Disney poncho randomly on the floor. Toyota Park's open stands afforded little cover from the elements, logical in the temperate south, but not in Chicago, famed for its extreme weather conditions amongst other things. Hence we got very wet.

It wasn't the greatest of spectacles. In the final round of matches The Fire needed three points to guarantee their place in the post season playoffs. Chivas, an LA-based offshoot of Chivas Guadalajara (Mexico's biggest club) had already qualified and were able to rest players. Chicago's squad boasted World Cup legend and all-round Mexican hero, Cuauhtémoc Blanco, alongside former Everton and Fulham striker Brian McBride. At half time, soaked to the skin and not exactly enthralled by events on the pitch, we returned to the suburbs. On our way out we heard the home contingent celebrating the evening's solitary goal, visiting Mexican striker Eduardo Lillingston put through his own net. Neither team ended up making it to the overall final. Chivas lost to runners-up LA Galaxy in the Western Conference semi-final, while Chicago were beaten in the Eastern Conference final by winners, Real Salt Lake.

It was easy to criticise the US football setup and in my opinion it had the worst structure in all the Americas. But considering the MLS was only conceived in 1993 to aid their World Cup bid, and the first season didn't begin until three years later, it's fair to say it'd come a long way in that time. Initially the authorities tried to create their own Americanised version of the game by introducing a number of gimmicks, the most ridiculous of which was decreeing no contest could be drawn. If scores were level at full time there was a shootout similar to penalties. The ball was placed 35 yards from the goal and a player had five seconds to score past the opposition keeper. Other ludicrous features included a countdown clock which stopped in-play, so there was no injury time at the end of the halves. They also allowed a fourth substitute; but exclusively for goalkeepers.

Even after acknowledging that the world's most popular sport cannot be improved upon, the MLS was still flawed. Participating clubs were franchises similar to other major US professional team competitions, meaning there was no promotion or relegation. Also the playoff system, similar to the one employed in many Latin American countries, diminished its competitive nature. At the time eight of 15 went through to the finals. This has since been extended with the

11

introduction of more franchises. Chivas had qualified for the post season before that damp night in Chicago when I saw them, and their performance reflected it.

However, there were lots of positive aspects to one of the world's newest professional football divisions. Over half the franchises played their home fixtures in purpose-built soccer venues and more were being constructed. The MLS featured sides from Canada, although they hadn't been particularly successful. There was an emphasis on developing future talent, especially since the introduction of a reserve league in 2005 provided chances for fringe and youth players. Sponsorship deals were becoming lucrative as television exposure increased, so the league was becoming more profitable.

The main reason I believed The Beautiful Game would continue to thrive was the presence of a squeaky former England captain. By relaxing their foreign players rule and salary caps it enticed European household names to the MLS, including David Beckham, Thierry Henry and Robbie Keane, along with Mexican stars Blanco and Marquez. This encouraged big European clubs to cash in on the sport's popularity by touring the country as part of their preseason preparations. Interestingly the US was competing with China and the Far East in this respect.

Soccer will never be more prevalent than traditional US sports like American Football with its average attendances of 70,000 per fixture. The future is still bright, reflected by the national team's improving World Cup performances. English fans certainly don't need to be reminded that it was the Americans who finished top of Group C at South Africa 2010, and progressed further in Brazil four years later.

As I had a pretty young southern girl to entertain for two weeks, football wasn't the only thing on my mind. I also planned to see some live music - obviously. Chicago had a thriving scene and its own famous version of the Blues. We spent time in downtown's dingy nightclubs listening to covers of Muddy Waters and Howlin' Wolf, as well as watching The Airborne Toxic Event at a venue next to the Cubs' Baseball Park, in vibrant Wrigleyville. A few hours' drive north found us in the funky student city of Madison, Wisconsin. There we saw English folk band Noah and the Whale playing a heart-breaking and beautiful set in a small theatre. It was autumn (or fall if you want to be an authentic American) and the leaves were a picture-perfect blend of yellow, orange and red. In a way it was an ideal time to see a bit of the Midwest. The scenery was colourful and the days were crisp and clear, but it was starting to get sufficiently chilly so I was keen to move onto a more tropical climate.

MEXICO

Population – 112 million
Size – 1.9 million km²
Time Zone – GMT ⁻6 to ⁻8
Currency - Peso
FIFA World Ranking – #17 (2009)
Best World Cup Finish – Quarter-finals (1970 & 1986)
Biggest Teams – Chivas, América, Cruz Azul, PUMAS

You might have heard of:
Benito Juarez, Pancho Villa, Hugo Sánchez, Cuauhtémoc Blanco, Rafael Márquez, Chicharito

Essential Spanish:
Clásico – Derby match
Taquillera – Ticket office
Dia de los Muertos - Day of the Dead
Salvador - Saviour
Cruz – Cross
Azul – Blue
Amigo - Friend
Chinga su Madre – F**k Off/F**k your mother
No mames wey – No way dude
Temporada alta – High season
Pendejo – Homosexual (Mexico only)
Navidad - Christmas
Idiota Inglés – English idiot
Cerveza/ Chela – Beer
Amor - Love
Playa – Beach
Libélula - Dragonfly
Alegría - Happiness

Game 2

Club América v Jaguares – (Primera División) - 1 v 1
Sunday 1ˢᵗ November 2009 – 16:00
Estadio Azteca, Mexico City

This was the first of several random games. To clarify my definition of random: I woke up on match day totally unaware there was a fixture I could attend. The reason for my ignorance was that I flew from Chicago a day earlier than expected. I'd planned to see the Mexico City (locals called it DF, pronounced dee-efay) derby on Thursday, but had neglected to research the weekend's schedule. As I was leaving my hostel on a sunny Sunday morning, the middle-aged, super gay proprietor enquired why I was in Mexico and what I intended on seeing in his country. Upon explaining my plans to watch the clásico he waltzed into his office, and with a little squeal returned to inform me there was a tie being played that day in the fabulous Estadio Azteca. Bonus!

With a metropolitan population of over 20 million, the largest in the Americas, I was quite daunted by the prospect of crossing such a vast city. My limited preparation prior to leaving England consisted of completing half a 'speak and read' Spanish course on my iPod. I had a far from confident grasp of the language, and this was the first time I'd actually have to attempt to communicate with a native speaker. It was a pleasant surprise to find that DF's Metro service was cheap, clean and really efficient. For less than $0.15 it was possible to traverse the world's biggest city in under an hour. This compared exceedingly favourably to the £4.80 I paid to go two stops on the London Underground a month beforehand.

Two line changes later and with minimal fuss, I was stood outside one of the largest and most historically significant football grounds in the world. A narrow bridge from the Metro station was lined with stalls selling fake replica shirts, banners, horns and other América-related paraphernalia. The bottom of the bridge opened out onto a huge market, which sold more replica items along with food and alcohol. I bought a badly stitched home shirt and in broken Spanish asked the vendor to take a quick picture of me. He looked slightly confused when I posed in front of an Estadio Azteca sign with a St. George's cross. Just as I settled in at a beer tent trying to soak up the atmosphere there was an almighty commotion from the Metro bridge. All of a sudden the whole area erupted into a cacophony of banging drums, waving flags and singing. The barra brava had arrived.

I'd been to my fair share of football matches in England and a few abroad, including a World Cup and a big game at the San Siro, but I had never seen anything like it in my life. The pure mass of human bodies moving in time to the beat of 20 drums was completely hypnotic. At the bottom of the bridge the procession came to a halt and formed a large circle, which for about 15 minutes sang, danced and jumped around, throwing one hand into the air at all times. As kick-off approached I followed the crowd towards the turnstiles, pausing briefly to buy a ticket. At the entrance the throng divided, went through security and regrouped on the other side effortlessly, whilst I was being searched, re-searched and asked incomprehensible questions in a language I barely understood. By the time I'd survived three lines of security checks the band had vanished and I was ushered up eight flights of stairs to the upper tier.

There's no denying how impressive Mexico's national stadium was, and remarkably considering its 105,000 capacity, it maintained the air of a real football ground. Although there was space between the pitch and stands, this was no Olympic-style, binoculars required affair. I was immediately struck by the sense of history you can feel in a place where two World Cup finals have been held, in addition to two of the most famous goals in footballing history. I was trying to figure out precisely where Maradona punched the ball past Shilton, when a man in a white coat approached me and started chattering away. Unable to tear my eyes from the glorious scene, I confirmed I wanted a refreshment. When I mentioned cerveza he opened two bottles of Corona and handed me the contents in a paper cup.

Once I'd awoken from my initial daze I realised the game had begun and my paper cup was curiously light. All I needed to do was glance at the same guy in a white coat, he pointed at me, I nodded and two minutes later I had a second cup brimming with beer. As incredible as Estadio Azteca was, when filled with only 20,000 spectators the atmosphere wasn't so great. The drummers were making a lot of noise, but much of it was lost due to the venue's sheer size. A cluster of approximately 500 fans from Chiapas (who'd made the commendable 750 kilometre excursion north) had been very vocal throughout, but it was impossible to hear them across the mammoth arena.

At half time the contest was goalless. I wandered round the concourse towards where the band was located. The environment changed rapidly from families buying snacks, to police in riot gear lining the bare concrete walls. I walked out behind the goal to experience the full impact of the noisy supporters. They were caged in by large mesh fences topped with barbed wire, which many were shaking and climbing. As the second period got under way the atmosphere became more intimidating, so I decided to play it safe and flee to the tranquil side seating.

Unfortunately the authorities had blocked all the exits, so it was impossible move between stands or leave Estadio Azteca. Feeling claustrophobic, I found a quiet spot to watch the action. After another double Corona had settled my nerves, I asked a teenager who'd been sitting peacefully next to me whether he would mind taking my photo. The appearance of my flag attracted a number of inquisitive youths who jabbered at me. Following a long and broken Spanglish conversation, during which I explained I was going to the clásico in a few days' time (and the teams traded goals) I returned to my hostel with a piece of paper. Written on it was: '30 minutos antes del partido. El árbol grande cerca de la taquillera visitante - ¡BARRA BRAVA!'

Game 3

PUMAS v Club América – (Primera División) - 3 v 2
Thursday 5th November 2009 – 21:00
Estadio Olímpico Universitario, Mexico City

The piece of paper handed to me by América's barra was an instruction to meet them by a big tree close to the visitor's ticket office. Well, that's what a dreadlocked politics professor advised me, whilst we were squashed next to each other in a VW van on the way to Estadio Olímpico. PUMAS was the club representing Mexico's largest university, which catered to over a third of a million students. It was fed by a single Metro station, from which a network of minibuses, vans, cars and scooters transported people to all corners of the enormous campus. This was why I had the fortune to be sat next a 35 year old lecturer who could speak decent English. He donated me a small bag of weed (which I was instructed to put in my shoe) and warned me about the barra brava. Apparently they were fanatical people who I shouldn't mess with.

    The tree by the visitor's ticket office was easy enough to find having been pointed in the right direction; unfortunately the outlet was closed. I waited in the darkness observing hordes of drunken, shouting supporters in yellow América shirts milling around. It slowly dawned on me that there was no way I'd be able to recognise the guys I'd met on Sunday. When stones and bottles started raining down and police pushed forward banging their batons against their riot shields, I elected to make a move. I reasoned home tickets were normally easier to come by, so jogged away from the melee.

    Once safely among the PUMAS contingent my first obstacle revolved around the fixture being sold out. Secondly, when you can't pronounce words in Spanish very well, taquillera sounds a lot like a famous Mexican spirit. Upon being directed to a third bar by different stewards I was on the verge of giving up. After a swift tequila (I'd got to the latest bar, asked the barman the location of the ticket office - his response was to pour me a shot) I pushed my way back through the crowds towards where I'd been dropped off. On the way I passed a man holding blue stubs in the air. A brief negotiation over prices (I knew Spanish numbers - ending up paying $15) and soon enough I was being patted down by the police as I entered Estadio Olímpico Universitario. Elated, I got a big cup of Corona and found space behind some drummers, at the top of the home end.

It turned out this was to be a clásico in both senses of the word. PUMAS took a two goal lead into half time, defender Darío Verón claiming his first and second goals of the season. Estadio Olímpico Universitario, a 67,000 capacity colossal curvy bowl, was rocking for this derby. Unusually the two terraced ends were fairly small, so the bulk of La Rebel barra were housed on the side opposite the main stand. Although I wasn't in the most animated section, I was still surrounded by drums, flags, balloons and bodies that didn't stop jumping. It was exhilarating, but looked nothing compared to the 15,000 souls packed in to my left, who managed the seemingly impossible feat of bouncing to the songs in unison. Up to that point in my life I'd not seen such a spectacular display of people supporting their club.

Mexico's football league, like the majority in Latin America, was divided into two annual tournaments. La Apertura (Opening) ran from August to December, and la Clausura (Closing) from February to June. PUMAS were current champions, but also bottom of the table after selling some of their star players. América's relatively expensively assembled squad boasted foreign stars such as Paraguayan striker Salvador Cabañas and Chilean midfielder Jean Beausejour, along with Guillermo Ochoa, the Mexican national team's second choice keeper. Ochoa played the role of pantomime villain for much of the contest, unnecessarily delaying goal kicks and feigning injury whenever possible.

In the second period América dominated. They levelled after Beausejour won two free kicks and Cabañas converted them both. The second was a screamer from 30 yards which nestled in the top corner. The final ten minutes were very tight and it looked like heading towards a draw. However a minute into injury time an América defender was harshly penalised for handling a cross inside the box. The referee theatrically pointed to the spot as he was encircled by protesting players. Argentine Martín Bravo stepped up to send the PUMAS faithful into raptures. Despite losing the visitors still qualified for the playoffs, but were eliminated in the quarter-final by Monterrey.

This wasn't the last bad day for América's two South Americans. Two months later, whilst Sunderland were finalising a bid for him, Cabañas was shot in the head by notorious drug lord 'JJ' José Garza, during an argument in a DF nightclub toilet. Doctors decided it was too risky to remove the bullet. Although he made a recovery of sorts, it was unlikely Salvador would ever play competitive football again. Beausejour had to wait a further seven months for his moment of misfortune. On 31st August 2010 he signed for Birmingham City.

Game 4

Cruz Azul v Puebla – (Primera División) – 4 v 0
Saturday 7th November 2009 – 17:00
Estadio Azul, Mexico City

My week in Mexico City was an eventful one. I'd witnessed a colourful Dia de los Muertos when families gathered together and decorated the graves of their deceased loved ones. There were numerous shrines of varying sizes around DF covered in brightly-coloured flowers, skulls and skeleton figurines. In a strange way it seemed like a happy time for many Mexicans, as if death was something to celebrate as opposed to mourn.

The central Zocalo area, flanked by its huge palatial and cathedral structures, appeared to be constantly covered with an eclectic mix of individuals, from happy-snapping tourists to groups of gospel singers. A few Metro stops away from the chaotic centre I found Coyocan's historic artistic suburbs. It was a lovely place, home to museums dedicated to the life and work of Frida Kahlo (one of Mexico's most famous artists) as well the Russian Marxist, Leon Trotsky, who sought refuge in DF after Stalin exiled him in the 1930's. I also took an hour-long bus ride out of the city to Teotihuacan, a massive archaeological site containing some impressive pyramid structures in a gigantic basin. This was the first of a handful of pre-Colombian historical sites I was to visit. It was a strangely overwhelming experience, and not just because I was tracing the same steps people had taken for 2,000 years. Standing on top of the tallest pyramid gazing at vast expanses of flat, undeveloped ground extending out towards towering mountains in the far distance; it was difficult not to feel a certain sense of desolation. I wouldn't recommend it to agoraphobics.

Obviously none of the traditional tourist attractions were as much fun as going to watch a local football match on a cloudless Saturday afternoon. Estadio Azul was one of the trip's less conventional venues. Situated right next to the world's largest Bullring (which could hold almost 50,000) the 35,000 capacity football stadium's pitch was sunk below street level, so it was overshadowed by its neighbour. As this was my fourth fixture I'd already started getting cocky and turned up only 15 minutes prior to kick-off. Faced with lengthy queues I saw the first 20 minutes on a TV in a bar, which was to become somewhat of a ritual. As the game approached half time I navigated the deserted streets. Whilst purchasing my $6 ticket I marvelled at how the fan noise echoed off surrounding buildings, and then made my way right into the middle of the home barra section.

I'd not missed anything significant. Cruz Azul opened the scoring ten minutes before the interval, prolific Argentine striker Tito Villa slamming in from a clever header back across goal. A couple of minutes later the former Derby County forward doubled the lead after Puebla's keeper spilled a routine shot into his path. It was effectively over in injury time, a lumpy pitch and bad goalkeeping allowed midfielder Ortiz to score a third. The second period was less lively as both sides looked happy to settle for the result. La Ultra Azul barra stepped the singing up a gear and it wasn't long until our packed end was bouncing to the repetitive beats. The blue cross added a late fourth, Paraguayan substitute Pablo Zeballos profited from some slack defending.

It was at this match I first noticed a strange free kick routine. When a set piece was awarded the referee designated the spot from which the kick should be taken, by marking it with a white spray dispensed from a cylindrical object he carried in a utility belt. He then walked the regulation ten yards away from the ball and drew a line on the field to specify where the closest opposition player could stand. A couple of minutes after open play resumed the mark had disappeared. I really didn't understand the point of this clever invention, which was a feature in many fixtures I was to observe over the next year and a half. I soon learnt that it was there simply because footballers from this area of the planet couldn't be trusted to stay where the referee indicated. The second it was perceived the officials weren't watching, players in the wall would inch forward, whilst the free kick taker would invariably attempt to move the ball closer to goal.

Once the final whistle sounded I hopped back onto the Metro, crossing DF to Palacio de Deportes where The Killers were playing a sold out show. A nice young lady sold me a spare ticket for $15, and even though I had a restricted view, they performed an entertaining hits-heavy set to a baying crowd. One of the things that had surprised me over the previous week was hardly any Mexicans spoke English. This was especially shocking considering their proximity to the US and the saturation of English-language, subtitled shows on their television networks. Nevertheless for two hours that Saturday night every single person inside the arena acted as though they could speak it fluently - they sang each song perfectly.

I left DF the next day to spend some time in the pleasant colonial town of Oaxaca. It was overrun with midrange tourists roaming round numerous historic buildings. I'd not had the easiest summer prior to my departure from England and what had kept me going through much of that time was the prospect of seeing the Pacific. It was an eight hour minivan ride to the coast, winding up, over and back down La Sierra Madre del Sur mountain range. During the journey a fellow passenger, a middle-aged US man, was being violently motion sick whilst his wife tried to keep him calm. Twice the van driver patiently stopped for him to get out and do his business, but on the third request he opened a window and continued driving.

By late afternoon, with streams of vomit splattered across the van, we'd arrived at San Pedro Pochutla, a dusty commercial town 20 minutes from the beach. Trying to get into the spirit of backpacking I ignored the taxi drivers trying to sell me a fare, and flagged a collectivo (a pickup truck with two narrow benches in the back covered by a tarpaulin roof). I didn't have to wait long to see the ocean. The setting sun combined with the smell of salt air was so intoxicating that before I knew it we'd passed my intended destination, Puerto Angel. Panicking slightly, I eventually managed to ascertain from a lady sitting opposite me we were going to Zipolite. Having read unsavoury things about the town and not knowing where to stay, I asked the local to recommend some lodgings. She shrugged her shoulders, rang a bell to get the driver to stop and pointed at the nearest hotel.

I was stood on a sandy road surrounded by residential dwellings, most of which were wooden shacks. Hotel Neptuno was the only available option, so I dragged my backpack through the front door. I was flabbergasted when my arrival was greeted by three Mexicans cheering at me. Fortunately one of them spoke English and explained they thought I was a guest at the upcoming wedding, but there were still tourist rooms available. Relieved that I had somewhere to sleep, I threw my bag into #10, took a quick picture of an amazing sunset, before gleefully plunging into the warm, thunderous Pacific waves.

I'd inadvertently stumbled upon an absolute gem of a location. Not only was the arc of yellowy/white sand stretching two kilometres from cliff to cliff one of the nicest beaches around, but the hotel itself, situated at the quiet end of the bay, was one of the best in town. The commercial 'centre' was a ten minute stroll along the shoreline and consisted of oceanfront bars, a handful of astonishingly good restaurants and some mellow backpacker-style accommodations. The site of an infamous hippy retreat since the 1960's also happened to be one of the rare nudist friendly public places in Mexico.

I soon made friends with the hotel staff - Oscar (a tall, thin fan of death metal) and Chucho (a slighter, more rotund aficionado of British trip hop) - kind of like a Mexican version of Laurel and Hardy. They were from DF and supporters of Cruz Azul and América respectively, so we instantly had some common ground. Although they didn't speak English, we established a level of communication that worked and after a few days they were taking me out to local parties. I had a lot in common with my new amigos. They, much like many Mexicans, shared my dark sense of humour. Also I was delighted when they played the brilliant Dummy by Portishead and Blue Lines by Massive Attack in the bar on my first night. I'd checked in on a Tuesday and there was a wedding on Saturday.

The guy who was getting married had used his government-funded marriage loan to hire Hotel Neptuno for three months. This meant he had a venue for his big day, and also covered the rent until the busy Christmas period. Oscar and Chucho, who'd already been there for five weeks by the time I arrived, were his mates from DF. His brother had initially spoken English to me and was staying after the nuptials to help run the business. By late Thursday night the whole wedding party had arrived, at which stage it dawned on me I was the only tourist sleeping in the hotel.

So in true Mexican fashion I was adopted by the family and invited to the big day. I had to return to Pochutla on Friday to buy a gift and some suitable clothes (God knows why I left my wedding outfit at home). At the exact same time Cruz Azul had kicked-off seven days earlier, I was stood on a wooden terrace overlooking the sun setting into the Pacific, the ceremony's sole foreign witness. I've never been a big fan of weddings, but this was the most natural, surreal and beautiful event I'd ever seen. Everyone held hands, then we all lit candles. After the blessing people took it in turns to speak about how much the couple meant to them. It was all a bit too much for me. I thought I'd got away with it, but during the reception the groom's mother came to our table with a big smile on her face, pointing at me, and then her eyes. She'd seen me crying.

Cruz Azul v Monterrey – (Apertura Final 2nd leg) – 1 v 2
Sunday 13th December 2009 – 18:00
Estadio Azul, Mexico City

At half time in the dramatic finale to my first season watching football in the Americas, I was sat on a beach not too far from where I'd attended a wedding five weeks beforehand. I was wearing my replica Club América shirt with pieces of paper taped to the front and back. In an attempt to windup one of my colleagues, I'd written various abusive messages about Cruz Azul and positive things about Monterrey. As I was sipping my beer a stray dog wandered up behind me, grabbed the piece of paper on my back in its mouth and ran off into the distance. It was another weird and wonderful day in the most delightfully bizarre place I've ever had the pleasure of staying in.

La Apertura's concluding game was goalless, with Cruz Azul somehow trailing 4 v 3 from the first leg, despite leading 3 v 1 at the break. Monterrey scored early in the second half. Although the side from DF mounted a spirited comeback by forcing an equaliser with a quarter of an hour remaining, the visitors sealed the championship in the 90th minute when Chilean forward Humberto Suazo scored.

Mexico's Primera División setup was almost as ridiculous as that of their northern neighbours'. At the time 18 clubs were divided into three groups. Everyone played each other once in la Apertura either home or away, and again in la Clausura when the fixture was reversed. The top two from each group qualified for the final stages, along with the two others with the most points. It was designed to ensure the competition's biggest names reached the knockout phase, maximising television revenue. Since my time in Mexico the football authorities saw some kind of sense, reverting back to a single league system with the eight highest placed participants making the playoffs.

Just over a month had passed and I was happily settled into Mexican beach life. After his celebration the groom (and hotel manager) had asked whether I'd be interested in helping out over Christmas. I negotiated a fair wage involving board and food in exchange for a few hours' work a day and spent six weeks prior to Navidad appreciating the laidback lifestyle. Catering had been part of my upbringing, so I endeavoured to make myself useful by identifying areas for improvement. It didn't take long, a cursory glance at the kitchen made me realise I could possibly have my work cut-out. Eight hours of tidying later, I was ready to start cleaning.

I established a daily routine which commenced at nine in the morning. I woke, put on my uniform (a pair of shorts and nothing else) and descended a flight of stairs to begin my chores. The day's first and most enjoyable job was tidying the front of house. This was a sandy terrace raised three metres above the seashore, with tables and chairs where patrons could relax, eat, drink and savour the stunning sea views. For two hours every morning I raked sand, cleaned furniture and made sure everything was in order. In reality I could have done this in a quarter of the time, but I was living on Mexico's only official 'clothing optional' beach. I genuinely tried to focus on the job in hand but was distracted by a stream of naked women parading up and down the shoreline, no more than 20 meters away.

Another of my assigned duties was to try and teach Oscar and Chucho some basic English so they could communicate with our European and North American clientele. As I had no learning material I resorted to using the solitary magazine in my possession (the fantastic Word publication) and my photocopied DF Lonely Planet pages. Fortunately we had similar music tastes and they were interested in reading a foreign view on their home city, so classes went far better than I expected. By spending an hour a day preparing lessons, researching the equivalent words in Spanish that we'd be learning; it wasn't long before my grasp of their language improved dramatically. This was a massive benefit and I'm confident I wouldn't have been able to write this book without it.

Whilst discussing topics with my pupils I quickly became aware how to define groups of people. My Mexican friends were keen to correct me when I referred to someone from United States as American. They rightly pointed out that this noun applied to every single person from Canada all the way through to Argentina. The US had monopolised the English word, which when used incorrectly could be quite offensive to Latinos, particularly Mexicans. In Spanish the correct term was the rather unnatural sounding Estadounidense, which was why Gringo was commonly used to describe North Americans and to a lesser extent Europeans. From my experiences the word rarely had negative connotations and was generally just used to label Caucasians. I had to accept it: I was a Gringo travelling on the Gringo trail.

It wasn't all graft, in fact reading my diaries from that period it seems we hardly ever worked. But is that not the Mexican way? Each night I ventured into what was essentially a little village called Roca Blanca (white rock - charmingly named after a large outcrop off the coast covered in seagull poo). Soon I became a regular in the chilled out bars, getting to know many locals. The place was an eccentric mix of Mexicans whose families had lived there for generations, and expats who owned businesses and had assimilated themselves into the community. The foreign residents, mainly Canadians and Central Europeans, all had the same reason for living there: they came on holiday and never left.

But it wasn't until I gate-crashed a party at the house next door that my social life started to get properly interesting. One night I could hear music coming from our neighbour's communal area. On closer inspection I was delighted to discover 20 or so European girls dancing and drinking. My horny Mexican colleagues didn't need much persuading to accompany me. It turned out that on the main road out of Roca Blanca there was a Nongovernmental Organisation which assisted local disabled children. Piña Palmera was sustained by a Swedish charity and relied on volunteers to staff their facility - chiefly female Scandinavian gap-year students. We'd stumbled upon one of the girl's leaving bash, and were warmly welcomed to an event where boys were outnumbered four to one. It was a raucous occasion which ended with Oscar and Chucho showing off their silky dance moves, as I stood on the side-lines cursing my two English left feet.

During this period the only thing that punctuated my peaceful existence was stepping on a stingray. Coming out of the ocean after an evening of body boarding, it felt as if something had bit me. Then it felt like my foot was on fire. Then for an agonising hour and a half I was convinced I was going die. The hotel manager drove me to the local doctor's surgery (a small room on Roca Blanca high-street) as I writhed around in pain in the back of his car. A couple of injections later and I was instructed to take a course of medication to ease the swelling. Upon my return I wasn't feeling better, so checked online whether the drugs prescribed were of any use to me. The tablets in question had been banned in Europe and the US as they'd been linked to 93 people dying. By this time the discomfort was easing sufficiently, so I could see the humour in the fact the sting was less likely to kill me than the drugs I'd been given to treat it.

The weeks leading up to Christmas had been pretty quiet and leisurely. I'd been told lots of stories about the town becoming overrun in the last week of December, but couldn't believe it. When I looked up and down my tranquil stretch of sand on a weekend and counted no more than 30 individuals, it didn't appear conceivable the accommodations could be so full that visitors had to camp on the shore.

Mexico v Europe – (Friendly) - 4 v 5
Saturday 30th January 2010 – 16:32
In front of a hotel, A beach on the Pacific coast of Mexico

I scored the winning goal in this game. Immediately after putting the ball through two t-shirts we were using as posts, a Serbian guy hurled me into the ocean while Oscar and Chucho pelted me with sand. The sun was setting on my time living in Hotel Neptuno, and in a way I was ready to leave.

The fortnight from just before Christmas to early January had been as chaotic, if not more, than had been predicted. In anticipation of the festive rush the hotel manager had arranged for three of his male student cousins to come and help out, as well as his wife (who'd returned to DF after getting married). To prepare for the influx of customers we'd successfully staged another wedding and an 80 strong student party. However absolutely nothing could have equipped us for the bombshell that was dropped days prior to the celebration of Jesus' birth.

The manager's 19 year old brother, who spoke English and had been there since my arrival, was a homosexual, and a bit of a screaming queen. He'd quit a lucrative entertainment position at a top Cancun resort to assist with the family business, and had been assimilating himself into the local gay community, which explicably was fairly prominent on a nudist beach. One morning before Navidad we had a staff meeting when it was announced the hotel was going to turn into a straight-friendly establishment. The idea behind the change was that gay people, without the burdens of children and other expensive accessories, had a greater expendable income. With an estimated gay population exceeding one million in Mexico City alone, the plan was that we were going to maximise revenue over the short high season by cramming as many of them into our hotel as possible.

This would explain why, on a Tuesday afternoon, I was listening to The Rolling Stones whilst painting the walls, ceiling and patio doors of a perfectly good guest bedroom, black. Well every respectable gay hotel has to have a Dark Room doesn't it? Apparently so. Just in case you thought we were going to set up a photography lab, I can confirm that our cuarto oscuro was a black room with minimal lighting, where men went to have sex. And thus started one of the strangest fortnights of my life.

It began with a visit to stunning Punta Cometa; a secluded rocky outcrop jutting into the ocean, which was one of the most spectacular locations I've ever watched a sunset from. A hippy had convinced the hotel manager he needed to bless his establishment prior to temporada alta. Armed with an array of strange items, the staff set out to perform a spiritual ritual. As the dazzling sun sank into the water, surrounded by a number other people who were enjoying the glorious scene, the manager, his brother and cousins lit a ceremonial candle whilst chanting and holding hands in a circle. The rite lasted about ten minutes, during which they doused themselves in special oil and waved small tree branches. I sat at a safe distance, taking pictures, trying to fathom how anyone in their right mind could consider this peculiar event as crucial to the future success of their business.

Our guests didn't really arrive until Boxing Day, so my colleagues seized their chance to party hard on Christmas Eve. Traditionally Mexicans ate Christmas dinner at approximately ten at night on the 24th. Ours wasn't ready until one in the morning, a sign of things to come. After eating we all went to the legendary Libélula bar which was only open to local workers. At four o'clock I called it a night and went to bed. Three hours later one of the cousins and Chucho were banging on my door, telling me I needed to get up. Naturally I assumed it was time to start work, but was wrong. They were still awake from the night before and wanted me to continue drinking with them. It took two hours and a lot of patience to get them all to go to bed and stop hassling the customers, who I was apologetically serving at the same time. When the last of the inebriated group had finally retired it dawned on me: I was left to run a 25 room Mexican hotel on Christmas Day.

Fortunately I had the assistance of a cook and a cleaner, and the guests who'd witnessed my ordeal were very understanding. When my colleagues eventually emerged from their beds with sickly expressions, the sun was setting. I immediately passed over responsibility and sat on the terrace reflecting on a unique 25th December experience. It wasn't until I was joking with the guys who'd got me out of bed that I realised the significance of what had happened. On Christmas morning I'd been woken by Emmanuel (the cousin) and Jesús (Chucho's real name) on Emmanuel's 22nd birthday. ¡Feliz Navidad!

No sooner had I survived Christmas than the gays arrived. For eight days our hotel was swarming with men of all shapes and sizes, mincing around in Speedos and the shortest shorts you could ever wish to see. Each night we hosted a super disco, which really just involved cocktail promotions and playing a David Guetta album repeatedly at an ear-bleedingly loud volume. The parties tended to run until six, just in time for me to begin work two hours later and get stuck into the clean-up operation. They created an unbelievable amount of mess, which I had to negotiate whilst serving the regular guests, most of whom were regretting their choice of accommodation. I'd like to clarify at this point that I was responsible for tidying the entire front of the house, apart from the Dark Room. On the mornings I was brave enough to peer inside the black curtain it wasn't a pretty sight.

In honesty I didn't really have too much contact with the gay clients. By the time they'd finished recovering from the previous evening it was normally late afternoon, at which stage I passed the money belt over to Oscar or Chucho who worked the late shift. The sexual debauchery wasn't limited to our hotel. At the beach's top end (near the self-righteous hippies in the Shambhala retreat) was an upmarket swinger's venue called Nudes. On the shoreline outside there were a handful of four poster beds where guests regularly had intercourse in full view of the passing public. At the other end was Playa del Amor, which was a prominently gay hangout. It's difficult to adequately describe the atmosphere of free love around this sexually-charged location, but perhaps an annual event that occurred between Christmas and New Year might help. A bonfire was lit outside Nudes and another on Playa del Amor, signalling the start of an all-night orgy: straight at the former, gay at the latter. Neptuno's manager didn't miss this business opportunity and sent his cousins (wearing only boxer shorts) to hand out flyers at the bottom orgy.

For high season I'd been evicted from my nice en suite room and was told to share with Oscar or Chucho. The prospect of bunking with a smelly Mexican (irrelevant of whether they were my good friend or not) wasn't extremely enticing, so I looked for somewhere more fragrant to sleep. My best option was a laundry closet where clean sheets and towels were stored. There was just enough space to fit a decent sized padded mat on the floor. My temporary accommodation was actually very cosy as the linen was insulation from the booming disco downstairs. Although I was content in my little room, I wasn't keen to share the situation with my mates back in England. I don't wish to think about the amount of abuse I'd have got if they knew that every morning I came out the closet, in a gay hotel.

New Year's Eve followed a similar pattern to Christmas: a late dinner, a night out and a few hours' sleep, before I was awoken by my wasted co-workers enticing me to party with them. On the first day of a new decade I staggered downstairs to the remnants of the previous evening's carnage. I figured the only way I was going to enjoy it was to start drinking, so I did. We went to a rave on the beach at ten in the morning with sunshine glaring upon us. It was overflowing with wide-eyed people, cherishing the last drags of their chemically enhanced New Year. Aware that I'd a job to do (and there was no service in the hotel) I rounded up a Mexican family and slowly cajoled them into returning to their beds at base camp. It was noon before I could even contemplate dealing with the mess, which seemed a rather easier task than on Christmas Day. Maybe the unrestricted access to a fridge full of Corona and Dos Equis helped as I had the best New Year's Day I could remember, although I couldn't really recall that much of it.

My early boozing ploy may have assisted me through my shift, but I ended up regretting it. For the preceding few days a stunning Argentinian girl (with cosmetically enhanced breasts) had been strutting around our establishment wearing nothing more than a skimpy thong. For some inexplicable reason she'd taken a shine to me, regardless of the fact she was a good four inches taller and clearly out of my league. Apparently it had something to do with my blue eyes, but I'm sure the lack of men in the vicinity willing to pay her the attention she was used to was a more plausible explanation. Anyway, on her way out to see friends on New Year's Day she gave me a big hug and said when she returned later she wanted to sleep with me. Or at least that's how I understood the conversation (Oscar and Chucho concurred). My problem was she didn't get back until gone 23:00, by which time I'd been drinking for 15 hours and was collapsed in bed. I woke in a panic at three the next morning and ran downstairs. Chucho was sat at a deserted bar shaking his head at me. 'Idiota Inglés' was all he said, pointing at Oscar's room.

By the second week of January things had reverted back to peaceful normality so my services were no longer required. I stayed on as a resident for a month, whilst lending a hand at a local backpacker bar with one of the two crazy Canadian girls who lived next door. It was a Sunday afternoon when I first met them. I caught a rolling wave on my body board right to where they were standing and introduced myself whilst they were bobbing up and down, topless in the surf. We were neighbours for two memorable months, along with a Swiss German couple and their amazingly intelligent three year old daughter who spoke three languages fluently.

Having never worked in a bar before I remained sober for the entirety of my first shift so I could get to grips with things. I was shocked to find when you're not even slightly inebriated, how unattractive drunken people look at half past one in the morning. It was certainly not something I ever wished to see again, so drank on every

31

shift after that. This practice was good in theory; especially as management encouraged staff to booze with customers to increase sales. Also I had two large fridges stocked with nine different brands of chelas to choose from. The major challenge was trying to calculate the shift's takings and lock everywhere up when I could barely see straight and there was a wild party in full flow.

I also found there was a rare phenomenon about serving alcoholic beverages: the later it was, the more attractive the barperson became to the opposite sex. It was particularly true if the ladies in question had done body shots off me at some stage in the evening, or if they'd consumed any Mezcal. This highly intoxicating liquid made from the maguey plant was an Oaxaca state speciality and tasted like you were swallowing petrol. The analogy wasn't too far from the mark as my bar purchased the spirit in green gasoline cans from a local vendor.

As January blurred into February, my body was telling me it was time for the party to end. I feared if I didn't leave soon I wouldn't at all (although in hindsight I'm not convinced it would have been a bad thing). I booked a flight from the nearest airport and spent a week as a tourist trying to see as many sights as I could. My last challenge was to cook a traditional British roast dinner for my colleagues, friends and neighbours. Making gravy and Yorkshire puddings from scratch with only the ingredients available at a local Mexican market was a colossal effort. After much perspiration and a little help I served 14 people on our terrace. The Europeans and North Americans were very complimentary, appreciating some home-cooked western food. The Latin contingent wasn't so impressed. They found it tasteless as I didn't put any chillies or hot sauce on it. None of them trusted the thick brown gravy enough to try any.

I left my corner of paradise exactly three months to the day after I'd unknowingly arrived there, with a brilliant tan and feet that had expanded from not wearing shoes for the entire duration. I also took with me a confident grasp of Spanish, nurtured through circumstances such as counselling an upset co-worker why his eldest cousin would send him to a gay orgy, distributing flyers wearing nothing but a pair of pants. It was undeniably the most enjoyable three months of my life. There was not one day, no matter how hung-over I was or whatever nonsense I was expected to do, that I wasn't thankful to be alive. And I still speak Spanish with a slight Mexican accent. ¡No Mames Wey!

Season 2

GUATEMALA

Population – 15 million
Size – 108,890 km^2
Time Zone – GMT $^-$6
Currency - Quetzal
FIFA World Ranking – #118 (2010)
Best World Cup Finish – Have never qualified
Biggest Teams – Municipal, Comunicaciones

You might have heard of:
Tikal, Lago de Atitlán, Semuc Champey

Essential Spanish:
Chapin – Person from Guatemala
Lago – Lake
Vamos Jaguares – Go Jaguars!
Gallo – Rooster (the name of Guatemala's national beer – the worst in the Americas)

Game 5

Heredia v Jalapa – (Liga Nacional) - 3 v 0
Sunday 7th March 2010 – 12:00
Estadio Municipal Julián Tesucún, San José, Petén

On a Sunday morning minivan ride around a lake it felt more like I was going to church than to a football match. I was surrounded by families in their best clothes going to visit relatives, and native Indians in traditional dress, clucking away in an indigenous language. In just under an hour I got from Santa Elena on the south side of Lago de Petén Itzá, to San José in the northwest corner. The van came to a standstill a block from the ground, at which point the plump driver turned to his passengers and shouted ¡Vamos Jaguares! With a good hour until kick-off I settled in at a stall set up on a piece of wasteland by the turnstiles, cracked open my first cerveza of the day and ordered a plate of unidentifiable meat from the BBQ.

It had been a rather convoluted journey from Mexico's west coast to north Guatemala. First I'd flown from Huatulco, via DF, to see Miss Arkansas in freezing cold Chicago. I spent a week wearing all the clothes I had with me (at the same time) and buying electronics I'd neglected to bring from England. From there I flew to Cancun to meet my parents in a five star all inclusive hotel. We spent a luxurious but overcast week in the least Mexican place in Mexico. The most exciting thing that happened involved me and my brother preventing a nurse from Michigan drowning in the sea. The rescue was much like you see on TV in programs like Baywatch – that's if you replace David Hasselhoff and Pamela Anderson with Morecambe and Wise.

Waving goodbye to my family, I caught a couple of six hour buses to Belize City, where I spent a daunting Friday night. Wanting to sample the social scene (and ignoring warnings in my guidebook) I went alone to a local bar. It wasn't long before a girl invited me to dance with her. Belize's population were mainly of Afro-Caribbean descent, thanks to the British claiming a part of North Guatemala and settling their slaves there in the mid 1600's. As a result their dancing was a lot different to that in Mexico. It wasn't fair, I'd only just managed to fathom how to move my feet and these women were shaking their top and bottom halves independent to each other. It took two songs for the men standing around the edge of the dance floor to ask me to buy them beer, and less than four songs for a fight to break out. In the ensuing chaos of overturned tables and smashing bottles I slipped out unnoticed and returned to my hostel.

A few sun-drenched days were then spent on the tourist enclave of Caye Caulker, a relaxed sandy island in the middle of the western hemisphere's largest barrier reef, about 35 kilometres from the mainland. Snorkelling and diving was considered world-class, and the chief attraction for those who love being submerged in water - the Blue Hole – was a karst-eroded sinkhole which dropped 124 meters to the bottom of a lagoon. This looked most impressive on postcards (which was as close as I got to it) although I did see a pair of nurse sharks and some pretty coral snorkelling off the Caye.

Back on the mainland I visited Belmopan, the world's smallest and arguably strangest capital. After a gigantic hurricane devastated Belize City in 1961 the government moved their administrative centre to the interior, building a city from scratch, basing the design on a traditional Mayan settlement. It wasn't very interesting so I headed to a village called San José Succotz, just off the tourist trail. It didn't take long to find the only other Gringos in town; three pasty paediatricians from Ohio were on work placement in the surrounding rural regions. Initially I was keen to lend a hand at the clinics they were visiting, but was discouraged by insurance issues and their pictures of the abject poverty they were witnessing.

Instead I explored Mayan ruins at Xunantunich, which was surreal as all the staff and guides showing me their proud national heritage were of Afro-Caribbean descent. Belize in general was a bit of a culture shock having spent so much time in Mexico, especially linguistically. Keen to practice my improving Spanish, the opportunities with natives was limited. The majority spoke their own distinct version of the English-based Creole language, called Kriol. A typical conversation went along the lines of: 'Da how yu di du. Mee naym Winston. Weh yu naym?' Consequently I found it easier to communicate with Latinos than Belizeans.

Crossing into northern Guatemala my first stop was the tiny, peaceful island of Flores. The weekend started with a 06:30 alarm to see Blues whimper out the FA Cup quarter-finals at Portsmouth. Although I was supposed to be getting a bus to Tikal later that morning, disappointed I went back to bed, waking in the early afternoon. The day's last service was now my only option, leaving me with less than two hours to negotiate one of the most famous historical structures in the Americas. It was actually more fun that way, kind of like a Mayan version of the Krypton Factor. Climbing four of the five towering temples and getting back to the transport in the time most people took to explore one of them was exhilarating. I'm not a massive enthusiast of traditional tourist sights. Nevertheless, jogging up stone stairs worn by centuries of footsteps was fairly awe-inspiring, as was the view from the temple tops across vast expanses of untouched rainforest. I'll be honest though, for me the main lure was to have my photo taken from the spot where the Millennium Falcon was 'filmed' landing at a rebel base on Yavin 4, towards the end of Star Wars IV – geeeeeeeeek!

Returning to Flores later that evening I stopped for a cheeky few in a bar. In the corner was a small TV with six men crowded round it cheering enthusiastically. The barman informed me they were watching a Guatemalan league match. During our ensuing exchange I discovered there was a local top flight fixture the following day.

All of which is how I arrived at sitting on a plastic chair in the late morning sun, at what could easily be mistaken for a family BBQ. After eating my brunch I was still unable to identify the particular type of meat I'd just consumed, but by the third beer it didn't matter. The queue at the sole ticket window began to grow, so I bought a replica shirt and got in line.

Entering Estadio Julián Tesucún's main stand I was struck by the view, as the side structure opposite was four rows high and the one at the far end wasn't much taller. The humble proportions gave a good vista of a pure blue Lake Petén Itzá with little sand islands, boats bobbing, settlements on the far shore and mountains rising in the background. It was the most naturally beautiful view from a football venue I'd seen. There wasn't too much time to dwell on the scenery. Within a minute of being inside hundreds of firecrackers had been ignited, heralding the player's arrival.

Guatemala's Primera División wasn't the most developed of all Latin American competitions. This was a basement battle between the hosts (bottom) and Jalapa from the south (second bottom) and it showed. I was surprised to see such a vocal barra section boasting drums, fireworks and flags. Early in the first half Heredia claimed the advantage, which prompted more firecrackers and a Mexican Wave - not so spectacular when there was only one populated area. The quality of the stadia's facilities was highlighted at the first substitution. Instead of an electronic board, the linesman held up a piece of A4 paper with a number printed on it and pointed at the player who needed to leave the field. Heredia scored another two goals prior to the break, causing the drumming and singing to increase. At the interval I decided to try and find somewhere relatively quiet to sit, and more importantly a cerveza.

I found both in the far corner, where a group of middle aged men were being served beers by an 80 year old lady. I stood close to them waiting to be attended and soon enough they wanted to know what a Gringo was doing on their patch. It turned out the guy next to me was mayor of San José and the other men were senior figures in the local community. By the time the second period had finished (with no addition to the score sheet) it felt like we were old friends. There had been lots of food and drinks passed around, photos with the Zulu Army flag and many jokes, most of which I didn't understand, but were probably at my expense.

They invited me to a bar one of them owned. It wasn't long before I was stood in a darkened room occupied by drunken men slurring along to songs on a blaring jukebox. The din was paused briefly to allow the stocky mayor to stand on a chair (to warm applause from everyone) and announce he wished to introduce his new English amigo. He told the expectant crowd I was David Beckham's brother, also called David! Luckily I'd consumed a sufficient amount of alcohol not to be too embarrassed when I had to replace the mayor on the chair, and say a few words of thanks for inviting me to their pub. For possibly the only time on the trip I was grateful when a jukebox was turned back on, so I could try and blend into the background. Eventually I emerged into blinding daylight, somehow managing to catch a minivan to my hostel on the other side of the lake, to fall asleep fully clothed at 19:30.

Game 6

Comunicaciones v Pachuca – (CONCACAF Quarter Final) -1 v 1
Wednesday 10th March 2010 – 21:00
Estadio Cementos Progreso, Guatemala City

'We're on our way, we're on our way, how we get there I don't know, how we get there I don't care, all I know is Blues are on their way.' This is what I was singing on the back seat of a bus pulling out of Río Dulce, which I thought was headed to Guatemala City. The barman in Flores had also told me there was a scheduled 'Champions League' game in the capital a few days after Heredia's match. I'd had so much fun by the lake I was really excited about seeing one of the country's two biggest teams, playing a Mexican side in the quarter-final of the CONCACAF Champions League (a tournament incorporating clubs from the Caribbean, Mexico, North and Central America.)

So excited, that I was on the wrong bus. It took two changes and an extra couple of hours to rectify that situation, but soon enough we were crawling through traffic and smog towards the terminal. Before kick-off I squeezed onto a local service for a half hour ride to the stadium. As we negotiated the compact but well organised one way system, I could intermittently hear singing and music. Stopped at a set of traffic lights, two buses pulled up either side of us. They were packed full of Comunicaciones fans hanging out the windows and doors, with drummers furiously pounding away in the back. As we progressed (with lots of over and undertaking) it was clear the buses were having a race, as well as some kind of singing contest.

Surrounding the ground were numerous informal stalls and bars, in and outside residents' front rooms. Despite being situated in an unsavoury area of the city, I felt safe drinking with the local supporters and observing their banter. Once inside (and after the Mexicans had taken a first minute lead) I was dismayed to learn beer wasn't for sale. But there were certainly other things available. An inspection of the main barra section revealed there were flags and a band, in addition to a large plume of smoke that seemed to hang over them as if they were creating their own smog. It rapidly became apparent that almost everybody was smoking very phat, Bob Marley-style joints.

As I settled in amongst an astoundingly active crowd, it wasn't long before I was in a circle of people all passing pure weed reefers wrapped in banana skins. When in Rome. Marijuana culture appeared to be a big part of this club; most the flags and banners had references to or pictures of cannabis. Also the songs they were singing all mentioned it at some point. Halfway through the second period I was starting to appreciate why this was the case. The host's football was so terrible I figured the fans needed as much distraction from events on the pitch as possible.

Pachuca, pretty much a mid-table Mexican side, were strolling around playing as if it were a preseason friendly, not the final stages of a major competition. A handful of visiting supporters were outnumbered by a line of riot police separating them from their Guatemalan counterparts. In spite of their meagre following they sang enthusiastically throughout. With 20 minutes remaining the entire contingent of 35 Mexicans packed up their flags and exited without warning. They left just before Comunicaciones scrapped an unlikely equaliser, sending the stoned faithful into raptures.

This goal must have been deemed to be fairly important - it was replayed on Guatemalan television for at least a week as an advertisement for the national channel which broadcast football. Accompanying a jerky slow-motion repeat was a tagline about witnessing priceless moments. The advert was soon removed when Comunicaciones exited the CONCACAF, although credit should be given to them as they put up a brave fight in Pachuca, only losing 2 v 1. They also had the dubious prestige of being eliminated by the eventual winners. Underlining who was the region's powerhouse, the semi-finals were an all Mexican affair; culminating in a Cruz Azul v Pachuca decider, which was settled on away goals.

I wasn't in Guatemala City exclusively to watch football; I was also meeting two friends from Coventry who were flying over to spend a couple of weeks with me. Paddy and Lenny could be described as two of my more intrepid amigos, but I knew they were both secretly a little apprehensive visiting a third world country they knew little about. I doubt any of their acquaintances said much to have calmed either of their nerves. My favourite comment was from one of Paddy's colleagues. He said, rather simply: 'I hear you're going to Guatemala. What the fook are you going to fookin Africa for?'

Keen to test the surfing skills I'd honed on my Mexican beach, we headed for tiny El Salvador. Opting for a cross-country route in a chicken bus (complete with a bullet hole in the window) within minutes of boarding we'd had a minor accident in a traffic jam. The victim of the collision was a motorist in an appropriately dilapidated vehicle. He stood in the road gesticulating at our driver before two men came over, handed him some currency and told him to get a move on - Guatemalan car insurance.

Chicken buses were prominent throughout Central America as a cheap mode of transport for the masses. The name originated from when backpacking around this part of the world first gained popularity in the early 90's, as it was commonplace for livestock to ride inside vehicles beside their owners. The presence of animals was unusual on a contemporary chicken bus; many were actually quite modern-looking. They were typically a retired yellow US school bus, sometimes with the name of the county and educational establishment of origin still on the exterior. Crucial modifications included garish images of Jesús or la Virgen María emblazoned across the bodywork, in addition to a stereo with one volume setting – deafening. It was a fun way of getting about, as the lads discovered when we were squeezed into the back of a packed bus speeding down a steep hill towards the coast, beers in hand, attracting curious looks from the locals.

As the smallest and least visited country in Central America, it was interesting to see how developed El Salvador was in comparison to Belize and Guatemala. Aided by adopting the US Dollar as its currency and a proud, resilient population, it had recovered from over half a decade of military rule to become relatively prosperous. Remnants of their violent past were very evident. Even the insignificant businesses were guarded by a man brandishing a firearm, generally an Uzi or a pump action shotgun. The abundance of weapons was largely attributable to former US President Ronald Regan supporting a military government in the early 1980's against their left-wing opposition. By supplying arms to the right-wing junta he was apparently suppressing the spread of communism in the region. Most historians agree that all this promoted was the rise of death squads, which killed an estimated 35,000 civilians in a three year period. Even when four female US Christian missionaries were brutally raped and murdered by the military, financial backing was only suspended for a month. Astonishingly, Regan claimed: 'The Soviet Union underlies all of the unrest that is going on'.

Reading El Salvador's history swinging in a hammock in the peaceful surfer enclave of El Tunco, the 20th century's social unrest seemed slightly improbable. To reflect the mellow vibe about town the men guarding businesses carried large machetes instead of firearms. El Tunco's gentle, beginner-friendly waves provided a perfect opportunity for my visitors to try their hand at a spot of surfing. Once I'd found a couple of English-speaking instructors they were soon out amongst the swell. Impressively, both Paddy and Lenny managed to stand on their first attempts, although very briefly in the case of the former. On the second go, Pads, who was already complaining how paddling was so tiring, caught a nice rolling wave, stood up, steadied himself and was in good shape to ride it to the shore. All of a sudden he looked around with a panicked expression on his face. Without warning he ran the entire length of his longboard and dived off the front into the ocean. I'm not sure the instructors had seen anything like it; they joined me and Lenny in fits of hysterical laughter.

Later that day we all watched the Champions League quarter-final together in a bar. Strangely almost all the local surfers (not a group normally associated with our most famous sporting export) had left the breaks to see Inter Milan dump Chelsea out of the world's premier club competition.

It wasn't too much of a surprise that El Salvadorians were football crazy, as my history books told me. This was a nation that went to war over a football match. El Salvador finished level on points with neighbouring Honduras in the 1970 World Cup qualifiers, so to determine who would be going to the finals in Mexico; they competed in a two-legged playoff. Relations between the two wasn't exactly cordial at the time. A few months prior to the contest Honduras' government had forcefully expelled El Salvadorian farmers who had illegally settled within their territorial boundaries, resulting in violent clashes. Honduras won the first leg at home by a single goal. They received a hostile reception in San Salvador, reports indicated visiting players and fans were attacked inside and outside the national stadium. The hosts won, meaning there was a decisive fixture. On the day of the decider El Salvador cut diplomatic relations with their opponents. Shortly after they invaded Honduras and bombed strategic targets, causing the deaths of roughly 2,000 people. A ceasefire was negotiated and a demilitarised zone was established along the border. It wasn't until 1992 that both sides came to agree on the issue, which was adjudicated by the International Court of Justice (ICJ). The tiebreaker staged in Mexico City was a thriller - El Salvador came out on top 3 v 2 after extra time to qualify for their first ever World Cup.

Game 7

Cobán Imperial v Dep. Achuapa – (Liga Nacional) – 5 v 1
Saturday 27th March 2010 – 20:00
Estadio Verapaz, Cobán, Alta Verapaz

After partying for over five months I'd had enough. I took a bus to Guatemala's mountainous central region to give my body a much earned rest from the abuse it had endured.

Prior this we returned from El Salvador and spent a couple of interesting days on the shores of stunning Lake Atitlán. This picturesque location was predictably a fixture on the Gringo trail as it was surrounded by volcanoes and large hills, while the water had a gorgeous pure blue tone. It was interesting to contemplate the impact tourism was having on places like San Pedro la Laguna. This was the most popular destination in the area for alternative types, reflected by a spate of Israeli restaurants and party bars. The backpacker invasion could certainly be deemed to have had a negative effect on this once rural community. Local youths were suffering from their exposure to the influx of alcohol and drugs brought to their town by westerners. Us three wanted to integrate fully with the Guatemalans, so as to purvey a positive image of Brits abroad. We achieved this by spending a lot of our time watching football and drinking pints in a Scottish-owned sports bar which served curry and roast dinners. Cheers!

My visitors' final day was spent in the colonial city of Antigua, amid pre-Easter celebrations. There was countless midrange, middle-aged tourists, happily snapping anything that looked remotely ethnic. In the month before Holy Week the main draw for crowds were colourful floral carpets intricately depicting scenes from the crucifixion, as well as purple-robed males parading through the streets with religious paraphernalia.

To facilitate an early flight I'd arranged for a shuttle bus to take the lads to the airport; situated an hour's drive away. Within minutes of saying our goodbyes they returned looking concerned. The bus company had informed them there was a general strike and roadblocks encircling Guatemala City. As nobody was permitted to enter or leave the municipal district, particularly tourists, it rendered their journey impossible. Fortunately for Cov boys money talks in poor countries. After a frantic search I found a driver in possession of a vehicle with blacked-out windows. He was willing to remove his taxi signs and find a way across the picket line - for a price of course. They made it home safe and sound and it pleases me to report that they've both been backpacking again.

Having drunk my way through Chicago and the Midwest, raved for three months on a Mexican nudist beach and covered three new countries in less than a month; it was time for a rest. I wanted to go somewhere I had the least chance of getting up to mischief, so settled on a quiet town called Cobán, set in the mountainous, misty tropics of la Alta Verapaz. In fairness it was a good choice as I had two relatively uneventful weeks, completing Spanish lessons I'd started in England and catching up on my diaries. Throw in a private room with a comfortable double bed, Wifi, plus a television with all the sports channels, I had the all the ingredients to stay static for a fortnight. My only problem was that by the end of the first week I began to get restless. I concluded that a Saturday night at the football might liven things up, so armed with an eight pack of beer I set off for the ground.

I'd stumbled upon the local club on one of my jogs during the week and was delighted to discover their two Easter fixtures were at home. I spent some time wandering around the tidy little open stadium surrounded by steep hills. Not wishing to pay the entrance price, I deduced a fool proof plan as to how I could watch the match for free. It was brilliantly simple: sit at the top of the hills encircling the venue and observe proceedings from a lofty vantage point, accompanied by a load of cerveza. Obviously nobody had ever considered such a cunning ploy before. I was therefore slightly dumbfounded when I climbed an access path, to be confronted by a security guard asking where I was headed. My response, about it being such a pleasant evening I couldn't resist going for a stroll, was undermined by the fact it was pitch black and I was carrying a plastic bag full of clinking bottles. I didn't even wait for his response to my ridiculous statement. I turned around, located a suitable hiding place for my cargo, before parting with the outrageous sum of $4.25 to enter Estadio Verapaz.

My punishment for being so stingy was missing four goals, all scored within the first half an hour. I arrived just as Cobán celebrated going 3 v 1 up. Although clearly semi-professional (and very much reminiscent of my teenage years following Folkestone Invicta) the game was more entertaining than either of the other two I'd seen in Guatemala. In the second period Imperial took control, a shaven-headed striker scored two goals of remarkable quality; the second was a dipping half volley from 25 yards which found the net via a post. Imperial's setup was quite developed bearing in mind the level. The main stand (entrance at a whopping $9) boasted a proper bar and restaurant, there was a sturdy side structure, and benches dotted along the grassy slopes.

Upon retrieving my beers and returning to my accommodation I was keen to go out partying. Some gentle persuasion convinced a lanky Canadian guy staying in the hostel to accompany me. According to my guidebook Cobán's hot ticket was an establishment called Ananda, described as an alternative bar, but was essentially somebody's house. It was a really interesting watering hole, situated in a large building with lots of little rooms containing groups of students. Soon enough two Gringos sitting at the bar attracted the attention of some drunken local men, as well as a couple of good-looking girls studying in town. After we'd shared a few rounds of shots – a spirit which set my throat on fire – the men collapsed in a room and my friend and I had paired off with the students. Rather embarrassingly we were kissing Guatemalan girls who were probably a decade younger than us.

A bottle of the nasty liquor later and the night ended back at our lodging, where we were unable to wake the security guard to let us in. After a while the enterprising Canuck climbed over a gate and opened the door from the inside. By this time our señoritas had got bored, allegedly one of their cousins came and picked them up. The next morning I was unable to recall much after the first round of shots. This probably explains why when I woke up I was fully dressed and had a piece of paper stuck to my face with a girl's name and telephone number written on it.

Game 8

Cobán Imperial v Deportivo Petapa - (Liga Nacional) – 1 v 0
Wednesday 31st March 2010 – 20:00
Estadio Verapaz, Cobán, Alta Verapaz

One of the foremost reasons for staying in Cobán for a fortnight was the celebration of Holy Week leading up to Easter. In Latin countries such as Guatemala, where Catholicism was prominent, Semana Santa was a big deal and brought the nation to a standstill. Processions, religious ceremonies and public festivities occurred in the week between Palm Sunday and Easter Saturday. They commemorated the Passion, Crucifixion and Resurrection of Jesus Christ. I'd seen part of the build-up in Antigua, but was unprepared for its sheer scale. Every day hordes of people took to the streets. Dressed in distinctive purple robes, white waistbands and cloaks, hundreds of locals paraded various images of Jesus and or la Virgen María on their shoulders.

Supposedly the statues embodied scenes from Jesus' final days on earth, but the variations between the sculptures were so subtle, that by the third time I ambled into town to eat lunch it felt very much like Groundhog Day. The vigils were organised by brotherhoods with each statue having its own group devoted to it. To be a member of a brotherhood indicated you had social status, and carrying a sculpture was a great honour, showing your dedication to the church. Men and women were separated; women wore white and had smaller floats to carry.

On a nondescript afternoon I followed a procession to its destination, which for some crazy reason was a church at the top of a steep hill. This was no mean feat as the statues could weigh in excess of 3,000 kilograms, hence there was a structured order as to who was selected and where they stood, based on individual's size and physical condition. As the week wore on I started noticing odd little moments in the events. The convoys were accompanied by four men dressed as Roman soldiers, carrying spears with hooks on the end. Initially I thought they were merely a decorative addition to proceedings, until they paraded down a street with low-hanging power cables. The soldiers used their spears to raise the wires so the statues passed safely underneath, negating any possibility of the worshippers injuring themselves.

During the week I attended another match in Cobán, a

forgettable affair decided by a penalty. Even on a quiet night, in a boring town in the middle of nowhere, I still managed to be adopted by a group of locals and ended up being led through street celebrations after the game. It involved going to a Cobán player's house, drinking at a bar (which was clearly someone's garden with some plastic tables in) and driving around in a pickup truck for hours.

Prior to getting back on the road I had time to visit Semuc Champey, where the River Cahabón cut underground, creating a natural limestone bridge and a series of gorgeous turquoise swimming pools. Situated in a relatively remote area of la Alta Verapaz mountain range, surrounded by groups of dark and mysterious caves, this was a pleasant day's excursion from Cobán.

Suitably refreshed and prepared for the next leg of my voyage, it was time to leave Guatemala and head for a new country.

HONDURAS

Population – 8 million
Size – 112,090 km^2
Time Zone – GMT $^-$6
Currency - Lempira
FIFA World Ranking – #59 (2010)
Best World Cup Finish – First Round (1982 & 2010)
Biggest Teams – Olimpia, Motagua, Real España, Marathón

You might have heard of:
Carlos Pavon, David Suazo, Wilson Palacios, Maynor Figueroa, Carlos Costly

Essential Spanish:
Barrio – Neighbourhood/District
Selección – National Football Team
Gratis – Free
Rico – Tasty
Leones - Lions

It took a whole day and five different buses to get from Cobán to Copán. As with a lot of travelling in developing nations, there was a fair amount of patience required. Much of the time was spent standing on a roadside, wondering when the next bus was coming and how far it was going to take me. Considering both my place of departure and destination were relatively remote towns, four changes was good going. Strangely the border crossing from Guatemala to Honduras was possibly one of the easiest parts of the journey, due to Central America's border control agreement (CA-4). This allowed people to move within any of the four countries signed up (Guatemala, El Salvador, Honduras and Nicaragua) without worrying about strict frontier formalities. Tourists were granted a 90 day visa to travel within the nations under this agreement, which was implemented to permit free trade amongst neighbours.

With a couple of exceptions borders hadn't been overly painful so far on the trip. Mexico to Belize had involved a large military presence, supervising an unsubtle scam which forced me to buy an exit stamp for $20. For my week back in Chicago after working in Mexico, my flight connected in Dallas. I was greeted by a fat ginger immigration officer who didn't take kindly to my passport's growing quantity of stamps. He sent me to an interrogation room for half an hour. Inside I was interviewed by an uptight official wanting to know precisely what business I had visiting the USA. My explanation of going to see Miss Arkansas for Valentine's Day didn't improve his mood one little bit. I had to field questions such as: 'What are your intentions with this girl?' and 'are you going to get engaged?' Also, upon explaining my longer-term travelling plans: 'what possessed you to go on this here.....errrr Walkabout.' All of which I had to endure without being able to apply any kind of sarcasm to my responses. I was well aware you do not mess with Homeland Security, especially not when you're in Texas. However, I did appreciate the inference that by going on a holiday for longer than two weeks, I could be likened to Crocodile Dundee and his forays into the Outback. The most amusing moment of the ordeal was him cross-examining my story about meeting Miss Arkansas. He couldn't comprehend that we bumped into each other on Koh Samet. But, from a country where over 60 per cent of its citizens didn't hold a passport, was it at all surprising?

I passed midweek in the charming colonial town of Copán Ruinas, before getting back on the football trail to watch la Liga Nacional's climax. The principal reason tourists flocked to this small settlement, a few kilometres away from the border, was its proximity to

Copán. These structures were the most easterly of all the main Mayan sites and marked the extent of their influence in Central America. Aztecs were dominant in Mexico around DF, whilst the Mayans were prominent in modern day South Mexico and Guatemala. Copán was one of the best preserved structures from this era, which was largely attributable to Honduras' government successfully promoting it as a tourist attraction.

Although not as visually stunning as the sites I'd visited in Belize and Guatemala, the intricate carvings were incredible. Disappointingly, in order to protect the elaborate stone artefacts, the more interesting parts were fenced off to visitors. Stories contained in the stonework spoke of Kings with names such as Smoke Serpent and Moon Jaguar ruling surrounding tribes, and the famous battles and events that took place. Copán's ultimate downfall was overpopulation. With over 28,000 people there in the mid 700's (AD) it was the most densely populated Mayan settlement. By the early 800's the city-state collapsed under the weight of its own numbers. Food and resources ran out and the once great metropolis was almost completely abandoned. It made me wonder whether there was a moral to these historical events we could take note of?

After three weeks of roaming around rural towns, witnessing traditional religious ceremonies and spending time in Mayan steam baths, it was time to head towards the bright lights of San Pedro Sula, Honduras' economic centre. I arrived in plenty of time for the big derby match being played there on Saturday night, and spent Friday wandering through the sprawling neighbourhoods.

Keen to reacquaint myself with some junk food, I followed signs for the golden arches situated on a dual carriageway that circled the city. When I got to the intersection I couldn't believe my eyes, it was more like a major US city than anywhere else I'd seen before. It was slightly surreal looking at the line of Wendy's, McDonalds, Burger King, KFC and other typical fast food outlets, all with bright signs outside illuminating the passing traffic. The half an hour I spent in an ultramodern, air-conditioned supermarket was enjoyable, as was purchasing cans of Budweiser for $0.50 apiece.

I sat on a well-trimmed lawn in front of Appleby's, sipping my imported beer, gazing on the neon wilderness. It begged the question why San Pedro Sula was so much more westernised than the rest of the places I'd seen in Central America and Southern Mexico? Sauntering back to my hotel I could make out bright lights on the hills that towered over the city. Considering the season I assumed they'd be illuminated crucifixes still in place from Easter celebrations. Upon closer inspection it turned out to be glowing letters promoting Coca-Cola.

Game 9

Marathón v Real España – (Liga Nacional) - 1 v 2
Saturday 10th April 2010 - 20:30
Estadio Olímpico Metropolitano, San Pedro Sula

Honduras' second city derby (el clásico Sampedrano) was an exciting prospect. I spent an afternoon Skyping with my Dad on his birthday in the ever reliable Pollo Campero, and playing Pro Evolution Soccer on an archaic arcade machine. On Friday I visited Real España's ground where they were holding a marketing event, and was impressed by how tidy and compact it was. Talking to locals they all echoed the same sentiments on el clásico. Firstly, it was a shame it was being staged at Estadio Olímpico. Secondly, the barrio next to the arena was dangerous after dark. Not one to heed good advice, once I'd bought my ticket at the venue I went for a stroll around the surrounding area. It wasn't that bad, a little menacing in places, but as a male tourist if you didn't look too conspicuous and could speak a reasonable amount of the native tongue, you were generally safe in most neighbourhoods. I found a quiet bar and sat discreetly in the corner. By my third beer a bunch of rough-looking inebriated people were trying to converse with me, so I made a brisk strut to Estadio Olímpico Metropolitano.

The 45,000 capacity Olympic-style stadium was pretty standard. Oddly Honduras' Selección played fixtures there, and not in the capital where there was a similar facility. The open bowl was deserted on this Saturday evening. On either side of the main stand were small bands of what could loosely be defined as barra, but much like Estadio Azteca, the dimensions prohibited any type of real atmosphere. The contest was quite lively. Marathón scored first, before España equalised and smashed a stunning winner from distance. As the interval approached I found myself hungry and holding an empty paper cup.

Wanting to beat the half time 'rush' I made my way to the concourse, which opened out onto a car park, refreshed my cerveza and sat at a food stall. The usual fare of rice, beans and meat was presented. I sat reading a newspaper unaware I was being watched by the employees. It wasn't until three girls stood right over me that I realised I was the centre of attention. My attempts at conversation were met with fits of giggles from the trio, whose ages ranged from six to ten. Their mothers preparing the BBQ weren't so shy, and we had a decent chat about living in Sula. By the time the first period was over I'd finished my dinner and sat observing as a production line was formed. The mothers handled money and plated meat, while the two elder daughters were responsible for rice and beans. Promoting their business to passers-by fell on the youngest girl's tiny shoulders.

Fuelled by a Salva Vida refill (their national beer was called Life Saver - brilliant!) I took it upon myself to help the ladies. At the top of my voice I proclaimed that their food was the best around and everyone should try it. At least that's what I think I was saying. My Spanish had improved leaps and bounds, but possibly wasn't at business promotional level yet. Everything I shouted was greeted with laughter, not just from my colleagues, but the punters as well. The novelty of a Gringo promoter seemed to be doing the trick as a queue began to form. I must have been fairly entertaining because a guy from a kiosk opposite came over with a big smile, patted me on the back and presented me with a Salva Vida, gratis. It was all going swimmingly until the riot started.

Whilst negotiating the entrance I'd noticed that both sets of supporters had their own turnstiles. Once inside the ground there was no segregation at all. During half time I'd been so preoccupied selling meals to bemused Hondurans that I'd not paid attention to the build-up of rival fans on either side of me. I did see the rock flying towards Marathón's contingent which sparked the confrontation. After a lot of shouting the two groups edged closer and closer to each other, until there was a skirmish in the car park behind where our stall was set up. All the diners grabbed their paper plates and headed for the safety of the stands, while the two mothers and three daughters sought shelter under their trestle tables.

Now I'd like to talk this up as a full scale riot, but honestly, it was just kids making noise, throwing things, exchanging a few tame punches and then backing off shouting insults. Initially it was captivating to be so close to proceedings, but soon became predictable, so I began promoting the food again. As rocks and bottles flew through the air and kids scrapped 20 metres away from me, I continued to shout about how rico our food was. The girls weren't laughing any more, they stared at me from their hiding places with looks of disbelief - what was this crazy Gringo doing?

When all the fuss had died down the ladies started packing up, so I said my goodbyes and returned to the terraces. Shortly after finding a spot a chubby Honduran guy asked for a light, in English. Delighted by the prospect of being able to have a proper conversation, we stood chatting for 45 minutes. At full time my new companion (who was the spitting image of Sean Kingston) offered me a lift back to the city centre in his pickup truck. First we had to drop his girlfriend and her mate home, to one of the most dangerous barrios in Honduras. Actually it was kind of his ex-girlfriend - a religious girl - as they were going through a breakup. Apparently it.... 'Started after dark, used chill in the park, oh then she took his heart, and that's when they fell apart, because they both thought, that love could last forever.'

The next stop was Sean Kingston's house, where I met his brother and their housekeeper. We drank some alcohol and smoked a joint they prepared using an A4 piece of paper. From there we went to his cousin's apartment, then briefly to a bar. At 01:15 sitting in a subterranean car park waiting for two girls to finish their shift at TGI Fridays; I questioned what the hell I was doing. But then they jumped in the back of the truck and our magical mystery tour continued. We ended up in a nightclub on the top floor of a crumbling building, where things got a bit hazy. I remember doing shots, dancing badly, and..... woke up the next morning fully clothed on my hotel bed. Slightly dazed and confused, I tried to recall the previous evening's antics, but could only remember as far as the club. A petrol station receipt in my pocket informed me I'd bought six beers and a packet of cigarettes at 02:43. Another sketchy football day.

Estadio Olímpico Metropolitano was to play an important part in 2014's World Cup. The competition's first game pitted Belize against Montserrat. A preliminary round first leg qualifying match was successfully staged in Trinidad and Tobago, to an audience of 100 supporters. La Copa Mundial looked like it might get off to a chaotic start as the second leg, scheduled to be held in Belize, was suspended due to severe interference by their government. FIFA and Belize's FA were unable to agree on a suitable venue as the mid July 2011 deadline approached. To negate a team being expelled from Brazil 2014 in its second fixture, San Pedro Sula was nominated as host city. Belize ran out comfortable winners 3 v 1 on the night, 8 v 3 on aggregate; watched by a marginally more respectable crowd, totalling 150.

Heading north towards the Bay Islands I stopped at a rowdy coastal town named Tela. It was a world away from Copán Ruinas' preened international tourist centre, and Sula's modern malls. Beachfront bars blasted music out from late morning to the early hours, and there was a distinctly wild atmosphere. This encouraged me to head towards a backpacker-infested island, Utila. Having caught a catamaran from La Ceiba, I settled into Caribbean life by renting an apartment from a geriatric couple of Garífuna descent called Norma and Will. Most visitors to this miniscule location were there for cheap, world-class scuba diving. Fringed by a coral reef boasting abundant marine life and clear waters, it was a perfect holiday destination. Scuba diving courses cost approximately $250, so it seemed appropriate to don a wetsuit and get involved.

As it was low season I shopped around the island's plentiful dive operators. At Utila Watersports I bartered a deal for one-on-one tuition and a free week's accommodation for under $300. The basic PADI wasn't particularly challenging, although it was rewarding to be gliding 15 metres underwater following Eagle Rays and shoals of brightly coloured fish, navigating coral walls. An attraction for divers was regular visits paid to the reef by Whale Sharks. These huge passive creatures favoured warm, tropical, plankton-rich waters. I didn't get to see one of these giants of the deep first-hand, which was a shame, as by all accounts swimming alongside such a large gentle beast was an awe-inspiring experience.

Game 10

Vida v Olimpia – (Liga Semi-final 1st Leg) – 2 v 2
Saturday 24th April 2010 – 20:30
Estadio Municipal Ceibeño Nilmo Edwards, La Ceiba

I was sat in a dive shop on a sun-drenched Caribbean island, blissfully unaware I would be seeing football that day. I'd just completed a weeklong PADI course and was waiting for a catamaran back to the mainland. Whilst checking Saturday's live scores on the BBC website Captain Chuck started talking to me. This was strange as he'd been the boat driver for all of my eight dives, but we'd exchanged no more than pleasantries. He glanced over my shoulder, saw I was looking at football and began chatting away. During the conversation he advised me there was a big game that evening in La Ceiba, the port town where I was headed. I was conscious that the Honduran championship finals were taking place, but FIFA's website listed incorrect dates, so thought I was going to miss them. Thank you Captain Chuck.

Ten hours later I was stood in the dark outside Estadio Nilmo Edwards wearing a silly red hat, wondering why all the ticket windows were shut. I wasn't alone. There were hundreds of locals in the vicinity, some drinking and dancing near stalls selling beer, whilst others loitered by locked gates. A circuit of the venue made me realise that not only were there no tickets for sale, they also weren't admitting anyone.

Rather deflated, I bought a cerveza and observed an increasingly restless group standing by the main entrance. Fireworks heralding the player's entrance sparked activity; it appeared as if the gates were moving. I went for a closer look and it became apparent they were trying to kick the doors down. All of a sudden I was being pushed forward by a surge of people around me. Then the gates sprung open and there was a loud roar. The crowd's momentum carried me to the entrance, where things got a bit tighter. All I could picture was the number of times I'd read about fatalities at football matches under similar circumstances. But I couldn't go back, so squeezed and barged my way forward through a suffocating heat and mass of bodies until, after what felt like an eternity, I popped out in the middle of a stand, still being pushed from behind.

The break-in hadn't gone unnoticed; police in riot gear were running over to deal with the disturbance. I quickly moved as far away from the entrance as possible, finding a mellow spot near some elderly folk. As I was doing so the visitors took an early lead via a diving header from Honduran Selección striker, Danilo Turcios. Although it was nine o'clock, the heat was so oppressive I was sweating just watching proceedings.

The contest compellingly swung from end to end. It was no surprise when Vida were on level terms on the half hour; Jerry Bengston raced clear and beat a sprawling keeper. Ten minutes later Turcios gave Olimpia the advantage for a second time, slotting home from an acute angle, sending the 2,000 travelling fans wild. Shortly after the restart it was all square once again. Olimpia failed to deal with an out swinging corner and the ball somehow bounced over their goalkeeper, who was stood on his line. Despite some good chances in the closing stages, chiefly from set pieces, neither side could take an initiative into the second leg, being played three days later.

Game 11

Olimpia v Vida - (Liga Semi-final, 2nd Leg) - 1 v 1
Tuesday 27th April 2010 – 20:30
Estadio Tiburcio Carías Andino, Tegucigalpa

La Ceiba's lively draw encouraged me to forego an expedition into Honduras' interior and head south towards the capital. I broke up my bus journey by stopping for a couple of days in a Brewery situated close to picturesque Lago de Yojoa. My excitement at staying in a place that made its own beer was swiftly extinguished within two mouthfuls of their homebrew. Fortunately the setting was pleasant. For most visitors to Honduras there wasn't much else on the agenda aside from Mayan ruins and scuba diving. This was understandable owing to the distinct lack of mainstream sights apart from these two. The area surrounding the country's largest lake was really diverse. There were small patches of cloud forest containing hundreds of species of birds and animals, which were overlooked by the Cerro Azul Meámbar Mountains.

On my way to a spectacular waterfall, I crossed paths with a middle-aged English bird enthusiast who'd moved to the region to study winged creatures. In a remote lakeside village, which wasn't really a popular destination for foreigners, it was a little weird to see a white-bearded Brit peering into binoculars strapped to his neck, scribbling in a notepad. Appropriately called Malcolm, he'd been living by the lake for some years and offered guided birdwatching tours. This sounded reasonably interesting until he mentioned they departed at 05:30.

On match day 11 I walked out of my room into a sunny wooded glade to the sounds of parrots squawking, a very different scene to the next morning. A local bus took me to a highway, where I flagged down an intercity service bound for Tegucigalpa (Teg-oo-ci-alpa). It was standing room only which seemed to make everyone sociable. Soon I was involved in variety of conversations with Hondurans, one of which, a weather-beaten man with silver hair in his mid-sixties, told me he was also going to the game that night.

Five hours later, through a torrential rain storm and choking traffic, we arrived at the terminal (a street corner with a bus company sign on the wall). It required five minutes of jostling and shouting to retrieve my bag from the hold, at which point the old man waved at me to follow him. Not one to question any type of randomness, follow I did. Onto a bus, across a pedestrian precinct and a busy cathedral square, down a couple of dingy alleys to the cheap accommodation he'd recommended. And at $3 it certainly was cheap. The main problem I could see was that we were housed in a terrace of sheds with filthy beds. Also the showers consisted of a barrel of cold water which you had to pour over yourself. Ah I almost forgot, within minutes of arriving it became clear that it also doubled as a whorehouse or sex motel.

Tegucigalpa's high-street provided some home comforts; I treated myself to a Burger King. My peaceful junk food fest was ruined by a crazy guy with a calculator, who was keen to show me statistics relating to the world's population on his miniature screen. At the outset it was quite impressive (he correctly entered figures for the United Kingdom's four members) but it became tiresome when he started on Eastern European nations. I'd no way of knowing if he was making it up and he kept putting his arm round me. Why do I attract these types?

Escaping back to the shed-come-brothel the old guy was ready to go. It was a 20 minute uphill hike to Estadio Tiburcio Carías Andino. Supposedly my amigo could get us free tickets, but by that time I'd spoken to him for long enough to predict what was going to happen next. So I sat outside a shop with a can of Salva Vida waiting for him to return with the bad news. Obviously I paid for his ticket too, which I didn't mind considering my lucky entrance to the first leg.

Purchasing a cerveza from a Domino's pizza stall, my companion found a group of his friends and left me to explore the venue. It was pretty sizeable, roughly 35,000 capacity and about half full. La Ultra Fiel barra were caged into a compact section at the ground's north end. Whilst the fireworks and pre-match fanfare was going on I photographed the bouncing white masses. A toothless man immediately warned me that if I took any more pictures my camera would be stolen. Not sure if it was advice or a threat I climbed to the top of the stand attempting to be as inconspicuous as possible.

The two legged format (with away goals coming into effect after 180 minutes) really didn't aid the spectacle. Olimpia, the country's largest and most successful team, were happy to sit back and allow the visitors to play football. Vida scored two minutes before the break, causing the boisterous home faithful to sing louder and jump higher. The atmosphere was even more raucous after the interval when Los Leones attacked in earnest. Less than 15 minutes in they equalised following a smart control and finish from a probing through ball. Then

59

they stopped pressing again, happy with their slender advantage. Vida nearly had the last laugh in the dying moments, but Olimpia's keeper made a smart save.

I'd been watching proceedings with a group of university students who were more interested in the $1 beers than events on the pitch. Not wanting to let our national reputation down I was matching them round for round, which came about alarming quickly. At full time I somehow managed to lose them and the old guy from the bus, so attempted to make my way back to the barn. An hour later rain started falling and I was nowhere near any recognisable landmarks, so I sought shelter in a karaoke bar. Via a taxi, lots of wandering in circles and directions from three different sets of people, I ended up outside my accommodation. At three in the morning, waiting for a security guard to let me in, a haggard old woman was unsuccessfully endeavouring to convince me I should pay $10 to spend the rest of the night with her.

Game 12

Motagua v Platense - (Liga Semi-final, 2nd leg) - 0 v 0
Wednesday 28th April 2010 – 20:30
Estadio Tiburcio Carías Andino, Tegucigalpa

The next day Olimpia's roommate and deadly rival, Motagua, hosted the second semi-final. They'd played their first leg away and had also drawn 2 v 2. I found myself at the opposite end of Estadio Tiburcio Carías Andino with half as many fans in attendance, nursing a Domino's beer. Unsurprisingly I was feeling sketchy after a skin full, an early morning bedtime, being woken by an old man singing four hours later, and a shower consisting of pouring a bucket of cold, dirty water over me. Disappointingly Los Revoluciónarios 1928 barra didn't come close to recreating the previous night's atmosphere and Motagua sat even deeper than their neighbours.

The evening's entertaining was provided by a linesman, who after giving a questionable offside decision spent an hour as target practice for spectators in the side stand. It was far more enjoyable viewing than the match, particularly due to the imaginative range of missiles aimed in his direction. My favourite was a half full bottle of water taped to a stuffed rabbit, which missed his head by mere centimetres. The cuddly toy got a touch of the ball 30 seconds later, before being thrown to the side-lines by a Platense player, who made an unsavoury gesture at the crowd.

In a way this was the most important fixture of all the 67 I attended. Sat at the top of an empty terrace wondering what the hell I was doing at such a terrible game; I came up with the ridiculous notion of writing a book about Latin American football. What a silly idea that was. Well that's what I told myself on a bus to Nicaragua. I really wanted to see the championship's conclusion, as capital city clásicos to decide a league title would've been good material for a football book. However, the prospect of staying in Tegucigalpa for another day, let alone ten, wasn't an enticing one. So I headed to the next country, and more alluringly, El Pacifico. For the record, Olimpia were crowned after beating Motagua 3 v 2 over two legs.

I was also keen to find a base to watch the upcoming World Cup, although Honduras would have definitely been an interesting place to have viewed it from. With one of their most successful generations of talent performing well in qualifying, La Bicolor found themselves with a realistic chance of participating in Africa's first finals. Perennial qualifiers USA and Mexico occupied the top two spots in CONCACAF's fourth round group, so Honduras was competing with Costa Rica for the last automatic berth. In the tenth and ultimate match Los Ticos were two points ahead of their less favoured rival. Fittingly Honduras was playing in El Salvador, and claimed the contest's only goal through Real España's veteran forward Carlos Pavón. A few hours later Costa Rica looked like they'd booked their place by taking a two goal advantage into the break in Washington DC. The USA rallied late on, forcing an equaliser deep into injury time. Honduras made it to the World Cup on goal difference but failed to win a game in South Africa, while Costa Rica lost in a two legged playoff with eventual semi-finalists, Uruguay.

NICARAGUA

Population – 6 million
Size – 130,000 km^2
Time Zone – GMT $^-$6
Currency - Córdoba
FIFA World Ranking – #158 (2010)
Best World Cup Finish – Haven't come close to qualifying
Biggest Teams – None

You might have heard of:
Somoza, Ortega, Argüello

Essential Spanish:
El Tren del Norte – The Northern Train
Agua - Water
Isla – Island
Por Fa – Thank you (the lazy way of saying it)
Árbolito - Small tree
Varas - Yards

I crossed the border riding over a long concrete bridge on a three wheeled bicycle with a passenger seat on the front, similar to the ones popular in Asia. I was greeted by ominous skies and strong winds blowing the bike precariously from side to side. Conveniently there was a minivan waiting for me at the bottom of the bridge as the heavens opened. By the time we'd arrived in Chinandega dark clouds and torrential rain had vanished, replaced by blindingly bright sunshine and an oppressive temperature touching the mid-30 mark.

I'd heard many positive reports from other travellers about Central America's largest country, and was keen to spend some time exploring what sounded like a geographically and socially interesting place. A brief stop in the former capital, León, started to educate me as to the turbulent history of this fascinating nation. Known as 'The Heroic City – The first Capital of the Revolution' this was the spiritual birthplace of Nicaragua's ruling socialist Sandinista party. León had also been the scene of a number of battles during the revolutionary years of the late 1970's. It was here I learnt about the region's political history and how each country developed its own character.

By the turn of the 20th century all CA-4 members could be described as banana republics. US companies established themselves and built infrastructure to facilitate the export of natural produce. Whether it was coffee in Guatemala and El Salvador, or fruit in Honduras and Nicaragua, corporations from North America made massive profits from producing and selling these goods. Inevitably with the investment of substantial sums of money comes corruption. Central America prior to the late 1920's was no stranger to big businesses influencing their governments.

The multinational company's grip weakened after 1929's Wall Street collapse, encouraging a rise of military dictatorships. These right-wing, US-supported regimes suppressed the general population through fear. They maintained profitable relationships with businessmen who were in cahoots with power mongers in Washington DC. This arrangement lasted well into the 1970's, at which point the populous began fighting the dictators. As unrest spread around Central America the US looked for a way to crush this rise in 'communism'. A base was founded in Honduras from which they looked to control the surrounding nations, as over the years their government had been susceptible to colonial overtones from the north. This cosy relationship could explain why it was possible to buy a Wendy Burger in San Pedro Sula.

The late 70's and early 80's were an extremely violent time in the region. USA was able to successfully assert its influence over each CA-4 country, apart from one. Nicaraguans revolted against their right-wing dictator, fought a bloody civil war, resisted attempted invasions from CIA-backed forces and had a socialist government in place more or less since 1979.

A few random twists and turns found me at a remote surf camp on the Pacific coast. The waves weren't really suitable and the place itself was overpriced and a bit underwhelming, but it was to have a large influence on my trip. A South African girl working behind the bar was teaching English on a part-time basis in Chinandega and advised there were plenty of positions available. Without really comprehending what was going on, a couple of telephone calls were made and I had an interview with one Central America's most prestigious private academies, based in the capital city, Managua. Four days later I was sat in Academia Europea's plush reception, wearing shorts and flip-flops. I wondered who was going to employ someone with no formal qualifications (I didn't finish my degree) and no experience in any form of teaching. Two basic questions later: 'Is English your first language?' and 'What country are you from?' I was hired; committing myself to a minimum three month stay.

Game 13

Real Estelí v Walter Ferreti - (Torneo Clausura Final, 2nd Leg) - 0 v 0
Sunday 9th May 2010 – 15:00
Estadio Noel Gámez, Estelí

I'd left Estadio Tiburcio in Tegucigalpa with vague ideas about writing an account of my travels with football, and a clear notion that it was my last fixture of the second season. On a short break in the mountain town of Estelí before my teacher training commenced, I discovered there was at least one more match to see prior to the World Cup. It was the climax of a thoroughly enjoyable weekend involving rock bars, a heavy metal concert, an air-conditioned nightclub (which looked remarkably like the one from Saturday Night Fever) and a 15 kilometre hike to a deserted waterfall.

On Sunday lunchtime (a few hours after Blues had lost at Bolton to finish in ninth place – our highest for 51 years) I was sat writing my diary in a bar opposite Real Estelí's deserted Estadio Independencia. I was surrounded by guys in baseball shirts, intently watching the live Major League coverage on a TV. I hadn't been in Nicaragua long enough to realise what kind of upside-down country it was, so, wanting to witness the climax to their domestic season, I'd come to the city's football ground. Naturally the game was being staged in a baseball park on the other side of Estelí. After some Toña's (my favourite beer from North, Central and South America) had settled my stomach, I hailed a taxi to Estadio Noel Gámez.

I strolled to a ticket window circumnavigating a herd of bison ambling across the car park, where they informed me it was sold out. I stood there inspecting the semi-circular main stand, wondering how on earth football was going to be played in a baseball park, when someone in a fluorescent vest tapped my shoulder and pointed to an administration office. As if I had been expected, they told me a ticket cost 50 Cordobas ($2.50) and I needed to go to the general entrance. Once the transaction was completed I asked why they weren't on sale to everybody. Their response: 'Because you are a Gringo' was to sum up both the best and worst of Nicaragua for me.

I was a little embarrassed entering the stadium, jumping a sizeable queue at the gate, most of who were trying, with varying degrees of success, to bribe the stewards to allow them past. Within minutes of being inside I found out the answer to my question - football should definitely not be played in a baseball park. For a start the playing surfaces aren't even close to being the same size or shape. They'd painted the pitch so first base was along the far touchline and second base was roughly on the centre spot. This meant there was a dirt line running diagonally down the field to the edge of the penalty area, where third base was ordinarily located. A large brown circle made it impossible for there to be any clear markings for the 18 yard box, which created at least two moments of controversy. From there the line from third to fourth base ran across the penalty area to the corner, which was just a mess of dust.

Fortunately the quality of football wasn't adversely affected by the inappropriate conditions. Even if they'd have been playing at Old Trafford it would have still been awful. Not that it really mattered because I couldn't actually see the contest anyway. The section I was in was a stretch of grass with a wire fence in front of it. Real Estelí fans were four deep at ground level trying to peer through the mesh. From what I could gather the home side, known as El Tren del Norte and the most decorated in Nicaragua's pitiful footballing history, were dominating proceedings.

There was cold Toña for sale so I wasn't all that bothered what was going on. I soon attracted the attention of some funny locals. Another Gringo was amongst them, a rugged Canadian student on his placement year specialising in farm animal's digestive systems. He enthusiastically proclaimed it was his first footballing experience; I was quick to assure him this wasn't representative of the sport in any way. A sunny afternoon passed chatting to various people, whilst a small band kept one of the two songs everyone seemed to know going throughout. There was even a tiny, vocal contingent supporting Walter Ferreti, housed on makeshift benches behind the dugouts.

All of a sudden the whistle was blown for full time and everybody began celebrating. As far as I could see nothing of any note had happened, apart from a couple of occasions when there were funny arguments between the referee and his assistant about whether the ball had gone for a throw, corner, or home run. As it turned out they were employing the same system as in Honduras; the first leg had been a 1 v 1 draw in Managua, meaning Real Estelí won the league with this dull 0 v 0 result.

So Ferreti's fans disappeared into the setting sun and out came a ridiculously large and rather phallic trophy. Fittingly it looked like it had been produced by a less than gifted GSCE Design Technology student. This was carried to both sides of the park, where a group of spectators perched on top of a wire fence got to hold the hideous piece of plastic, to much cheering and applause all round. Estadio Independencia didn't host the final as it was being prepared for CONCACAF's Champions League the following season. By winning La Primera División Real Estelí qualified for the competition, but their venue didn't meet the necessary standards, meaning there was no Nicaraguan representative that year.

My day ended on a reflective and strangely educational note. After an amazing fried chicken dinner had sobered me up, I found my way to a bar called Rincon Legal. During the civil war Estelí, a staunch leftist stronghold, witnessed much of the fighting and was comprehensively bombed by the ailing right-wing regime. Shelled-out buildings were visible scars of the violence in a city where more than 15,000 lives were lost. The bar had a sombre atmosphere and displayed murals and pictures of the destruction that took place. It was undoubtedly a world away from winning a football final in a baseball park.

Returning to the capital I started my teacher training. This consisted of reading from a text book, and practising how to repeat phrases r-e-a-l-l-y s-l-o-w-l-y. I was suspicious as to why a school would take me on so suddenly, especially considering I didn't have any previous experience or qualifications. A week of living in Managua explained it. To be honest a cursory look at my guidebook should have warned me. Its description of the city was so well worded and accurate that I incorporated it into my lessons:

'Hotter than an oven and crisscrossed by anonymous highways there can't be a more visitor unfriendly capital than Managua. Less a city in the conventional sense than a conglomeration of neighbourhoods and commercial districts, Managua offers few sights and cultural experiences – in fact most visitors are so disturbed by the lack of street names and any real centre that they get out as fast as they can.'

I'd committed myself to three months in this place. But, much like the British city I resided in for a decade prior to setting out on the trip, Managua was cheap. I found a compact en suite room situated at the rear of a pharmacy for $80 a month, and settled as best as I could into daily life.

The early signs weren't particularly positive. At the end of my first shopping spree at one of the city's large markets I had to fight two teenagers who tried to mug me. Whilst waiting to cross a dual carriageway to catch a bus home, a couple of youths made simultaneous attempts to snatch the contents of my pockets and rucksack. Rather worryingly my immediate thought was for the safety of my iPod, so I squirmed away from the pair shouting obscenities in English with my fists flying. The skirmish lasted less than 30 seconds, after which I found myself barefooted in the middle of the road as two lanes of traffic hurtled towards me. Returning quickly to the pavement, I regained my composure while some elderly locals came over to make sure I wasn't injured. The scruffily dressed duo made no effort to escape the crime scene in any hurry. They ensured I'd seen they were both carrying knives before casually standing at a snack stall on the opposite side of the road, throwing me an occasional threatening glance.

My accommodation proved to be worse than I had initially hoped, although it encouraged me to have a quiet period. In fairness to la Señora who ran the place she told me the quarters were normally for female students only, which sounded good at the time. My room was set around a courtyard which I shared with six teenage undergraduates, who spent the majority of their waking hours running about, shouting, screaming and playing music on their mobile phones. It might not sound that bad, but any interactions were met with fits of giggles and whispering amongst themselves.

Following a week's training the Academy deemed I was capable of teaching English to a class of Nicaraguans (or Nicas as they liked to be known). Bright and early one Saturday morning, dressed in a second-hand shirt and tie, armed with a text book and some hastily scrawled notes, I attempted to educate Central Americans how one should speak my language.

Game 14

Walter Ferreti v Real Estelí - (Grand Final, 2nd Leg) - 1 v 1
Sunday 16th May 2010 – 15:00
Estadio Olímpico, Managua

Teaching my first class the day before had been an exhilarating experience. Trying to capture and maintain the attention of a group of children and adults for four hours on a Saturday morning was a real challenge, particularly when you're not 100% convinced what you are teaching is correct. The next day, suitably hung-over after a night of rewarding myself for surviving the first lesson, I set out for a second sunny Sunday football final.

Outside the capital taxi fares were set dependant on the city's status. León, a sizeable tourist trap, charged $1 for most journeys, compared to Estelí's charming $0.50. Managua's rates depended on how local you were. As a Gringo I'd already been overcharged on more than one occasion, hence I found myself on a bus that day and pretty much every one after. The main problem was that there was no way of discerning their route or destination. Buses in other notable Central American cities listed the necessary information on a windscreen plaque. In Managua there were just numbers and no guide anywhere as to what they signified. The fact that locals had a very limited knowledge didn't help either. This is why I was walking through the wrong neighbourhood whilst game 14 was kicking off. In the end I relented and paid $3 to be dropped off at the venue's entrance.

It was disappointing this fixture was played in a real football stadium. After the preceding weekend's farce, I was hoping we could test the effects of a horseracing track or tennis courts on the outcome of a domestic football final. Not that I'd describe Managua's Estadio Olímpico as a good ground. For starters it only had two functional stands and the running track encircling the pitch was so wide it was difficult to see the players. I wasn't complaining because the sun was shining, the Toñas were cold and I'd found my way into the visitors section with Estelí's faithful - some of whom recognised me from the previous Sunday.

At least we were graced with a couple of goals on this occasion. Walter Ferreti took the lead before half time, prompting their 2,000 spectators crammed in the main stand to respond noisily. The contest suffered from long delays as they hadn't employed any ball boys. In

70

order to retrieve the football when it went for a corner or goal kick, a player had to negotiate a long jump pit, a group of hurdles, and traverse eight lanes of running track to the grass by the concrete boundary. This may not sound like much, but when you then have to wait for him to return to resume play, successive corners were taking five minutes.

Real Estelí nicked a goal with roughly a quarter of an hour remaining, to hand them the advantage on away goals (the first leg held at the baseball park a few days earlier had finished goalless). The 200 fans from the north celebrated in style. First they let off purple flares, which the wind blew into our faces, leaving us all coughing. Then came their water celebration. A group of 20 lads bought up a vendor's agua supply (they cost $0.05 for a 200ml bag) bit holes in the corners and sprayed the crowd. The game ended with a whimper as Estelí were crowned double winners with another oversized, ugly trophy, paraded in front of us and then briefly given to the travelling contingent.

Slowly but surely I adapted to Managuan life. After seven chaotic months my body was grateful for consecutive nights of sobriety, and a routine of working six days a week. Academia Europea was only a ten minute mooch from my pharmacy, although the journey could be tricky as it was rainy season. Nicaragua had a tropical climate; temperatures whilst I lived there regularly reached 35 degrees. Thunder storms arrived almost on a daily basis, casting darkness over the city and unleashing vicious lightening and rain, which turned roads into rivers. The weather wreaked havoc on my teaching schedule. A storm before class generally meant none of my students could get to the Academy, whilst a heavy downpour during lessons would cut the power, leaving me trying to amuse a room of people in near darkness.

Teaching got easier with the more experience I gained; the process was like learning my own language all over again. For me the problem was that we don't label our word groups as readily as most foreigners do. For example I knew the meaning of: myself, yourself and ourselves, but I had no idea these were called reflexive pronouns. Prior to my arrival in Nicaragua I was aware that a noun is a word for a thing, an adjective describes a noun, and a verb defines an action. Perhaps I'd fluked my B grade at GCSE English and hadn't paid any attention to what I'd been taught, but does anyone know what a gerund is?

Despite struggling to identify things like possessive nouns, it soon became crystal clear that we speak a simple language. Compare it to Español and you realise how easy English really is. Spanish nouns are either masculine or feminine. Therefore, as well as remembering vocabulary, you have to be able to identify whether it is a boy or girl

71

word. The sex of a noun then defines how the adjective is formed, as the endings of most change depending on whether the preceding word has a penis or not. Then you get to verbs. Whenever one of my students complained about how difficult learning English was, I would write this on the whiteboard:

I, You, You (formal), They, We – want
He, She, It - want*s*

Yo quier*o*
Tu quier*es*
Ustede quier*e*
Ustedes quier*en*
Nosotros quer*emos*
El/Ella/El quier*e*

When it comes to the principles of languages, ours is somewhat basic in comparison to Spanish, which is fairly easy in contrast to German. I believe this, combined with the fact that English is the most internationally spoken language, makes it harder for us to learn how to communicate in a foreign tongue. Apply that rationale to football and it's logical to conclude European players in the Premier League automatically have an advantage over their British colleagues - they can speak at least two lingos. In reality the majority of footballers from the home nations struggle to converse effectively in one, let alone two. This could go some way to explaining why it is uncommon for British players to settle in European leagues.

My teaching lifestyle may have been mundane, the hours antisocial and weather oppressive, but the guarantee of at least two amazingly good-looking female students in each class motivated me to turn up every day. The Academy was a private institution run by a family from El Salvador who had an assortment of schools all over Central America. As the fees were fairly expensive (although this wasn't reflected in my $3.30 an hour salary) only the relatively elite sections of society had the financial means to attend classes.

An interesting thing about spending so much time with wealthy students was their sentiments about the Sandinistas. Politics in Britain has no appeal to me; I'm not ashamed to say I have never voted. I was vaguely aware of Nicaragua's left-wing government upon arrival, but wasn't in any way prepared to live for four months under what could loosely be described as a socialist dictatorship.

Nicaragua's ruling party was, and probably still is, Frente Sandinista Liberacion Nacional (FSLN or Sandinistas). The organisation's roots can be traced to the 1920's, when Augusto Sandino led a guerrilla campaign against a US military presence in his country. Much like other CA-4 nations, Nicaragua had been little more than a US colony at the turn of the 20th century. Once the Great Depression set in Sandino fought for independence; rallying against weakened US control. The North Americans responded by forming a National Guard to protect their interests, before installing Anastasio Somoza Garcia as a de facto dictator in 1937. In order to maintain beneficial trading conditions, the National Guard was responsible for crushing anyone who opposed their regime. This led to Sandino's assassination in 1934, instantly creating a national martyr.

The Somoza family ruled for over 40 years while Nicaragua flourished economically. It became the richest country in Central America and was dubbed the 'breadbasket of the continent'. Death squads were active throughout this period, controlling the populous with fear and intimidation. In 1961 the FSLN was formed by nationalistic students, and gained popular support after a seismic event in 1972. On 23rd December an earthquake hit Managua, killing approximately 8,000 people and leaving a quarter of a million homeless.

Capitalising on unrest caused by the government's sluggish response and embezzlement of international aid funds, the Sandinistas became more prominent, principally in rural areas. In 1974 FSLN rebels invaded the Minister of Agriculture's house, took hostages and negotiated the freedom of a number of their prisoners, giving them much prestige. Somoza's power decreased as the decade wore on. When famous journalist and pacifist, Pedro Chamorro, was assassinated the country was edging towards a civil war. Eventually León was taken by FSLN guerrilla groups. US military funding was withdrawn, and leading up to July 1979 the Somoza family and National Guard were isolated in Managua, as the Sandinistas led by Daniel Ortega marched on the capital.

Sundays were my only full day off, so I endeavoured to make the most of them by exploring as much of the city as possible. Statistically Managua was the second safest capital in Latin America. Theoretically I shouldn't really have had any problems as I'd already negotiated dangerous places such as Mexico City and Guatemala City. I'm not sure whether it was attributable to my experiences at the market, but I always felt uneasy walking the streets. Consequently

Sunday was spent on public transport. I'd ordinarily have breakfast, potter about for a while and by lunch it was time to find somewhere to enjoy a cold Toña. The obstacles I faced were: there really wasn't anything of interest to see, and even if there was I had no way of discerning which bus went there. Hence I invented Random Bus Day. My idea was to pick the first one that passed my local stop, ride it to a barrio where it looked as if I might not get stabbed, and go for a wander. After a few cervezas flag down a different one, repeating the process until it was dark or I somehow managed to get back to my pharmacy. One Sunday I found myself outside an eerie and deserted National Palace, bathed in late afternoon sunshine.

It was here the Sandinistas scored an important victory against Somoza's regime. In August 1978 commandos disguised as National Guard soldiers entered the building and captured members of the National Assembly. This daring coup d'état was one of the key events in the FSLN's eventual success. The palace occupied one side of La Plaza de la Revolución opposite a glistening modern Cultural Palace, and flanked by the crumbling remnants of Managua's old Cathedral (which was condemned after the earthquake). It was unnerving to see how the area was devoid of any kind of human life. A handful of people I saw were lounging on the surrounding expanses of grass, acting a bit sketchy, casually watching me.

A brisk strut along a dual carriageway, on which there were more horse and carts than cars, and I was at the shore of Lago Managua. There were families milling around a small fair and collection of buildings, so I braved one of the drinking establishments - a cavernous affair with waiter service. The Reggaeton music was deafening and the temperature whilst seated was uncomfortable. I slugged my beer surveying a packed dance floor, full of sweaty bodies gyrating in time to the repetitive beats. As it was such a nice Sunday afternoon in the centre of the nation's capital, home to a million and a half citizens, I couldn't fathom why so many were indoors.

It wasn't the only inexplicable thing about this eccentric city. During a morning lesson a student wrote his address on the whiteboard, inviting the class to a party he was hosting. The literal translation was: Dorado Cinema, two blocks to the lake, one and a half blocks down, red door, blue car. I thought he was joking, but remembered the address I'd been given by the Academy when I came for my interview had been written in a similar fashion. At the time I concluded it had been described that way so a silly Gringo wouldn't get lost. I was wrong. The truth was Managua didn't have any street names, so residents identified their address using the most ridiculous system imaginable.

To locate properties in their capital city, Nicaraguans defined its position in relation to a famous landmark. This may not sound too complicated (and in theory it shouldn't be) but that wouldn't be the Nica way. Commonly used landmarks were businesses that existed prior to the earthquake in 1972, and had changed since. These included: cinemas, petrol stations and chemists that had been closed for almost 40 years. I asked all my classes to outline the point of reference from which they based their address, and received some hilarious responses. The best was 'white water tank' sparking a debate in the room as to which one they were referring to – loads of water tanks in the city were painted white. My personal favourite was 'El Árbolito' an insignificant-looking shrub in the middle of a crossroads, not far from the lakeshore. This was so integral to Managua's address system that it had remained in place despite the fact it was clearly a traffic hazard. Due to the amount of times people had driven into it (causing the authorities to regularly plant a replacement) they built a concrete wall around this little tree to protect it.

But it doesn't finish there. Once you've found your point of reference you need to work out where your destination is in relation to it. Traditional compass points were far too logical, so they dreamt up their own names. North was 'to the lake' - south 'to the mountains' - east 'up' (as in where the sun rises) - and west was 'down' (where the sun sets). Now you know where you are and which direction you're going in, you need to discern how far to travel. Usually this was measured in street blocks, which would be fine if the city was built on a US-style grid system, but the roads were all higgledy-piggledy, so one block might consist of two houses, whilst another 35. Alternatively you could measure the distance from the landmark, but even this was flawed as there was no uniform measuring system, some used metric while others used varas.

If by some miracle you find yourself on the correct street, because properties weren't numbered it was necessary to identify how each house was unique to its neighbour's. To achieve this, brilliantly accurate descriptions were employed, such as 'the one with a tree outside' or 'the one with a large iron gate' or (my favourite) 'the one with a brown dog in the garden'. In this case surely the poor animal couldn't be taken for a walk, because the second it left the premises there ceased to be an address. Unsurprisingly there was no postal delivery service, residents paid for a deposit box and collected their correspondence.

Living in Managua was an infuriating experience, but at times it was the peculiarity that made it bearable. The pharmacy I lived behind was situated between an affluent neighbourhood (containing opulent houses protected by sturdy metal gates and security guards) and a rough barrio. The wealthy zone's US-style bars weren't really to my taste, so I drank in the barrio's salubrious establishments. I adopted someone's house as my local. They served clients through an iron grill attached to their front window, and if there was space you could relax on the luxurious concrete blocks on their porch. For the sake of decency I'm not going to describe the toilet facilities. It was unlike any pub I'd previously frequented, although similar to many others, the quality of the night was dictated by which pissheads were in attendance. I had some memorable evenings, singing and dancing when people brought instruments with them. Equally there were forgettable ones when I endured drunken Nicaraguans trying to hug me on a regular basis, whilst covering me in spit in their vain attempts to communicate.

A lot of my frustration with the lifestyle was due to cultural differences and reluctance on my part to accept them. This extract from my diary, recounting an hour I spent in the main post office, was representative of the patience required to reside in Managua:

'So I wanted to post some of the junk I've collected in the last nine months to my parent's house. A simple task you would think. A lady at the window marked 'overseas packages' informs me I need to get a box. I go to a room which says it handles packages to Cuba, as it's the only place with any boxes. Return to the window with a cardboard box and a bill for 10 Cordobas which I will settle in a minute when I pay for everything (snigger). The nice young lady proceeds to cut parts of the Cuban box so it fits the contents of my HH Gregg bag tightly. She starts sticking bits down and taking bits off, which takes about ten minutes. Fair play to her. Right, ready now? Nope. I need to stick the address on the box somehow – apparently the woman over by the door has what I need. Cool. Errr which woman? That one - pointing in the direction of reception. I waited a few minutes as the employee was occupied, but realised she just passed calls around, so I spied customer services. They pointed me back in the same direction. But I don't think reception can help. No, not reception, the elderly woman in a wheelchair in front of reception. Really? When I entered the humongous building I'd noticed her but figured she was a charity collector, if she was even alive at all. Yes she could help. She pointed towards the Cuban box suppliers and began moving laboriously in said direction. No, no, no, really I know

76

them so you don't have to wheel yourself over, plus you need to stay and continue collecting for Nicaraguan Guide Dogs or something. Back into the Cuban office I went, where they reminded me I still hadn't returned a paid receipt for my box, but the disabled woman who was tortoising her way across the hall could help me locate a sticker. So I waited as she made her way over (perhaps I should have offered to push – how rude!) She gave me a key; well a set of keys with one specifically selected, and directed me to a cupboard. Off to the cupboard I trot, down and back up a couple of sets of three steps, noticing by a door there was an archaic wheelchair ramp. In hindsight I should've moved the ramp and pushed her down, moved the ramp again and pushed her to the bloody cupboard. Suffice to say there were eight locks and she shook her head for two minutes as I tried them all until the last one worked. Obviously there were no stickers in the cupboard, which I discovered after five minutes of scrabbling around with stuff falling all over the place, whilst the head shaking continued. Eventually another member of staff came over, established there were no stickers, relieved me of the keys and found a blank white envelope that could be stuck on my package. Triumphant, I returned to the window to find the attendant occupied. Patiently I waited, wrote the address, handed over a completed label and took my wallet out. How much do I owe? Don't be so stupid, you need to cover the parcel before you can stick anything on it, or indeed send it. So what the hell do I cover it in? Brown paper of course, don't you know anything about Nicaragua's postal system? Well actually... I knew exactly where to get the paper from as I'd been juggling it ten minutes earlier in some weird little cupboard. Back round to the other side of the colonial building I go, where the wrinkled woman is trying to direct someone how to open a locked fridge so she can sell him a can of Coke, which for some stupid reason was also her responsibility, even though she was unable to get within 20 meters of it. Wait for the Coca-Cola ordeal to run its course, take ownership of the keys, swiftly procure paper of the right size, lock everything up, return the keys to the lady (who'd spent the last half an hour spectating idiots messing about with a business she was very protective over) paid 10 Cordobas and returned to the overseas packages window, only to find a 'gone for lunch' sign sitting there. Fortunately the nice lady was still around. She efficiently covered my box and stuck the address on it (during which time the Cuban box lady came over to advise me her receipt was an hour old). Finally sealed and stamped, I gratefully paid $35 to ensure the passage of my smelly clothes and random pieces of paper to Cranbrook. I passed the paid receipt to the box seller and left in fits of laughter shaking my head. Clearly I could have turned up with my stuff already in an addressed and covered box (they still would've wanted to check the contents for security reasons). But where was I going to get all of those items from, apart from maybe.... a Post Office?'

Remarkably the parcel made it to England in one piece and in an implausibly timely manner, nine days to be precise. Socialism has its advantages.

Holland v Spain – (World Cup Final) – 0 v 1 (AET)
Sunday 11 July 2010 – 12:30 (Nica Time)
FNB Stadium, Johannesburg, South Africa.

There can be no denying that it was an average World Cup, even if you could ignore England's embarrassing failure. Spain was the tournament's best team, and when they rightly secured victory over a gallant Dutch side, festivities on the streets of Managua commenced. The country had been divided as to who was their favourite Selección because many Nicaraguans were of German descent (which explains why Toña was one of the most amazing beers I have ever tasted). Up until the semi-finals the majority had rooted for either los Españoles or die Deutsch. When the former eliminated the latter, pretty much everyone lent their support to the nation that first arrived on Nicaraguan shores in 1522. After Andrés Iniesta's extra time winner, the owner of the Gringo bar where I was watching the game celebrated by distributing complimentary crates of Toña to his grateful clientele, signalling the start of a very messy afternoon/evening. My lesson at seven the next morning was not at all fun.

With no kitchen facilities available and a McDonald's meal costing more than two hours wages, I was reliant on buying food from the barrio. Nicaragua's speciality was a dish called Gallo Pinto (painted rooster) consisting of rice and beans fried together. A normal Nica diet was: breakfast of Gallo Pinto and egg, a stew lunch with rice and beans cooked separately, and meat for dinner, with guess what? Gallo Pinto. It didn't take long for me to get sick of rice and bloody beans.

Pollo Campero was undeniably my favourite fast food chain in Latin America; they served slightly healthier fried chicken than the famous US brand. This business, created by a Guatemalan, was one of the only places on the continent I was guaranteed a reliable internet connection. Hence I spent a lot of time eating chicken and speaking to friends and family via Skype. In fact my parents have seen the interior of more Pollo Camperos than a junk food obsessed Hispanic teenager. It was waiting for my mum and dad to come online one afternoon when I read about how Nicaragua won a famous international legal case.

After the Sandinistas had claimed power on 19th July 1979, the US was keen to overthrow the left-wing government. From their strategic position in Honduras, they assisted a group called the Contras in their attempts to achieve this. Chiefly anti-Sandinistas and former members of the National Guard, the Contras engaged in covert operations and guerrilla warfare in an effort to overthrow the 'communists'. They were funded, trained and controlled by the CIA under President Ronald Regan's orders, and led by future Fox News host, Oliver North. It was acknowledged that even if they were unable to defeat the FSLN using military means, it might be possible to bankrupt them by being involved in a conflict so soon after taking power. The US poured millions of dollars into supporting a group their commander-in-chief once described as: 'the moral equivalent of our founding fathers'. Even when Congress outlawed sponsoring the Contras, Regan continued to provide financial backing through third parties, predominantly Colombian drug lords and Iranian arms dealers. The turning point came in 1983 when US-backed forces bombed oil installations and laid mines in three of Nicaragua's harbours.

The Sandinistas responded by raising a case at the International Court of Justice so the North Americans would be held accountable for their actions. In 1986 the court ruled Regan's administration had breached Nicaragua's sovereignty and illegally invaded their territory. The US was ordered to pay damages, but they refused. Despite signing the ICJ treaty (meaning they were legally bound by its decisions) and employing the court on previous occasions, no money was ever paid. This landmark case was eventually closed in the 1990's, when a newly-elected Nicaraguan democratic government stopped seeking to have the judgement enforced. It certainly wasn't the first time the United States of America showed itself to be above international law that it believes everybody else should be subject to, nor the last.

Celebration of the Anniversary of the Revolution
Monday 19th July 2010 – 14:00
Plaza de la Fe Juan Pablo II, Managua

The most interesting event during my time in Nicaragua (and possibly the entire trip) was on a Monday afternoon in a gigantic park, surrounded by socialist 'revolutionaries'. The exuberant celebrations of the country's proudest day were not like anything I've witnessed before, and feel it's unlikely I ever will again.

My involvement began not long after arriving in Managua. Academia Europea was located a couple blocks off the capital's main highway, Carretera Masaya. This was particularly handy as there were a variety of businesses dotted along the road, including a relatively well-stocked supermarket, a modern mall and a row of fast food restaurants. Crucially there was also an internet café with a strong enough connection to download music. I visited la carratera at least once a day, either on my way to or from classes. A few weeks into my daily routine construction started to widen and resurface it. Initially this didn't disturb the flow of traffic. As 19th July approached, the project's centre piece – a large statue of Nicaragua's most famous sportsman – closed a big junction for a fortnight. This caused absolute havoc in a city not renowned for its free-flowing traffic. Horrendously congested roads around the Academy were the reason many of my students suspended their classes (not that the majority needed too much of an excuse to do that).

The syllabus I was employed to teach was shoddy to say the least. I was once reprimanded on a Saturday for not sticking to the scheduled discussion topics, which was talking about abortion and adoption with a class featuring ten teenagers and two nuns. Grateful for a subject of conversation incorporating a local hero, I asked each member of my classes to stand at the front and give their opinion on Nicaragua's sporting champion. The results were astounding.

Alexis Argüello was born on 19th April 1952 and died on 1st July 2009. He was a famous boxer in the 1970's and 1980's, at one point considered by some to be the world's best pound for pound fighter. He had a record of 82 wins, 8 losses and 65 knockouts. Known as the gentleman of the ring, Alexis was inducted into the International Boxing Hall of Fame, and carried his nation's flag at the opening ceremony of 2008's Beijing Olympic Games. In his later years he ran a boxing school and bred cats. The Sandinistas, looking to benefit from his celebrity status, sponsored him as their candidate for Major of

81

Managua - a prestigious position, as over a quarter of the country's population lived in the capital. This move could be adjudged to be a little strange, because Argüello had fought with the Contras against the FSLN during the civil war. A narrow victory was confirmed in November 2008, amid allegations of fraud and intimidation. He committed suicide seven months later.

These were the facts, although apparently not the whole story. One afternoon I asked a class of outspoken mid-20 year olds why they thought their top sportsman and Major would take his own life. The unanimous verdict was that he didn't commit suicide, he was murdered. Latin Americans tended to be advocates of conspiracy theories, so I was sceptical about their outlook. However, the more classes I asked, the more convinced I became.

Argüello's demise wasn't widely covered on the internet. There were articles that questioned the circumstances, but nothing concrete to indicate the actual cause of death. Local television coverage had shown the body as it was taken from his home in Managua, allegedly covered in bruises. The coroners reported that he'd died from a shot through the chest, fired by the deceased using his left hand. Alexis was a right-handed fighter. To summarise the official line: he committed suicide by beating himself up and then shooting himself with the gun in his weaker hand. I'm no expert on these types of things, but that does seem suspicious. Not to Nicaragua's police, the case was closed within 24 hours. Verdict: suicide.

Unsurprisingly in the weeks leading up to the tragedy, Argüello and President Daniel Ortega had a high profile disagreement, after which the Major threatened to leak a story to the national press. I'm not too sure how the Sandinistas thought they were going to have a working relationship with Alexis, especially as they had radically different political ideals. I guess they were happy once the problem had resolved itself. To commemorate this brave Nicaraguan, a year after his sad departure from this world, the least they could do was build an enormous statue of him in the middle of their busiest thoroughfare, causing weeks of disruption. Surely that would prove to the sceptics they couldn't possibly have had anything to do with his death.

I may not have too many positive things to say about the FSLN, but I must confess that I met a lot of party members who were genuinely lovely people. The dodgy local barrio was a Sandinista stronghold. Despite not being a massive fan of their absence of a work ethic and how content they were to raise children in squalid conditions, they were all very friendly to me. The neighbourhood's most prominent socialists were a large family that lived next to my favourite bar, who always chatted to me as I passed to buy litre bottles of Toña. The head of the barrio FSLN association was a good pal of la señora who ran my pharmacy, she regularly enquired as to how the teacher from England was getting along. This would explain why, on a Monday lunchtime I was sat on a chicken bus wearing various pro-Sandinista items, surrounded by familiar faces.

The streets were a sight to behold. Red and black flags and bunting covered the barrio, whilst everyone was out the front of their dwellings showing support for the government. The area's most important party members were chosen to represent the neighbourhood at the main event. Apparently I was one of them.

I was a bit intimidated at first and felt rather stupid wearing a Sandino T-shirt, complimented by a red and black bandanna. Fortunately my best friend – Miss Toña – was also on the bus. A couple of cans later I started getting into the swing of things. The journey to the centre was spectacular; we passed all manner of vehicles full of flag-waving, singing Sandinistas. Strangely, for a city that was so outrageously disorganised, everything went without the slightest hiccup. Even though there were hundreds of thousands of people all turning up to a location which was accessed by a fairly basic road system, there were no traffic jams and we parked without any fuss.

Not allowing the people I recognised to leave my sight, I followed the group as we made our way through the crowds to a spot inside an immense grassy plaza. We were all told what time to be back at the bus and to enjoy the festivities. A blanket was set out; I established my bearings and went to find some refreshments.

Out amongst the seething masses the Toña wore off and a feeling of panic set in. The people I passed tended to fall into two categories: family groups or drunken men, the former being in the minority. A distinct lack of a police presence added to a feeling of lawlessness about proceedings. My sense of unease intensified when I found a vantage point to gaze over the vast crowd, which exceeded a quarter of a million. There was only one way I was ever going to relish that experience. I purchased as many cans as I could carry and a bag of ice, before returning to the sanctity of my comrades.

After an hour or so I felt less overwhelmed and began to relax and joke with those around me. No matter what their political stance, Nicaraguans were enthusiastic and generally intelligent conversationalists. It didn't take long for a token Gringo in Sandinista gear to attract curious locals, an experience not too dissimilar to attending a football match wearing the home team's colours. On a scorching afternoon, as beer flowed, the music on stage became increasingly entertaining, although by the time they'd played it for the fifth time, I was getting a little sick of John Lennon's 'Give Peace a Chance'. Having said that any song by the overrated scouser would have been preferable to the long, tortuous speeches from senior party members that interrupted the music. It was during a laborious discourse that I struck up a conversation with a professor from Managua University.

We had a very interesting discussion focusing mainly on politics. The gaunt, bearded lecturer was intrigued to hear a European view of the FSLN, so I broached the subject of Alexis Argüello. Not wanting to offend him (or those in the vicinity) I approached the topic cautiously, apologising for the information I'd been given by my students, but stating I was keen to know whether he felt it was true. He responded by telling me Daniel Ortega was a friend of the people and had Nicaragua in his heart. I figured that in my tactical approach the question had possibly been misinterpreted, so queried whether he thought Alexis' death was in anyway suspicious. He launched into a sermon about education and how strong their universities were because of government funding. Just to be sure I wasn't being completely stupid I asked the question a third time, but in my native tongue, which he spoke almost fluently. Not constrained by others understanding our exchange, I stated bluntly: 'Was your greatest sportsman murdered?' He replied in English that he was proud of his party and his country.

Needing a refill, I left him to enjoy the visceral rhetoric coming from the stage, disappointed that an academic would be so coy about such a relevant issue, especially as we'd been having an informative debate up to that point. A few more cervezas later and it was time for the man himself to impart his wisdom to the expectant masses. In the socialist scheme of things Daniel Ortega was relatively restrained, his average Revolution Day speech lasted between 45 minutes and an hour. This was bliss in comparison to Venezuelan President Hugo Chávez's three hour tirades.

Slightly bored and possibly feeling the effects of a day drinking in the sun, I set out to find someone who'd accept Alexis Argüello hadn't committed suicide. I can distinctly remember being polite (not at any juncture saying the FSLN had anything to do with his death) and everybody being equally amiable in their responses. Yet not one of them even acknowledged my question, which I felt was open-ended: 'What happened to Alexis?' I got similar replies from the dozen I asked, telling me how Ortega was building hospitals and helping rural communities. Eventually, as I was getting tired and frustrated, the leader of our barrio Sandinista group approached me. She recognised we had freedom of speech in Europe, but warned me that saying the wrong things in Nicaragua would get me into trouble. I reluctantly agreed to behave myself. Once the speech and fireworks were over we all returned to where we came from in a ridiculously efficient and organised manner.

That was pretty much it for my time in Managua. The Academy cut my classes a fortnight earlier than agreed, which I was secretly grateful for. I spent my last three weeks appreciating the plentiful tourist attractions this geographically diverse country had to offer. These included surfing a number of the good Pacific coastal breaks, expeditions into the beautiful green mountains covered in coffee plantations around Jinotega, and spending time on remote Isla de Ometepe. This island was incredibly striking, its twin volcano cones rising out of mysterious Lago de Nicaragua, purported to be the habitat of rare freshwater sharks.

At August's Hipica celebrations in the capital (a weird kind of horse parade which was just an excuse to get drunk) one of my former students - who was employed as a promotional dancer for a mobile phone company - invited me to dinner the following day. This was the start of a brief but interesting liaison which gave me an insight into Managua's social scene. Originally from Estelí, her family were all FSLN members. On our first official date we attended a pro-Sandinista heavy metal concert. The frontman entertained us by screaming about romantic topics such as child prostitution and capitalism raping the proletariat.

Now there is a large distance between me and Nicaragua I do look back on my time there with a great deal of fondness. After three months working on a Mexican nudist beach my next job was always going to pale significantly in comparison, and most weeks I did struggle to enjoy my daily life. On the positive side I left with my internal batteries fully recharged, ready to take on South America.

In my opinion it was an amazingly complex and at times contradictory place, but also fairly raw and undiscovered. The Sandinistas controlled the main institutions since they seized power in 1979, so democratic governments were never really able to effect positive changes. When Daniel Ortega has not officially been in power

85

he 'rules the country from below' via FSLN-controlled bodies. Whilst he is alive I don't envisage much altering in this regard. Also, it's hard to see any major foreign companies investing in a nation governed by socialists who haven't bothered to complete the simple task of naming their capital's streets. Maybe that's a good thing. After all there aren't many countries in Latin America that stood up to US colonialism and theoretically succeeded.

Season 3

COSTA RICA

Population – 4 million
Size – 51,000 km^2
Time Zone – GMT $^-$6
Currency - Colón
FIFA World Ranking – #69 (2010)
Best World Cup Finish – Quarter Final (2014)
Biggest Teams – Deportivo Saprissa, Ajaluelense, Herediano

You might have heard of:
Paulo Wanchope, Bryan Ruiz, Keylor Navas, Joel Campbell

Essential Spanish:
Puerto Viejo – Old Port
Copa – Cup
Libertadores – Liberators

Game 15

Deportivo Saprissa v Marathón - (CONCACAF CL) - 4 v 1
Thursday 26th August 2010 – 21:00
Estadio Ricardo Saprissa Aymá, San José

My third football season in the Americas began in Costa Rica's capital. Saprissa were the country's most decorated side and CONCACAF champions on three occasions (the only non-Mexican team). The Purple Monster dominated their domestic league, and was one of the most successful Central and North American sides. Consequently I was quite excited to see them play Marathón, who'd been fairly abysmal when I'd seen them in the San Pedro Sula clásico.

The new season's curtain raiser was the Copa Libertadores final, which was staged later in the year than usual due to the World Cup. Brazilian heavyweights, Internacional, took a goal advantage into their second leg home tie against Mexico's Chivas de Guadalajara. The visitors, without Chicharito following his summer transfer to Manchester United, stunned their hosts by taking an early lead. After the interval Inter dominated and won by scoring three goals in the last half an hour. The match finished on a rather unsavoury note as Chivas proved they were in no way sore losers by trying out various lucha libre wrestling moves on their opposition.

As I set out into the humid San José night it started raining, not drizzle but a torrential, tropical downpour. During a short taxi ride to Estadio Ricardo Saprissa Aymá I discovered they didn't sell cerveza inside Costa Rican venues. Hence I watched the opening exchanges in a bar by the ticket office, observing a lively affair which saw both teams attacking with pace. Against the odds and run of play, Marathón were the first to register, through a deflected 40 yard strike. It was all square at the break, Saprissa equalising from a set piece. The evening's decisive moment came just before half time, whilst I was wandering around getting wet trying to buy a ticket. Superbly named Honduran winger, Randy Diamond, was shown a red card for kicking Saprissa's goalkeeper in the head.

The 24,000 all seated stadium's size and design, boasting three tiered side stands, was similar to an English ground. It was unique because the grass pitch was replaced with synthetic turf in 2003, the first of its kind in Latin America. Following their traditional national arena's demise, Costa Rica's Selección played at the home of Saprissa in 2005. They hosted the first World Cup qualifying match ever to be contested on an artificial surface.

When the game recommenced I sat in the sheltered upper tier, as Saprissa pressed and went ahead early on. The goal was greeted by ecstatic celebrations from La Ultra Morada barra in the south end. It was quite a spectacle seeing 500 drenched lunatics huddled together, jumping from side to side in time to their banging drums. Even with a numerical disadvantage Marathón threatened on the counterattack and were unlucky not to equalise. In the end they lost heavily, Saprissa scored two simple goals in the last quarter of an hour.

Although relatively uneventful off the field in comparison to other fixtures I'd seen, all in all it was a good start to the new season. It was a year that saw Saprissa make it to the CONCACAF semi-finals, where Utah's Real Salt Lake eliminated them 3 v 2 on aggregate. Predictably a Mexican club lifted the trophy; Monterrey won the final by the odd goal in five.

I didn't spend much time in Costa Rica, after Nicaragua it seemed too sanitised and developed. Central America's richest nation had many interesting tourist attractions and had successfully marketed them to foreigners for decades. It had strong ties with North American countries and benefitted from a long period of political stability, aided by not having a standing army for over half a century.

A couple of nights regularly hearing Yankee accents whilst trying to avoid the advances of San José's numerous prostitutes inspired me to take a bus to the Caribbean coastal town of Puerto Viejo. Expensive accommodation and an over-infested Gringo population encouraged me to cross the border as quickly as possible. I spent four months in Nicaragua and five days in Costa Rica.

PANAMA

Population – 3.5 million
Size – 75,500 km^2
Time Zone – GMT $^-$6
Currency – US Dollar
FIFA World Ranking – #64 (2010)
Best World Cup Finish – Have never qualified
Biggest Teams – Tauro, San Francisco, Árabe Unido

You might have heard of:
The Panama Canal, Manuel Noriega, Luis Tejada

Essential Spanish:
Bien hecho muchachos – Well done boys
La Marea Roja – The Red Tide

Game 16

Panama v Costa Rica - (International Friendly) - 2 v 2
Friday 3rd September 2010 – 21:00
Estadio Rommel Fernández Gutiérrez, Panama City

Panama revitalised my travelling spirits after I'd found Costa Rica wasn't really to my liking. Situated close to the border and appropriately named David, the nation's second largest city was a relatively unspectacular place. Nonetheless it had lively sports bars, friendly people and cold Bud in the supermarket for $0.65.

An eight hour bus ride through fairly mundane scenery to Panama City was very comfortable. Upon arrival I flagged a local service to a recommended centrally-located hostel. It took almost an hour fighting choking traffic and then another half an hour on foot, sweating and going round in circles, trying to find a place that'd closed the previous month. It wouldn't have been too bad, but it was the third time that week I'd attempted to stay in accommodations listed in my guidebook; only to discover it was shut. Defeated (and smelling like a French person on a good day) I hailed a taxi to the old colonial district of San Felipe.

I spent the best part of a week in Panama City trying to organise a boat to Colombia whilst seeing the sights. Considering its distance from any other significant civilised centre, it was like a strange urban oasis. Its location on the Bay of Panama facing the Pacific Ocean, with skyscrapers and Spanish forts within walking distance of each other, undoubtedly made it one of the most individual capitals I'd ever visited. The population was a cosmopolitan mix, consisting of a large concentration of Asians and a strong European influence.

The isthmus connecting North and South America had historically been of international strategic importance, but this intensified after the Panama Canal was completed in 1914. The basis of the country's economy was truly an astonishing accomplishment; it provided a passageway from Atlantic to Pacific. In 2010 the average toll was over US$50,000, making it one of the world's most expensive waterways. As there were approximately 50 transits per day, it was certainly a very valuable facility. So guess which nation had its grubby fingers all over it for a century? It wasn't the French, who launched the project but abandoned it 1893 after losing over 20,000 workers to disease.

Uncle Sam was the one to take up the mantle. Eventually construction was concluded just before the First World War started. In doing so the Canal Zone was formed, an area of eight kilometres on either side of the channel, which was to all intents and purposes US territory. For 60 years tensions between Panama and the US fluctuated, until 1977 when Democratic President Jimmy Carter signed a treaty promising to handover control at the turn of the century. But that didn't work for Ronald Regan, who loved meddling in Central American affairs. In a bid to maintain control over this valuable asset whilst also fighting their Cold War enemy - communism - he vetoed the instillation of a military dictatorship, headed by the delightful 'General' Manuel Noriega.

Having been on the CIA's books since the 1950's and trained by George W Bush senior, Noriega's appointment was regarded as one of the biggest foreign policy cockups ever, in a rich history of US gaffs. He allowed free presidential elections in 1984, and seeing his chosen candidate losing by a substantial margin, stopped the voting, made a few adjustments and announced victory. His rule was characterised by violently suppressing public protests, murdering anyone opposed to him and assisting Colombian drug cartels trafficking their goods to North America. When he refused to hand over power after 1989's elections, the US, by then under Noriega's old chum Señor Bush, ousted the dictator by invading Panama City. The self-proclaimed General was captured and shipped off to Miami, where he stood trial for his crimes and was incarcerated for 18 years. In cleaning up the mess they created the US were responsible for the deaths of over 100 Panamanian civilians, and left more than 20,000 homeless. ¡Bien hecho muchachos!

As weird and wonderful as exploring Panama City was, I also wanted to see football. In this case it was the only full international fixture of my trip, and between neighbouring countries, the term friendly couldn't have been less accurate. My journey to Estadio Rommel Fernández Gutiérrez lasted an hour and a half. The bus filled up, emptied and filled up again, whilst there was a torrential rainstorm outside. Once I'd reached my destination the skies had cleared and it was a pleasantly cool evening. Initial signs weren't good, there were long queues snaking all the way around the ground and a distinct lack of tickets for sale. It took a lap to work out the tie was a sell-out. A little deflated, I sat in the forecourt of a nearby petrol station drinking beer with the employees, watching the opening exchanges on an antique TV.

Resigned to the fact that I'd not conducted my research properly and was bound to miss a few matches on the trip, I returned to the main entrance to take photos. As I stood at a gate trying to make my camera zoom, a bulky dark-skinned guy ambled past waving tickets in the air. Within a matter of minutes I'd paid $20 (twice face value) and was in the stands next to delirious Panamanian football fans.

What a scene it was. The 32,000 capacity, partially-constructed huge bowl of a venue was full to the brim with jumping bodies. I tried to locate my seat, but there really wasn't any kind of order to proceedings and nobody was sitting anyway. At the petrol station I'd seen La Marea Roja (as Panama's national team were known) getting off to a poor start. With less than ten minutes on the clock Costa Rica scored a soft free kick, the keeper managing to dive over the ball from a standing position. I'd entered the fray at just the right time. On the half hour mark, following a passage of uncharacteristically incisive football, Panama equalised - star striker Luis Tejada pounced after Costa Rica's shot-stopper had parried. The crowd erupted. By the time everyone had calmed down and the scorer had finished a lap of honour, I found myself four rows away from where I was prior to the goal. Ten minutes later Tejada was presented with a second, a free kick rebounded off the post straight into his path, allowing him to gratefully slot home. This time the celebrations included supporters invading the field, requiring riot police to restore order. When the game eventually got back underway the remaining five minutes of the half was a crescendo of noise, all manners of drums and horns, shouting and screaming blending together in joyous rhapsody. Consequently I had a splitting headache at the break when I strode across the concourse, trying to find some refreshments.

When St. Andrews' bar opens at half time I'm normally good at getting served quickly. Being relatively slight in stature I can usually squirm my way to the front easily, which is exactly what I did here. I stood at this bar for 15 minutes but didn't even get close to purchasing a cerveza. Firstly, I wasn't shouting loudly or aggressively enough at the bar ladies. Secondly, I wasn't throwing enough polystyrene boxes about. Within minutes it dawned on me the guys with the boxes were selling cups of Balboa for an inflated price. They were bribing the bar staff so they got priority service. What fascinated me most (and the reason I stood observing the chaos for so long) was the way ordinary punters were trying to get served. It was a complete range of emotions from pleading to threatening, and a pointless exercise as they were only selling to the vendors anyway. Having more than two operational barrels for a whole tier of spectators would have made sense, but then sensible wasn't a word I often associated with Latin American football. A simple solution was to buy a cup of overpriced beer from the vendors, who weren't even leaving the concourse before selling out.

The second period was marginally less exciting on the pitch, but was full value entertainment in the stands. I changed ends, and my new companions were busy choreographing a group dance move when I arrived. Approximately 30 people in front of me were shuffling four or five steps from left to right, throwing their hands in the air, singing and repeating the movement in the opposite direction. This was accompanied by a guy with a snare drum and much handclapping from the dancers. It was rather repetitive, but soon got inside my head. I found myself clapping and shuffling with them, but in a reserved, English way. The dance was then interrupted by a 20 minute Mexican wave, which circled the stadium numerous times with total crowd participation. In the midst of all this Costa Rica equalised. Although Panama had the best chances, a draw appeared to be a fair result.

I ended up crossing paths with a number of Panama's Selección on show against Costa Rica, later in my trip, playing for various clubs. At right back that night was Luis Moreno, who caused uproar during his short stint at Colombian side Deportivo Pereira. Whilst attempting to clear his lines - as his team were losing 2 v 1 to Junior in Barranquilla - the ball took a deflection off a grey owl which had found its way onto the pitch. Not particularly pleased with the bird's contribution, Moreno walked up to where it lay on the floor (dazed after being hit by a football) and kicked the creature into touch. Unfortunately for the Panamanian defender the owl in question was Junior's unofficial mascot and the incident was broadcast live on national television. Moreno had to issue a public apology, he was fined, banned for two games and endured chants of 'murderer' from opposition fans wherever he went. The owl died the day after the match.

Next on my tour was Colombia. I'd travelled all the way from Cancun to Panama over land and was keen to go as far as possible without resorting to flying. For the majority of my journey I'd been on the Pan-American Highway, which had taken me from Guatemala City to Panama City. This road continued south from the Panamanian capital for a short distance, but abruptly ended in an area called the Darién Gap, a wild region of uncultivated rainforest stretching over 100 kilometres between Panama and Colombia. Whilst it was possible to cross from Central to South America through the Darién Gap, it wasn't a safe expedition. There had been all too frequent stories of robbery, extortion, kidnapping, murders and individuals simply disappearing. This was not surprising considering it was the frontier between one of the world's most prolific narcotic producing countries, and a pivotal shipping lane. Wanting to avoid a 'Proof of Life' situation, I decided to opt for a less dangerous route and sail on a private yacht.

This was a well-established excursion. My hostel presented me with a variety of vessels, all sailing on different days. The timing was key as I wanted to attend the friendly and arrive in time for Colombia's north coast derby the following weekend. My options were fairly limited, which is why I found myself on a tiny boat crewed by a Spanish captain and a Colombian first mate. Joining me aboard the SY Frederica was an English couple and a Swiss couple.

It was all pretty civilised to begin with; setting sail from a fishing village 30 kilometres outside of Panama City, to the backdrop of a fiery sunset. We spent a few peaceful days moored around the San Blas Archipelago - an arc of small tropical isles inhabited by the native Kuna tribe. Local villagers seemed quite welcoming to the tourist presence and the revenue stream that accompanied it. Each afternoon a handful of wooden canoes passed the collection of anchored leisure craft, happily selling their day's catch, including large lobsters for $2 apiece.

The reefs weren't in the same league as the Bay Islands or Caye Caulker, but still provided some good snorkelling opportunities. I found it sad that there was no real regulation of the boats that passed through the area, as on more than one occasion our captain destroyed sections of coral whilst dropping anchor. Ecotourism is big business, but as far as I'm concerned it is almost a contradiction in terms. The impact of tourism, no matter how minimal, is generally negative on the environment, irrelevant of whether your shower is solar-powered or not.

The last 36 hours of our four day voyage was a straight sail across the Caribbean. We obtained our exit stamp from a remote immigration post, the captain turned on his autopilot, and we sat back as the boat chugged along at 15 kilometres per hour. It was a strange day and a half surrounded by nothing but water. I completed the first lookout shift from dusk to the early hours, sitting on the bow starring out into pitch black nothingness, making sure we didn't collide with any of the non-existent obstacles.

By the next afternoon cabin fever set in, my fellow passengers were getting restless. This was mainly attributable to the Swiss guy

96

finishing off a massive bag of cocaine on his own prior to reaching Colombian customs. He stalked the short deck with a crazed look in his eyes, complaining about the quality of food available (not that he was in a fit state to eat anyway). Fortunately the arrival of a pod of dolphins calmed the mood on board. A group of grey mammals splashed and played around the craft for 20 minutes before swimming off into the distance.

As darkness fell on our final evening the night sky was illuminated by Cartagena's bright lights even though we were 12 hours from our destination. The closer we got the more passing traffic we saw, which was comforting after a whole day of not seeing another vessel. I volunteered for first watch again, but quickly handed over the responsibility when an autopilot glitch sent our boat careering towards an oncoming oil tanker. A hasty manoeuvre, some urgent shouting between captain and first mate, and a lot of bobbing up and down later, we were back on course.

COLOMBIA

Population – 46 million
Size – 1.1 million km²
Time Zone – GMT ⁻5
Currency - Peso
FIFA World Ranking – #48 (2010)
Best World Cup Finish – Quarter Finals (2014)
Biggest Teams – América de Cali, Millonarios, Atlético Nacional

You might have heard of:
Pablo Escobar, Andrés Escobar, Faustino Asprilla, René Higuita,
Carlos Valderrama, Hugo Rodallega, Radamel Falcao, James
Rodríguez, Símon Bolívar

Essential Spanish:
Costa – Coast
Juventud – Youth
Ciudad Perdida – Lost City
Blanco – White
Somos – We are
Dios – God
Entrada – Entrance/Ticket
El Astronomo – The Astronomer
Como No – How Not?
Violencia – Violence
El Mono – The monkey
Yo No Sé Mañana – I don't know tomorrow

Game 17

Real Cartagena v Junior – (Liga Postobon) - 1 v 1
Saturday 11th September 2010 – 20:30
Estadio Olímpico Jamie Morón León, Cartagena

Down the rabbit hole I went. I'm not sure whether it was when riot police covered the crowd around me with pepper spray, or when two vicious teenagers tried to drag me off a bus, I realised: watching football in South America was going to be a wholly different prospect to what I'd already experienced.

Saturday had started with SY Frederica's bedraggled crew sailing in glorious sun towards a hazy collection of skyscrapers which represented our destination, Cartagena. Once docked and on dry land, swaying after four days at sea, the five passengers shared a taxi to a hostel. Upon discovering the fixture was that day I was slightly relieved (and not at all surprised) when my companions decided they didn't want to accompany me. Some good food and a nap later, a minibus driver was telling me to sit next to him in the front seat, as I couldn't count a new currency and was delaying his departure. After much coin inspecting and a half hour journey, I was dropped-off at a set of traffic lights and pointed in the right direction. My route took me through the middle of a shopping centre, which was enjoyable due to the abundance of Colombian girls; I shall revisit that subject later. Following a 20 minute march along a boulevard past strolling families, I arrived at the compact Estadio Jamie Morón León. Against the advice of people I was chatting to in a bar, I purchased the cheapest ticket available, in with La Revolución Auri-Verde Norte barra brava.

I'd been looking forward to this game as not only was it my first in South America; it was also el clásico de la costa. Cartagena were taking on their larger and more successful rival from Barranquilla, located a two hour drive up the coast. Junior, known as the Sharks, resided in an imposing 50,000 capacity arena and were reigning champions, after winning 2010's Apertura. I was therefore not expecting Real to open the scoring inside 20 minutes. The goal prompted a reaction from the home barra the likes of which I'd not seen outside Reading Festival's mosh pit. There were approximately 1,500 of them moving up and down the terracing, pushing, shoving and grabbing each other. Although I'd bravely opted to go in the fanatical section, I was drinking flat cerveza in a passive area close to a big family (there wasn't many members, they were really fat).

At half time I went to refill my cup with the stale syrup that was being sold under the pretence of beer. I noticed several of the barra were posing for pictures next to impressive-looking banners. Keen to get a good Zulu Army shot, I sauntered along the front row and within seconds I was approached by a guy trying to communicate in English. I responded in Spanish and soon our conversation evolved from the games I'd attended to English football hooliganism. During the exchange I made the mistake of getting my wallet out to show him ticket stubs from Panama and Costa Rica. When Colombian flags were brought out and we were all having photos taken, a kid tried to snatch the wallet out my front pocket. He slipped as he leant forward, missing his target; instead he groped my arse to balance himself. Shocked, I turned around. He just looked at me expressionlessly and returned to where he'd been sitting seconds beforehand.

I have to say the reaction from the barra (all of whom knew him by his first name) was outstanding. Some of them were swearing, telling him off and the guy who had originally spoken to me gave him a slap. Another lad produced an identification card and shepherded me away. When he took me to an official and described what had happened, I figured he was a police cadet who wanted me to point out the perpetrator so he could be arrested. Not wishing to create any more of a scene, I thanked him and explained I'd already caused enough trouble. He understood, and the officer had very little interest in either of us. We made small talk whilst some of his friends came over to proudly show me their tattoos - rather bizarrely one had 'Skinhead' in large letters across the top of his back.

I returned to the comfortable companionship of the obese family and spent much of the second half shaking my head thinking about what had occurred, whilst Junior equalised from a corner with a quarter of an hour remaining. At full time I was looking to get out of there as quickly as possible, but was blocked by a line of riot police. In a move unfamiliar to me at the time, the authorities were letting the visiting fans leave whilst retaining the home contingent. By the time the barra had untied their flags, organised themselves and started their procession out of the ground, we'd been waiting patiently for ten minutes to be allowed past. But the barra wouldn't be stopped. A column of sweaty, shirtless bodies pushed right through the middle of where we were standing and began confronting the officers.

It took 30 seconds for me to realise that this was not going to be pretty. The barra at the front were remonstrating with the men in uniform, whilst those towards the rear were pushing everyone forward, forcing the officers to retreat. I squeezed my way out of the throng to take a position at the top of the uncovered stand just in time to observe the police shouting a warning (to a response of insults) followed by streams of red liquid being shot into the air. That was when all chaos broke loose. Initially the scene was one of people covered in a red dye, coughing, crying and reeling away from the exit. Within minutes the group had recovered enough to be angry. All of a sudden the police were backing off at a modest pace as the hordes surged forward. Seeing this as a good an opportunity as any, I jogged along the top of the terrace to the gates. There was no immediate backup, so I slipped down and out the exit.

As we streamed out I asked an inebriated young guy next to me why they'd kept us inside for so long. Apparently it was because the juventud were going to cause trouble. He wasn't wrong. The dual carriageway outside the ground had already turned into a mini battlefield between the police, Real and Junior thugs. It appeared to me the rival barra had joined forces to fight the authorities, although my account at this point is not entirely accurate. I was too busy running to catch a bus frantically doing a U-turn to escape the mayhem.

On the opposite side of the road a retreating driver kindly opened his doors to allow me aboard. I'd taken two steps onto the vehicle when I felt someone grab my shirt. I spun around to be confronted by the teenager who I'd just been speaking to. I'm not quite sure what his intentions were, but he was very keen for me to leave the bus. Aided by an accomplice, they struggled to drag me back out onto the street. Much like the incident at Huembes market in Managua, I spent half a minute fighting the pair whilst trying to maintain my position on the steps. I believe the driver was the one who saved me. Once he saw I had a grip on a handrail, he accelerated sharply, causing the two youths to lose their hold on me and fall backwards. I gratefully thanked him and gingerly found a seat, while the other passengers enquired about my wellbeing. They were all really nice and despite not going to the centre, the driver made a slight detour to ensure I safely hailed a taxi. I returned to my sailing companions, visibly shaken, but with the unmistakable pulse of adrenalin rushing through my veins.

It was a shame I didn't have more time to spend exploring Colombia's north coast. Cartagena was a gorgeous city of cobbled streets, colonial buildings and an interesting history as Spain's main Caribbean port for centuries. Pirate raids, buccaneer sieges and impregnable fortifications were part of stories about this modern metropolis and tourist resort.

Attractions further north such as Ciudad Perdida and Tayrona national park's paradisiacal beaches seemed enticing, but it would have required backtracking to continue south. Plus I'd no interest in going anywhere near the socialist lunatic asylum that was Venezuela.

This country had some stunning natural features including the world's highest waterfall, Salto Ángel. However, I'd spent too much time in Nicaragua where the governmental worship of their President, one of the most outspoken men in world politics, bordered on obsessional. Hugo Chávez's regular public speeches, which at times were better defined as tirades or rants, involved describing President Bush (junior) as the devil who leaves a satanic smell of sulphur behind him. He perceived himself as a Latin American David, fighting the North American Goliath. If he wasn't the leader of a major oil producer, I'm convinced he'd have gotten a fraction of the attention he craved. In any case, I had no interest in taking a huge detour to visit a place controlled by someone who'd created his own time zone. By putting Venezuela's clocks back half an hour, Chávez ensured he was theoretically in a different zone to his bitter enemy, the US. Also taking money out of Venezuelan banks cost twice as much as exchanging US dollars on the black market. What's more, in this wonderland of a continent, I had a footballing white rabbit to follow.

Game 18

Itagüí Ditaires v Atlético Nacional – (Copa Postobon QF) - 4 v 0
Wednesday 15th September 2010 – 20:00
Estadio Atanasio Girardot, Medellín

At 19:53 I was stood on Itagüí Metro station, kicking myself for not checking the venue's address or listening to the receptionist at my hotel. Itagüí was a small town on the outskirts of Medellín. As they were the home side, I'd attempted to get to their ground in time for kick-off. Upon arrival a taxi driver informed me the tie was being played at Nacional's stadium, in the city centre. It was testament to Colombia's public transport system and a helpful 'paisa' couple (people from Medellín) that I was stood on the terrace at 20:36.

It was the Copa Colombia quarter-final, which at the time was titled Copa Postobon. The Primera División, second tier and national cup was sponsored by a drinks manufacturer, Postobon. This match was billed as a clásico due to the geographical proximity of the two teams. On paper it was an intriguing encounter between the second division champions elect and Medellín's struggling powerhouse. Fortunately after I'd arrived at the correct Metro station (cunningly named Estadio) downed a cup of beer, jogged to the entrance, was searched on three separate occasions and taken my place in the stands, I'd not missed much. Nacional had been awarded a questionable early penalty, but it remained level following a smart save. Within minutes of my arrival Itagüí scored the only goal of the half, a neatly clipped finish over Nacional's keeper.

Estadio Atanasio Girardot, a beast of a massive open, curvaceous, two tiered Olympic-style stadium, was sparsely populated. I was in the vocal Los del Sur barra section with the majority of the supporters. Both sides and the other end were almost empty. It looked like there wasn't any visiting faithful – well none that were brave enough to celebrate their goal. After my experiences in Cartagena I was a little wary of the barra, so stood on the periphery. I was just acclimatising myself to the new surroundings, wondering where the unmistakeable smell of weed was coming from, when a group of five youths in front of me pulled out a 12 inch hunting knife. Before I could say 'please don't rob me' they'd distributed a bag of white powder onto the blade, cut some rough-looking lines and were passing it around. In a weird way it was quite satisfying to see this stereotypical image of

Colombia unfolding before me. What puzzled me was: how did they manage to get a weapon that size past three lines of police searches?

Whilst wandering about at the interval I worked out who was smoking marijuana... everyone! The smell was present in all corners of the terrace. I spent the early part of the second period nervously trying to determine the best place to have my Zulu Army photo, without attracting too much unwanted attention. I eventually opted to ask a reasonably sensible-looking guy with glasses. It was a funny shot because within seconds of pulling my St. George's cross out, a 12 year old (who'd begged a bit of kebab off me at half time) suddenly appeared with a green Nacional flag, posed and disappeared - all in the space of a minute.

The 'home' side ran riot after the break, scoring three more goals, including a glorious 30 yard free kick. Both teams finished with ten men; Itagüí's goalkeeper was sent off under comical circumstances for timewasting. What astonished me was the way Los del Sur barra were completely unfazed by the poor performance. They sang and danced constantly throughout, in fact Itagüí's fourth goal triggered the most vociferous song involving throwing umbrellas and pushing people. There wasn't even booing or jeering at the final whistle, which I found remarkable.

But not as remarkable as the return leg. Six days later the second fixture was held at Estadio Atanasio Girardot, observed by a similar-sized crowd. Itagüí took the lead in the first half, increasing their advantage to five on aggregate. Nacional pulled two back prior to the interval and scored three more afterwards to take the tie to penalties. Itagüí went on to win 5 v 4, their keeper impressively saved Nacional's 5th penalty and then stepped up to dispatch the decisive kick himself. The minnows were soundly beaten by Cali in the final, but gained promotion shortly after.

Nacional, along with Millonarios and América, were considered to be the nation's biggest three clubs. One of their famous former players was a name synonymous with Medellín – Escobar. Andrés was born and raised in Colombia's third largest city; he signed professional terms with the green and whites aged 21 and was a key member of 1989's Copa Libertadores winning squad. He was capped 51 times, scoring his only goal against England at Wembley. After a stint at Young Boys in Switzerland he returned to Nacional, and was part of the highly rated Selección which arrived at the 1994 World Cup finals. His unfortunate own goal in the second group match saw them eliminated from the competition. Drug cartels, who'd staked a lot of cash on Colombia qualifying, didn't appreciate Escobar's contribution to their failure. Two weeks later he was shot 12 times in the car park of a Medellín restaurant. The assassin, a crime lord bodyguard, admitted his crime and was released from prison after serving an 11 year sentence.

Game 19

Independiente Medellín v Envigado – (Liga Postobon) - 2 v 2
Saturday 19th September 2010 – 16:00
Estadio Atanasio Girardot, Medellín

I was back at Estadio Atanasio Girardot on a grey, miserable Saturday afternoon for Independiente Medellín's league game against local adversaries Envigado. Following my idiotic midweek detour I arrived with plenty of time to spare. In terms of organisation, football clubs in South America were a lot different to their British counterparts. Each one generally tended to be a sporting association which sustained a football squad, in addition to a range of other sports teams competing at the top level, most prominently volleyball and basketball. Meandering around the complex on match day I'd not expected to see so much activity. On another football pitch there was a well-attended women's fixture, in a cavernous sports hall was a national juvenile gymnastics meeting, and in the stadium's bleachers, a provincial judo tournament. There were even groups of bare-chested men and bikini-clad women playing beach volleyball in the rain, next to an Olympic swimming pool.

For the second time in four days I was witnessing a clásico of sorts, as Envigado's ground was less than 20 kilometres from Medellín. In Colombian terms (a country approximately the same size as France, Spain and Portugal combined) this was considered a short distance, although yet again there wasn't a visiting contingent. As the city's two clubs shared their home it made sense that either set of barra had their own end. Independiente were the less successful side, their five domestic titles and lack of international trophies paled in comparison to Nacional's achievements. The support for this league tie was numerically inferior to that of their rival's midweek cup disaster.

La Rexixtenxia Norte barra still had a strong presence, including an array of banners, flags, umbrellas and an energetic band. In addition to the pounding of numerous drums, there was a dominant horn section that elevated the mood in the terrace. After ten minutes they set the tone by breaking out a version of 'Rivers of Babylon' with lyrics subtly questioning the parentage of Nacional's fans. Even in the persistent drizzle, wearing what could only be described as a large plastic bag, I couldn't resist moving about a bit. I was a little dismayed I'd left my Mickey Mouse poncho (found on the floor at game 1) at my hotel, as 15 rows in front of me were two spectators wearing the same hideous yellow jackets. At least theirs appeared to be adult size. It took the stupidly dressed pair nearly until half time to get up and dance with the rest of the crowd, a flawless version of Culture Club's 'Karma Chameleon' did the trick.

It wasn't a bad contest; the hosts went one up from a corner after a quarter of an hour and the visitors responded just before the interval with a cleverly headed free kick. The second period didn't really come alive until the 90th minute. Independiente midfielder Barahona went down in the area under a soft challenge and was awarded a spot kick. After a lengthy delay to proceedings (during which an Envigado player was sent off) Barahona, a Panamanian international who'd been influential in game 16, stepped up and converted confidently. This sparked wild celebrations both on and off the pitch, which continued for the remaining two minutes of injury time. While everybody was jumping around Envigado equalised straight from the restart. It was a strange end to a gloomy afternoon.

I spent the best part of my week in Medellín exploring its modern commercial centre and strolling next to families in public parks. It was difficult to imagine that less than 20 years ago this was one of the most dangerous urban areas in the world. The man people ordinarily identified with the city's violent past was Pablo Escobar. At the height of his powers he was believed to be one of the world's ten richest men, and the most affluent criminal ever. Born into poverty, he fast-tracked his way from petty thief to drug baron. There were so many myths surrounding Escobar it was very difficult to discern fact from fiction. He garnered a public image of being a Robin Hood-style character, building homes and football pitches in underprivileged neighbourhoods. Escobar was obsessed with animals and built a zoo on his Hacienda Nápoles estate, paying millions of dollars to import hippos and other exotic creatures. Once he even offered to settle Colombia's foreign debt.

But there was also a dark side to Pablo. He was at war with a variety of bodies such as Cali's cartels and both the Colombian and US governments. His rival drug lords from the south built their operations comparatively unobtrusively, often pretending to be legitimate businessmen. While the Cali organisations tended to use the threat of death as their tool, Medellín was renowned for violence and brutality. In the north there was a time when Escobar paid hit men $1,000 for each police officer they killed, and his involvement in national politics saw three presidential candidates murdered in the same campaign.

107

He ultimately negotiated his own surrender on the understanding that he would be incarcerated in his own luxurious jail, called 'The Cathedral', but this didn't stop him from continuing his business ventures. Public opinion turned against him and he was targeted by the families of his victims, as well as his aforementioned enemies. Pablo Escobar's life came to an end in December 1993 when he was gunned down by Colombian police on a suburban rooftop.

There was undoubtedly a seedy side to certain areas I visited in Medellín, including an open red-light district where sex and drugs were flagrantly for sale. Nevertheless, I didn't ever feel unsafe at any stage. To me walking the streets of Managua was a more precarious pastime, and I was surprised at the abundance of proud and affluent people roaming around. Geographically it was quite an imposing place, encircled by steep hills which enclosed the metropolis into a long valley. To get a panoramic view I climbed the narrow streets, past tall tower blocks clinging precariously to the slopes, up to a lookout. The first thing I noticed from my vantage point was small to medium-size aeroplanes having to manoeuvre sharply to negotiate the airport's tight runway. It was interesting to think how much airborne traffic in the 1980's and 1990's was funded by Señor Escobar. This lofty perch gave me a good perspective on Medellín and Colombian life in general. Urban and green spaces blended together much like the wealthy and impoverished sections of society, at times they were indistinguishable.

As there was a whole week until my next fixture I looked to spend time touring La Zona Cafetera, where Colombia's other famously exported crop was grown. It was at this juncture I discerned that this country was different to others in the Americas - it was necessary to barter the price of your bus ticket. My fare from Cartagena (even though it was a 20 hour journey) had seemed excessive. It wasn't until I was at Medellín's main terminal I gathered the tariff was approximately a third cheaper than advertised; it was all about haggling. Luckily there was a nice Kiwi couple wandering around, equally as confused by the situation. We teamed up, and after some firm bargaining got a private minivan for half the original price. Bizarrely the chirpy New Zealanders' were dental tourists. One of the many things cartels poured their illicit earnings into was universities; so Colombia boasted some of the world's cheapest and best dentists. Apparently the root canal work recently undertaken was the most comfortable and painless procedure they'd ever endured.

We spent a few days in the picturesque, Swiss-looking student town of Manizales, home to Once Caldas FC. I visited their stadium one afternoon. As it was under reconstruction for the upcoming Under 20 World Cup, I ambled through an open gate and sat writing in the stands. I was annoyed I didn't get to see a match at Estadio Palogrande as it looked to be incredibly atmospheric. In 2004 it was the setting for el blanco's finest hour, winning the Copa Libertadores on penalties against Argentina's Boca Juniors. To be honest it was an uneventful week of travelling through the coffee region, so I was kind of glad when I was staring out a bus window, on a treacherous road winding up the side of a rain swept mountain, towards the capital.

Game 20

Millonarios v América de Cali – (Liga Postobon) - 2 v 0
Saturday 25th September 2010 – 18:20
Estadio Nemesio Camacho (El Campín), Bogotá

I was really enjoying my time in Colombia, but had been disappointed with the attendances at the three clásicos I'd been to. It appeared the term didn't hold as much significance for Latinos as it did for us in Europe. To put this theory to the test I went to el clásico con mas estrellas (the derby with most stars) between the country's two most decorated clubs. Possessing a record 13 titles each, it would be fair to describe these two old foes as the Manchester United and Liverpool of Colombian football. However, both were out of form coming into the game and were more concerned about relegation than adding to their collection of championships.

Negotiating Bogotá's complicated transport system to get to the venue took a little while. In the end following people wearing football shirts paid dividends. Arriving disgustingly early I drank beers in a café, dividing my time between watching a live televised fixture and Los Comandos Azules barra with their band, theatrically entering El Campín as if it was some form of religious ritual. The drummers held their instruments high above their head, while youths manically waved flags behind them. Slowly and deliberately they climbed a large external staircase to the upper tier's concourse, singing the same song throughout. They generated a hell of a racket as it was clearly audible across a sizeable car park, main road and over the television commentators. Then without any warning they vanished into the ground.

As skies darkened and the players mimed their way through the clubs' anthems, I bought a replica shirt and a ticket (combined cost $15) before braving the security checks. It was the tightest controls to date, three lines of riot police intent on preventing anything even resembling a weapon from getting past them. I had to plead for five minutes that I needed to keep my metal belt buckle - it was the only one I owned and I'd no desire to remove it from my belt and throw it as my jeans would fall down. Eventually they let me past with all my items of clothing intact.

Within five minutes of being inside I realised the atmosphere was finally going to live up to my expectations. I couldn't get into the lower tier, the crowds spilled back so far it was impossible to see the pitch. In the upper tier I squeezed into an entrance and managed to push along a row to where there was enough space to stand without treading on anyone. Then I had to jump up and down. It wasn't through choice or passion for Millonarios that I was pogoing like a jack-in-a-box on speed, but complete necessity. Everyone around me was bouncing to such an extent that unless I joined in it was impossible to see anything. At the opposite end of El Campín was a smaller and more vocal section of home faithful, and along the side a red army of 5,000 América fans. This was the first game where I was in the middle of the barra brava and it was exhilarating.

The intense atmosphere generated by an incredibly loud support seemed to inspire the players, who produced a captivating football match. América pressed early but couldn't find the net, denied by the woodwork and some great goalkeeping, including a one-handed penalty save. Millonarios undeservedly took the lead by capitalising on some slack defending, sending the locals into delirium. Trying to stay on my feet after the goal was always going to be an impossible feat. I ended up on the floor, desperately clinging to a metal barrier to prevent myself from being crushed.

At the interval the bouncing was temporarily put on hold. Those around me turned their attentions from the pitch and onto the Gringo in their midst. It wasn't long before we were discussing English football and having photos with my Zulu Army flag. Whilst most were friendly enough, the atmosphere was still intimidating. For a start I was the only person without a visible Millonarios tattoo. What was also making me uncomfortable was the half time entertainment. This consisted of a troupe of scantily clad teenagers (some of whom looked well under the legal age) performing an erotic dance routine in front of the barra. The unsubtle moves included squeezing their pubescent breasts together whilst shaking them at the baying crowd, followed by bending over and waving at the whistling masses through their open legs.

By the time the second period was a quarter of an hour old I was beginning to get tired of jumping. I tried staying still, feeling confident enough that those closest to me knew I was foreign so didn't need to blend in. I found myself standing there like a plum, watching other people bouncing and only being able to see half the action. When the hosts got a decisive second shortly afterwards, it was necessary to clutch onto a blue banner in an attempt not to be swept down the terrace with a tide of barra. At that point I'd had enough and went to observe

111

the remainder in a bar. But I wasn't permitted to leave the stand, let alone the stadium. Riot police had every exit covered and weren't even allowing anyone to go to the toilet. Reluctantly, I continued to hop like an injured kangaroo for the remaining 25 minutes, whilst América squandered a plethora of chances. Just before full time an announcement was made via the public address system - the Millonarios fans would be detained for 40 minutes after the final whistle. Not the best news I'd ever heard.

América's defeated contingent left their side quickly while those around me bounced and celebrated. After the home side had done a lap of honour things calmed down, so I decided to find somewhere inconspicuous to hide until we were released. In fairness it wasn't that bad. The result helped the mood of Los Comandos Azules, who divided their time as captives between throwing handfuls of paper at each other, debris at the officials and visiting players, and trying to impress the significant number of attractive women in attendance. We were held prisoners for almost an hour, at the end of which everybody was too tired / thirsty / hungry / in dying need to urinate, to want to cause any problems. It was the first time I'd properly seen this type of crowd control. Although I didn't like waiting, it was an effective way of dispersing large volumes of opposition supporters from a match without complications.

Millonarios was the centrepiece of an enjoyable weekend in Bogotá. My initial impression of the eight million inhabitants was a very positive one. Climbing aboard a crowded minibus from the main terminal to the centre, I was told by the driver there wasn't enough space. As I strained to get my bag back onto the pavement, a passenger tapped me on the shoulder and offered me his seat. Apparently he wasn't in a hurry so he'd catch the next service. When it's late at night in an intimidating place and you are tired and hungry, acts of kindness like that really do warm your heart. As did the Friday evening I spent in historic La Candelaria district with a group of students.

Whilst exploring the city during the day I saw youths drinking heavily in the bars and queuing to enter nightclubs. This appeared a little odd considering they were drunkenly staggering through the streets while I was eating lunch. I assumed it might have been a graduation party. Later, whilst writing my journal in a shop/bar, I was invited to join a packed table of students. They explained it was a normal Friday, they just knew how to party!

After we'd shared some surprisingly agreeable Aguardiente (a sugarcane-derived aniseed flavour spirit) I began to appreciate the booming reggaeton and made tentative steps onto the dance floor. I was met by a swaying young lady making some very unsubtle advances and whose left breast kept popping out of her vest top. To tell the truth I'd dismissed Latin pop music during my time in Central America, but had been slowly warming to it since landing in Colombia. It was interesting that throughout Latin America the most universally popular music played on the radio was the rap / reggae / romantica / dancehall / salsa crossbreed. This predominantly originated from Puerto Rico and Panama. One of the successful artists at the time was Nicaragua's Luis Enrique, whose hit: 'Yo No Sé Mañana' I heard in every single country I visited.

Just to clarify: I succumbed to the drunken girl's overtones and didn't manage to get her boob to stay inside her top despite my repeated efforts, but did ensure she got home safely, before somehow chipping a tooth whilst swigging a bottle of cerveza on my bunk bed. All which meant that I, like the Kiwis, would have to be a Colombian dental tourist.

Game 21

La Equidad v Real Cartagena – (Liga Postobon) - 2 v 1
Sunday 26th September 2010 – 15:30
Estadio Metropolitano de Techo, Bogotá

Following the previous night's tiring antics I was ready for a slightly more sedate football experience. Again I struggled with the buses, crossing a city that had a permanently cool climate on account of its 2,600 metre altitude. Eventually I found my way to Mundo Adventure TransMilenio station in time for kick-off. I figured it'd be easy to purchase a ticket for a small game inside a 8,000 capacity stadium, but like many of my Colombian footballing assumptions, I was very much misguided.

Upon arrival the stewards pointed me to a ticket office which was supposedly part of a nearby supermarket complex. Strutting with purpose I ignored the touts as I was too busy concentrating on a large theme park situated directly behind the football venue. A group of riot police sat idly by the supermarket told me I had to buy entradas at the theme park ticket booth three blocks away. Within a block I got frustrated, bought two cans of beers, downed them and reluctantly handed a tout some cash. I negotiated the turnstiles muttering unpleasant things about jumping through hoops to get into a shit ground. Whilst delivering my tirade of expletives I paused to wonder why there was a group of roughly 40 yellow-shirted Cartagena fans standing patiently by the entrance.

Once settled amongst the visiting spectators opposite the main stand I'd missed La Equidad's opening goal. Not that I would have seen it anyway, the backdrop of fairground rides was far more enthralling viewing than proceedings on the pitch. The most exciting thing I saw prior to the break was a wayward shot narrowly missing a swinging pirate ship, to loud groans from the crowd. At half time I chatted to the lads sat near me. Our conversation drifted to why there were a bunch of Cartagena supporters stood outside. Their explanation was quite puzzling.

La Rebelión Auriverde Norte barra had trekked from the north coast to watch their club, but didn't have enough money to pay for a ticket (not that they could have found the bloody ticket office anyway). They were waiting until the second half when it was free to enter. I couldn't comprehend their logic: these people were travelling at least 25

114

hours each way to see less than 45 minutes of football. Lo and behold, shortly after the interval, in they came and hurriedly tied their banners to the fences. When their paraphernalia was in place the singing and bouncing commenced. Some friends of the guy sat next to me interrupted their brief stint inside Estadio Metropolitano de Techo to come over and talk to him. I was introduced and took photos of them with my St. George's cross.

After meeting the followers who journeyed two days to see three quarters of an hour of football, I was hoping Cartagena would muster a second half display to match their devotion. Unfortunately the hosts scored a second and ran out winners despite a late goal and subsequent flourish from Real. La Equidad, an association funded by an insurance company, didn't have the best vocal backing, although the folks in the main stand with two drums were doing their best to make some noise. This win left the side from Bogotá comfortably on course for a place in the post season championships. Talking to locals in a bar afterwards I was keen to learn how a team with such a tiny fan base could be more successful on the field than their illustrious neighbours. They were of the impression that a smaller organisation (especially with corporate patronage) was easier to run than a giant like Millonarios (who had shady connections with narcotic traffickers).

Next day I was at Bogotá's transport terminal waiting for a connection to the Tatacoa Desert, when I heard someone shouting: 'English football hooligan'. I looked up to see the smiling faces of the Cartagena barra I met at half time and had a picture with my flag. They bounded across the large hall, shook my hand and after a minute chatting proudly informed me they were late for their bus home. Apparently they had to hurry otherwise wouldn't get back in time to start work the next evening. 'Somos Cartagena' they chanted at me, whilst jogging towards their gate.

I quickly became aware that Colombian supporters were the craziest I had ever encountered. This was reinforced by a story I read in Argentina, six months after leaving the country. A 17 year old member of La Barra del Indio from Cúcuta (in the north east) was killed in a drive-by shooting, on the eve of his club's Primera División fixture against Envigado. La barra arranged a good send-off by taking him to see his beloved team play one last time. With 20 minutes remaining in a low-key affair in which the away side had scored the only goal, the stewards opened the exits to allow spectators to leave. Without warning 200 Cúcuta fanatics surged into the stadium carrying their fallen comrade's coffin, catching the officials off-guard. By the time the police and stewards were conscious of what had happened, the casket was in the middle of a large group of bouncing barra brava. Cristopher Sanguino's final visit to Estadio General Santander lasted less than ten minutes, but that was just enough time to 'witness' Cúcuta-born substitute Diego Espinel profiting from a fortuitous deflection to score the equaliser.

As the next match was six days away, I reverted back into tourism mode to see some of the sights this fascinating country had to offer. After a six hour ride down from the mountainous capital into flat cattle territory, I found myself on the outskirts of Desierto de la Tatacoa. This spectacularly open landscape, encircled by towering peaks, cliffs of multi-coloured sand and sprouting cacti, was pretty much off the beaten track. It was a pleasant change to be the only guest at the family-run hotel I was staying in. An old man in an even older looking car drove me on a little tour of the landscape, stopping at swimming holes and sites of apparent geological interest. The climax was after sunset in an observatory run by an eccentric man known as El Astronomo. This desert was a particularly good place to gaze at stars, due to its proximity to the equator and the absence of light pollution. For an hour I was captivated as Xavier Restrepo used his laser pointer to identify each of the most visible constellations. Astronomical words must be fairly universal, because I understood his explanations without any real difficulty. At the end of the display he setup a homemade telescope, through which I got a clear view of the passing planet Jupiter.

Game 22

América de Cali v Atlético Nacional – (Liga Postobon) - 2 v 0
Saturday 2nd October 2010 – 18:20
Estadio Doce de Octubre, Tuluá

I arrived in Cali the night before a big game between two Colombian footballing titans. However, I should have learnt my lesson from seeing Itagüí in Medellín - just because a team is at home, doesn't mean they are playing in their own stadium. In this case América's Estadio Olímpico Pascual Guerrero was being reconstructed for the upcoming Under 20 World Cup. Until it was habitable again the town of Tuluá (Too-l-wah) an hour and a half's bus ride away hosted their fixtures. So on Saturday morning I left my backpack at a hostel in Cali and set off for a weekend in the country.

Pulling into Tuluá the first thing I noticed was the number of supporters already milling around Estadio Doce de Octubre. Since Honduras I'd gotten accustomed to fans, mainly in their teens, standing outside ticket offices begging for their entrance money. The presence of these pleading barra hadn't been too prominent in Central America, but in Colombia it was rife. There were hordes of them banging on the bus windows expectantly, over four hours prior to kick-off.

La Señora at the hotel I checked into had an interesting bartering technique. Initially she attempted to charge me 35,000 Pesos a night. When I thanked her and turned to leave she offered me two nights for 30,000. The evening's entertainment began with a lukewarm four pack in a park by the venue, flanked by riot police and armoured vehicles. A $7.50 ticket was the cheapest in the ground (but the most expensive I'd bought in Colombia) and allowed me to enter with El Baron Rojo Sur barra along the side facing the main stand. My flag was inspected and questioned by the stewards; fortunately América's colours were also red and white so I managed to talk my way round it. In order to verify that I had a genuine entrada, a steward burned my ticket with a lighter. It singed to his satisfaction so I was admitted to the arena - who needs barcodes?

Within seconds of being inside I gathered this was a game I needed to be anonymous for. The barra were all very rough-looking and really angry. I hid at the opposite end to which América were shooting, in amongst some comparatively reasonable individuals. The hosts dominated early on, agonizingly hitting a post before scoring; John

117

Lozano headed home a free kick. Nacional, having won the Medellín derby in front of a packed Atanasio Girardot three days earlier, responded but couldn't capitalise on their possession and set pieces. In stoppage time the contest was settled. An out swinging Nacional corner was cleared to an América striker. He ran the length of the pitch and unselfishly squared it for a teammate to tap in. Even though the visitors mounted an all-out assault in the second period they returned to the northwest empty-handed.

Obscurity was key, and I survived the first half unscathed. With the idea of writing an account of my football experiences gaining momentum, I was determined to get as memorable a photo with my St. George's cross as possible in each stadium I visited. This being my 22nd game, I'd developed a sense of who, where and when to take the picture. In Colombia I'd been lucky enough to get some decent ones. But there was no way of guaranteeing a good image as the process was a little convoluted: first I had to pick an appropriate local, ask politely in Spanish if he or she would mind taking my photograph, point out the correct button, walk down the stand to where I deduced was the best place and angle for it, pull the piece of cloth out of my back pocket, ensure it was the right way up, face the camera (as well as thousands of people trying to watch the match) and wait until I got a thumbs up signal.

For this tie the quiet section I was trying to hide in also seemed to be the flag area. I was enthused about getting a snap with the other banners until I saw a kid in an América shirt trying to take one on his mobile phone, only to be chased away by barra who didn't take kindly to the exposure. It was all rather hypocritical. Five minutes later the same group were jostling round an old lady, trying to purchase a Polaroid of guess what? Yep, it was them with the flags.

Not many fans had switched ends at the interval. In order to select my cameraman I started talking to some guys near to me. I identified the most articulate of them and struck up a conversation. On the hour mark I was going for it, but swiftly retreated when the linesman correctly ruled an América goal out for offside. He was rewarded by El Baron Rojo Sur throwing presents in his direction. There was also a handful that tried to scale the relatively small fence, presumably to congratulate him on such good officiating. Time was running out and play was stopped for an injury, so I made my move. Asking permission from the lad who owned the flag directly behind me, I passed my camera to my new friend, pulled out the St. George's cross, and within a matter of seconds it was over.

Or so I thought. The camera and flag returned to my pocket, I thanked the photographer and stood casually staring at the pitch as if nothing had happened. Within moments a group of teenagers descended like vultures saying I had to pay for the picture. I coolly clarified that I'd been given consent and didn't have any spare cash. Following some swearing and gesticulating the youngsters returned to where they came from. In injury time another teenager (who'd not been in the mob trying to extortion money) approached me and asked who was being substituted for América. Unfamiliar with the players' names, I said I didn't know. After asking where I was staying he wandered off with a vacant look in his eye, clearly high on something. When the game was over I was keen to get out of there as soon as possible. I offered to buy those that had been friendly a beer; they declined as they needed to get back to Cali. I thanked them and bid farewell.

By the time I'd left the terrace all but one exit gate was locked. As I ran to the only remaining opening it closed. I stood there weighing up my options; not too enthralled by the prospect of being locked in for almost an hour. Out of nowhere, the wasted youth who'd asked me about substitutes minutes earlier ran over shouting something barely comprehensible about me not being an América fan. Before I could respond he produced a large glistening knife and held it to my throat, glaring at me psychotically. With my heart racing I backed towards the gate, explaining I was English, I was there to watch América and he was right - I wasn't a true fan because I support Birmingham City. He paused for a second shaking uncontrollably, and as quickly as he appeared, ran off. Stunned, I frowned at him as he vanished into the darkness.

Regaining my senses I realised that I was surrounded by other barra who were keen for me to prove I wasn't a rival supporter. Having to again maintain my composure, I asked precisely how I was supposed to do that, to which they responded: 'show us your tattoos'. I removed my shirt to display a distinct absence of body art, at which point I was thankfully rescued. A female police officer on the other side of the fence had observed my ordeal. She tapped me on the shoulder, beckoned and announced she was going to let me out. The protests were met with a simple 'como no' from her, and all of a sudden I was on the safe side of the gates being checked for injuries.

Once it was established I was unharmed the lady and her colleagues asked what the hell I was doing in such a dangerous place. My response of: 'watching football' didn't go down too well. She told me I was an idiot, I should have been in the main stand as it was the only safe place for Gringos, emphasising her statement by slapping me on the head. I strode back to my hotel with adrenaline pumping through my veins. For the record it was all worth it - the Zulu Army photo was one of the best!

Game 23

Cortuluá v Millonarios – (Liga Postobon) - 1 v 2
Sunday 3rd October 2010 – 17:20
Estadio Doce de Octubre, Tuluá

My impromptu outing to Tuluá had an unexpected bonus, on Sunday the local club were playing Millonarios. After Saturday night's escapades I wasn't really in a boisterous mood for this one as I'd not had much sleep. High on adrenaline until the early hours, I went boozing in la zona viva until dawn. This was a mismatch of bars bundled together along a 500 metre stretch of road, blaring out everything from salsa to heavy rock. Suitably late, I arrived just in time to hear Millonarios' fans celebrating their opening goal. Wanting a tamer experience than Saturday, I resisted the temptation to jump about with the supporters from Bogotá and headed towards the main stand's ticket office. On my way I was intercepted by a middle-aged man and his eight year old son; they had a spare ticket for $2.50. Slightly warily I followed them through the gates (no burning verification on this side of the ground) and we sat together near the halfway line.

Cortuluá were a classic yo-yo club. After they'd been promoted as Primera B champions they struggled in la Apertura (finishing second from bottom) and weren't doing much better in la Clausura. Millonarios, buoyed by the victory against América, looked more confident, but were pegged back by a moment of genius. Defender Carlos Terranoba stepped up and bent a gorgeous, dipping 35 yard free kick high into the top corner past a sprawling keeper. The home faithful celebrated jubilantly, not least my new amigo. He ran over to the preferencial section, abused two Millonarios officials, returning to hug his son and shake my hand. The rest of the half passed without incident, but in honesty I was more interested in gazing at the spectacular backdrop of tall mountains radiating in the sunset.

At the interval, whilst a group of high school cheerleaders performed, I started chatting to the father. He'd lived in Tuluá all his life and was positive about the temporary presence of América fans. Notwithstanding their disruptive and occasionally violent episodes, it had given the local economy a bit of a boost, and Cortuluá were profiting from a percentage of their gate receipts. We also discussed the upcoming Under 20 World Cup and the positive impact this could have on Colombia's image, if they were able to hold it without any security problems.

He left ten minutes before full time, missing Millonarios' late winner. The goal sparked a local exodus which left Estadio Doce de Octubre practically empty for the remaining few moments. An animated travelling support ecstatically celebrated their first consecutive wins of the season. It was a case of too little too late for Millonarios, who in spite of their late revival finished in mid table. Cortuluá sadly lost their relegation battle and returned to Primera B.

I ambled back through Tuluá's pleasant tree-lined streets to my hotel, comparing my two football experiences that weekend. For me it was further evidence of how two sides of Colombian society - whilst being so far apart in terms of their behaviour - could coexist so closely that in plain sight it was sometimes difficult to differentiate between them.

2011's Under 20 World Cup was a big event for Colombia. The country's preceding international tournament, 2001's Copa America, was initially cancelled due to perceived security issues. Although authorities eventually went ahead with the competition, both Canada and Argentina refused to participate - the latter claiming their players had received death threats from Colombian gangs. The hosts went on to win the cup, but they'd been unable to shed their negative international image.

Domestic football was one of the countless areas of Colombian society that had been affected by fluctuations in narcotics trafficking. In the 1980's and 1990's drug cartels poured money into their favourite teams. This not only aided the youth development, but also gave clubs the ability to keep hold of their home-grown talent. The illicit funding was so prevalent, that in 1995, América de Cali was placed under watch by what was known as: 'The Clinton List'. This froze all the organisation's assets in the US as a result of its connections with, and financing from cartels. Governmental action against drugs lords since the mid-1990's meant the illegal revenue stream had mostly dried up by the time I got there. Unfortunately so had attendances at domestic games, and it wasn't exclusively the local leagues that suffered. Their Selección hadn't qualified for the World Cup since 1998.

The government had devoted hefty amounts of public spending to develop eight of their largest stadiums, so they conformed to FIFA's international standards. During the month I spent there I had numerous discussions with natives about the event's significance. They were aware the U-20 World Cup wasn't prestigious internationally, but were happy they'd been elected as hosts. Many repeated the same statement: it was their opportunity to show the world Colombia was a safe place to visit. I'm pleased to report that's exactly what happened. It passed without any major incident and was very well attended, with an average of 25,000 per match.

With a week to kill in Colombia's second city I decided it was time to confront one of my greatest fears head-on. My inability to dance had been a stumbling block on plenty of occasions, so I checked myself into a hostel with a salsa school onsite. It seemed as though every Latino, no matter what their shape or size, had natural rhythm and the propensity to move gracefully in time to music. Generally the only occasions I'd partaken up to then had been when so inebriated I couldn't remember how I performed. I booked private lessons, and each evening there was a complimentary group session open to all residents.

The first few days were a frustratingly painful experience. I stomped around sulking that I couldn't count four simple beats and make my feet move in time to music. Slowly but surely it started to come together, thanks to the patience of my effeminate dance teacher. By the third day I was ready to practice with a partner, the randy receptionist in her mid-forties was happy to help out. As my confidence grew I joined the teacher and other backpackers on outings to local salsa clubs.

I was really impressed with Cali's thriving social scene, its nightclubs and friendly drinking culture. Dubbed the 'capital of salsa', it really did live up to its billing. The handful of places I went to in my brief stay were packed full of gyrating bodies. Some traditional salsa venues were Cuban-looking with their sparse décor, large dance floor and lack of air-conditioning. Other locations were no more than small bars where dancing spilled out into the street. Cali's inhabitants had their own unique salsa style, which was quicker than most. Watching an experienced couple on the dance floor was a truly captivating sight. I gingerly took my first steps on the last night, and once my initial nerves had faded, I loosened up enough to genuinely believe that, finally, I didn't look like I belonged in a wheelchair

Cali was obsessed with salsa, a fact that was emphasised when I went to withdraw cash from an ATM one midweek afternoon. Standing outside a branch of Santander (one of my former employers) waiting for the machine to dispense my currency, I noticed some commotion inside the bank. Upon closer inspection there was a couple in their late 30's, skilfully performing a complex-looking salsa routine whilst the customers were clapping along keeping time. The display lasted two minutes, at the end of which the duo took a bow to generous applause, walked around to the other side of the counter and began serving the people they'd just been entertaining. I worked in the banking industry long enough to be confident that type of thing does not happen in England.

Another reason why I held Cali's nightlife in such high regard was that the female residents of the city (and the country in general) were without doubt the most attractive I'd ever seen. To put it bluntly, I wanted to marry a Colombian girl! I appreciate I'm generalising at this point, but their body shape was fantastic - all the right curves in the right places. The majority had a backside donated to them directly from Dios himself and they definitely knew how to shake it. The clothes they wore deliberately accentuated their curvaceous physique. I have no idea how some of the ladies I saw managed to squeeze into their skin-tight jeans, but I'd sure as hell like to. Also they didn't appear to be bound by the same Catholic guilt which noticeably restrained other Latin girls. It was a sexual nation, reflected in the hot, up-close moves of the salsa. The locals I came into contact with were aware of their sexuality and how to exploit it - not in a brazen way like you would see in a British nightclub - but more subtly and sensuously. Colombian women knew what they were doing and did it very well. I was a big fan.

Game 24

Deportivo Cali v América de Cali – (Liga Postobon) - 6 v 3
Sunday 10th October 2010 – 17:20
Estadio Deportivo Cali, Palmira

El clásico de Cali was the climax of my month in Colombia, and much like game 3 it turned out to be a clásico in more than just geographical terms. The day had been spent at a free salsa concert, after which I checked out of my hostel and said goodbye to everyone. Of the six backpackers who'd expressed an interest in the match, only a Mexican guy actually wanted to go. Two girls from Oregon declined due to safety concerns, but then went to Nacional v Millonarios in Medellín. At the end there were violent scenes which resulted in them being covered in tear gas.

Estadio Deportivo Cali, boasting the largest capacity in the country, was in the middle of nowhere. From Cali's bus terminal it was a half hour drive along a highway, followed by a five minute motorbike ride down a dusty road. It was still a lot closer to Cali than Tuluá, so why didn't América share Deportivo's home until theirs was ready? It wasn't a question of security because it was bordered by a mass of open fields. The answer was the same as why there were no América fans allowed to attend that fixture: hatred. Deportivo's faithful explained they'd rather abandon their own club than permit their city rivals to set foot inside their ground. But two foreigners weren't a problem. They only charged us $2.50 and after a little arguing let us keep our belt buckles. And there were nine goals.

The first thing I need to mention about this particular 90 minutes of football was that it changed my view on Olympic-style stadiums. I'd always been of the opinion that this design took people away from the action and diluted the atmosphere. Estadio Deportivo Cali was a relatively traditional rectangular venue with wide sides containing a disproportionately large number of director's boxes, and an open single-tiered stand behind each goal. The issue was that when the statutory array of flags and banners had been hung on the tall fence separating you from the field of play, the end wasn't steep enough to afford a view of the goal frame in front of you. In this case we were unable to properly see six goals because our view was obstructed by pieces of green cloth. Not that the barra were bothered about this. For them the event was more about singing and bouncing to support their team, whilst cursing the opposition and officials.

Another advantage of an oval shaped arena was that the game wasn't interrupted by objects thrown by spectators. For some reason football fans in Latin America thought it necessary to take rolls of toilet paper to matches, so they could lob them onto the pitch. In Olympic stadiums it created a scene behind the goal in which the Andrex puppy would thrive, but didn't affect proceedings. In regular stadia it created havoc.

My Mexican amigo and I attempted to gain the best vantage point amongst La Frente Radical Verdiblanco barra, without getting too close to the ones that looked like they needed rabies vaccinations. The hosts started brightly and seized the initiative on 18 minutes. Andrés Escobar (a Cali striker - not the ghost of the Medellín defender) ran clear before beating the keeper and streams of white toilet paper. Shortly after it was level as América's goalkeeper scored from the spot. With ten minutes to the interval Deportivo regained the lead, Argentine Martín Morel fired in a low 25 yard free kick. Minutes later Morel bagged his second, neatly controlling a cross, flicking the ball in the air and dispatching a delightful overhead kick. The second touch appeared unnecessary at first glance, but repeated viewings show that he was merely trying to knock the ball away from a large wad of bog roll. Deportivo went into the break three goals ahead, courtesy of an injury time penalty.

Martín Morel completed a spectacular hat trick just after the restart, whilst I was still waiting to use one of the three Portaloo's on offer. The Argentine intercepted an América pass in his own half and with his second touch chipped the keeper from inside the centre circle. The stunning finish had shades of a young David Beckham scoring from the half way line against Wimbledon in 1996. América got one from close range, but any thoughts of an unlikely comeback were quashed in the last ten minutes. A visiting defender received his second yellow card, followed by Deportivo scoring a sixth. Commendably América continued fighting and got a consolation with two minutes remaining, before having an effort ruled out in the dying moments. This win for Deportivo took them above their enemy on goal difference, but it was a fruitless tournament for both Cali teams. They failed to qualify for the post season competition, which Manizale's Once Caldas won.

I spent the best part of five weeks travelling from north to south of Colombia; it was a pretty eye-opening experience. The outside perception was predominantly of drugs and kidnapping - for the entire time I was there my mother had sleepless nights worrying about my security. Like other Latin American nations it had a turbulent history after becoming part of Spain's Empire in the 16th century. Following the French Revolution Napoleon invaded Spain, and in 1808 made his brother king. Sensing a weakness, some key Colombian cities declared independence. Led by the dashing liberator, Símon Bolívar, the natives won important battles against the colonists. Napoleon's defeat at Waterloo prompted the Spanish to recapture some fallen regions, but Bolívar (with a helping hand from the British) fought and won independence in 1819. He formed Gran Colombia, a massive territory including modern-day Ecuador, Venezuela and Panama, but lost control due to its size. Civil wars broke out in the late 1800's, the most damaging was the 1,000 Day War. This conflict claimed over 100,000 lives and gave the US the opportunity to establish Panama as a breakaway republic.

The first half of the 20th century was a comparatively peaceful phase in their history, but violence returned in the late 1940's. A new civil war broke out and infamous guerilla groups formed, each with their own objectives. They were founded by left-wing 'revolutionaries' inspired by Bolívar to fight their conservative government, which in contrast to many Latin countries at the time, wasn't a military dictatorship. During the period known as La Violencia militants were driven by alleged electoral fraud, in addition to social and political injustices. Chiefly consisting of poor farmers and peasants, the groups (of which FARC was the most prominent) controlled rural provinces, vast areas with ideal coca growing conditions. A few decades later white gold became popular in North America and the cartels exploited its money-making potential.

Although it had calmed down significantly since the last 20 years of the previous century; there were plenty of horror stories coming out of Colombia on a regular basis. Whilst I was there the Obama regime assisted in killing of one of FARC's senior commanders, El Mono Jojoy. However, the guerillas still sustained a substantial amount of power. Great steps had been taken to succeed in the war on drugs, but supply lines had remained fairly consistent to valuable North American and European markets. It is thought that in the early 21st Century Peru and Bolivia overtook Colombia in terms of production. The authority's attempts to eliminate the problem at its source created a vicious circle. By spraying coca fields with harmful chemicals underprivileged farmers suffered, which encouraged them to support the guerillas. In a nation where civil war had simmered for decades, and there were more internally displaced citizens than anywhere else in the world (except Sudan) there wasn't a simple solution.

Despite its turbulent past I felt relatively safe in Colombia. Much like Mexico, tourists didn't see the worst of it, although there were still some rough edges as my encounters at football proved. From my very limited experience most residents seemed to be civilised, proud and resilient. In the majority of nations I'd visited on the trip there was a feeling of the inhabitants being grateful for tourism. I felt Colombians were less interested in their visitors, even though everybody I met (with a few exceptions) was warm and welcoming. I think it's because they were an attractive people in a stunning country - they were cool and they knew it!

ECUADOR

Population – 15 million
Size – 272,000 km^2
Time Zone – GMT $^-$6
Currency – US Dollar
FIFA World Ranking – #53 (2010)
Best World Cup Finish – Last 16 (2006)
Biggest Teams – Barcelona, El Nacional, Emelec, LDU Quito

You might have heard of:
Christian 'Chucho' Benitez, Antonio Valencia, Augustin Delgado,
Ulises de la Cruz, Jefferson Montero, Enner Valencia

Essential Spanish:
Arriba – Above
Tenemos cerveza – We have beer
Bien fría – Nice and cold
Ladrón – Thief
Bodega – Store Room
Salud - Cheers
Concha tu madre – Your mother's vagina
Pendejo – Idiot
Puto/puta – Bitch/whore
Oscura – Dark
Sur – South

Game 25

Universidad Católica v Independiente – (Primera A) - 1 v 2
Saturday 16th October 2010 – 10:00
Estadio Olímpico Atahualpa, Quito

Game 26

Deportivo Quito v El Nacional – (Primera A) - 1 v 0
Saturday 16th October 2010 – 12:00
Estadio Olímpico Atahualpa, Quito

The day began in a backpacker's hostel in the centre of Quito, jumping around the common room, swearing at events taking place some 9,200 kilometres away at London's Emirates Stadium. Shortly after Nicola Zigic had scored his first goal for Blues, Arsenal's Marouane Chamakh clearly dived to earn a spot kick (not the last penalty controversy against the Gunners that season). One of the advantages of being in Latin America was ESPN and Fox Sports had tremendous coverage of our Premier League. It was possible to watch up to four different live Saturday 15:00 kick-offs simultaneously, and there was more top class English football on Ecuadorian television than Sky Sports. Not that I was grateful for the footage on that occasion, as Arsenal ran out 2 v 1 winners. When the final whistle sounded in England's capital I set out into a pleasant Ecuadorian morning.

My initial reaction when I arrived and saw the fixture list was: who the hell holds back-to-back games in the same ground? Then I thought: why on earth would any professional football match start at ten in the morning? I suppose the second question was answered by the first, although this didn't ease my rum-induced hangover on the bus. A brief ride later I arrived at the venue for this football bonanza, Ecuador's national stadium, Estadio Atahualpa. There was a strange mixture of people in replica shirts milling around as the teams on show that day all had similar home kits. The entrance system was very relaxed and slightly confusing, especially considering there were four sets of supporters coming and going. Ignoring the numerous touts and far too hanging to buy any memorabilia, I purchased a ticket and climbed the nearest set of steps.

At the top I was greeted by two middle-aged gentlemen selling refreshments. In my delicate state I opted for a bottle of water, and as they chattered away I sat down and engaged in conversation. My footballing Midas touch struck again. I'd arrived to witness the final quarter of the first game, which apparently contained most the content of note. Independiente were a goal ahead from the first half, but the hosts, who were playing with ten men, crashed in a free kick via the underside of the crossbar to equalise. Shortly after the visitors had a man sent off for a reckless challenge and then immediately reclaimed the lead. There was enough time left for an 18 man brawl (without any disciplinary action from the officials) and a last minute penalty for Católica - which was acrobatically saved, to the jubilation of a pocket of Independiente followers.

At the changeover it was time for a cerveza, although I declined a large chunk of ice they offered to accompany it. Whilst the coin was being tossed three Gringas (female Gringos) sporting Deportivo shirts bought a beverage from us and went to sit at the top of our deserted north stand. With the alcohol flowing, myself, Manuel and Patricio sat in the sun witnessing a lacklustre second contest. Not that it mattered because we were all too busy acting like children to care. The jokes were flying around about las Gringas arriba (the girls at the top of the stand) and La Madrina (Patricio's wife) who was trying to keep the pair of them in check. Business was slow despite my efforts to entice punters with cries of 'tenemos cerveza bien fría' similar to the night selling dinners in Honduras. The small quantities of fans in attendance were situated either in the side terraces or at the opposite end, which gave my colleagues ample opportunity to consume their merchandise. They were sharing a cup and going through the litre bottles of beer at a ratio of one for customers - one for the workers.

At the break, Manuel (the more animated of the duo and the one most interested in las Gringas arriba) went to sell badges on the other side of Estadio Atahualpa. The half time entertainment consisted of promotional staff throwing complimentary footballs into the sparse crowd. This attracted one of the ginger haired Gringas who didn't catch a ball, but fared better than a lady in the main stand who fell down a whole flight of stairs in her excitement. After lengthy treatment she was driven round the running track to a waiting ambulance, in a golf cart used to take injured players off the field. Her departure was accompanied by sarcastic applause from the other spectators. Well my applause was sarcastic anyway.

A brief lull after the restart was broken by the returning Manuel. He was jesting with a weather-beaten 70 year old salesman, who'd been appearing intermittently pretending to sell his ice-creams, but really just wanted a swig of our drinks. Crisis struck midway through the half when we inexplicably ran out of booze, even though there were only roughly 50 people in our section to account for our eight empty crates. It wasn't a problem, Manuel's son worked in the main stand's storage room, he could steal some more for us. A phone call and less than five minutes later we were all at the fence separating the stands, receiving two crates of beer, a bottle at a time, under the wire mesh. I resumed my sales pitch with 'Tenemos cerveza del ladrón de la bodega,' which caused La Madrina to cry as she was laughing so much, and Patricio to run off to the toilets as he was going to wet himself.

All of a sudden folks started to leave, which surprised me as I'd forgotten there was a game taking place. I helped tidy up, thanking the exiting Gringas arriba for providing us with some amusement, and before I knew it we'd all hugged, shook hands and I was staggering back towards my hostel at two o'clock in the afternoon.

For the record Deportivo won by a single goal which came after 33 minutes, their victory assisted by a red card to a Nacional defender five minutes prior to scoring. Deportivo and Nacional ended the tournament respectably in mid-table positions, whilst Católica and Independiente didn't fare so well, finishing second bottom and bottom respectively. Católica were relegated to Primera B due to an equally poor showing in the first half of the year.

My first experiences of Ecuadorian football were obviously very different to those in Colombia, not exclusively because of the welcome presence of alcohol for sale inside the ground. God bless my three amigos - they were generous, welcoming and funny. Fair play to the two guys, who looked like they were approaching their 60's, they must have drank at least 8 litres of beer between them whilst I was there. ¡Salud!

Game 27

LDU Quito v Unión San Felipe - (Copa Sudamericana) - 6 v 1
Tuesday 19th October 2010 – 20:00
Estadio de Liga Deportiva Universitaria, Quito

For my trip's only Sudamericana tie I had a companion. A guy staying in my hostel from Georgia, USA, was unexpectedly keen on soccer, so off we went. Whilst walking to the bus stop on a nippy Tuesday evening, I explained that I only ever took three things with me to Latin football matches: wallet, camera and flag. He responded in his slow, southern drawl 'Aah did naart think it was a good aahdeah to bring maah camera, but aah do haave maah naahfe' emphasising the statement by pulling out a six inch flick-knife. You just can't take bloody Yanks anywhere. It didn't prove too much of an issue as the security at Ecuadorean games was relaxed; he concealed it in his large football socks. The ticket office closed as we arrived, but as usual the touts were more than happy to make a dollar off us.

La Copa Sudamericana was Latin America's second most important international club tournament, it only allowed participants from the southern continent and was contested from August to December. It's older and more prestigious sister, Copa Libertadores, consisted of teams from South America and Mexico, and ran throughout the first half of the calendar year. These competitions could easily be compared to the Europa League and Champions League respectively. We were attending the octavos de final (last 16) second leg, between one of Ecuador's most successful sporting associations and their opponents from the highlands of Chile. The gap between the two was emphasised by the fact that in 2009 LDU won la Copa Sudamericana; whilst San Felipe were in Chile's second division, only qualifying for 2010's edition by winning La Copa Chile. Interestingly, the visitors had a two goal head start after winning 4 v 2 at Estadio Municipal de San Felipe the previous week.

Within minutes of entering the reigning champions had levelled the score on aggregate, a neat volley and a penalty evening things up. Assisted by the wind at their backs and a partisan crowd inside an impressively steep and enclosed Estadio de Liga Deportiva Universitaria, Quito forced the newly promoted Chileans to defend deep in their own half. But San Felipe hadn't read the script and scored just before the interval.

My well-armed amigo and I watched the first period from the safety of the upper tier, which although it afforded a very good view, wasn't generating any real atmosphere. This was mainly attributable to being surrounded by a pocket of subdued away fans, families, and sickeningly, other Gringos. At the break I decided we were going to mix it up with the barra brava. Equipping ourselves with some ammunition (a couple of pints and a disgusting rice dish) we set out into the middle of the standing masses.

The south concourse's bare concrete walls were covered in graffiti, from pictures of Che Guevara and socialist propaganda, to slogans proclaiming how feared La Muerte Blanca barra were. This, combined with the booming noise created by the flare-wielding white-shirted masses, had led me to believe it would be similar to Colombia. Instead we found a bunch of students. They weren't even tough or intimidating students. What's more they were singing from photocopied hymn sheets. I pushed my way to centre of the throng to ask a guy holding a corner of a flag where the barra were located. He waved his arm focusing on a shirtless group bouncing enthusiastically. But they were nothing like those I'd seen previously. Whilst I was trying to determine what was going on, LDU scored a header from a set piece. The academics around me hopped up and down clapping politely. Then, referring to their sheets, they began a new song.

Slightly bewildered I forced my way back to the bar trying to reconcile the white death barra brava with their Latin American counterparts. These weren't the ragged, crazy looking youths I'd encountered from Mexico through Honduras to Colombia; they were working toward law degrees. It reminded me that another university club (PUMAS from game 3) had created a stunning atmosphere and yet their most passionate fans were incredibly civilised.

After a swiftly consumed pint my attentions returned to the remainder of a compelling game. LDU ran away with it, two Argentines and a Uruguayan scoring to seal a 6 v 1 victory; 8 v 5 on aggregate. As we left the stadium I was still muttering how confused I was, whilst my confederate cohort was waxing lyrical about how it was the best soccer experience of his life. LDU didn't retain their Sudamericana crown. They bowed out in the semi-final to eventual winners, Independiente of Argentina. Despite racing into a three goal lead after an hour of their first leg home tie, they lost on away goals.

LDU's barra were representative of my experiences in Ecuador up to that point. Gone was the unpredictability of Colombia to be replaced by a tourist-friendly country. Perched almost three kilometres above sea level, Quito was a stunning metropolis, squeezed into a valley encircled by Andean peaks. The centre was full of Gringos whilst I was there; scores of tourists explored its colonial old town and partied in modern El Mariscal. An hour's bus ride took me close to the middle of the world. In the 18th Century a Frenchman built a monument where he deemed the equatorial line to be. His calculations were approximately 300 meters out, although it was a remarkable achievement bearing in mind the age in which it was accomplished. It was sufficiently accurate for me to be able to stand with my feet on either side of a yellow line and genuinely feel I was straddling the hemispheres.

Ecuador's modern history had been fairly stable in comparison to others on the continent, but that was a very relative statement. Since gaining independence from Bolívar's Gran Colombia in 1830, the government had changed hands on a regular basis. In 2010, roughly half their Gross Domestic Product was based around oil. The population's psychology was divided between the conservative highlands and liberal lowlands.

Although Ecuador had a better international reputation than Colombia, the political situation was more unstable in Quito than its neighbour. Two weeks prior to my arrival the police force had called a nationwide strike over their salaries, despite President Rafael Correa's attempts to negotiate an agreement. When talks inside the constabulary's hospital broke down, the President made to leave, only for officers to fire tear gas and hold him captive for 12 hours. They then seized control of airports and bus stations in addition to blocking roads, making it virtually impossible to travel anywhere. The Ecuadorian people reacted by taking to the streets, clashing violently with the police, who responded by breaking into a national television centre to stop them broadcasting pro-governmental material. This tense deadlock was resolved when the military rescued the President from captivity, killing two officers in the process. It happened in a nation which had seen four military coups since the mid 1990's. I suppose it goes to show reputations can be misleading.

Game 28

Macará v Olmedo – (Primera A) - 0 v 1
Wednesday 20th October 2010 – 16:00
Estadio Bellavista, Ambato

It was my one year anniversary of being on the road. How else could I celebrate, other than getting a bus to the countryside to watch an Ecuadorian football match? On a lovely, sun-drenched day with the backdrop of snow-capped peaks, $1 beers and charmingly small sets of enthusiastic barra representing both sides, I couldn't envisage many better ways. I shall ignore that I had to pay $7 to enter Estadio Bellavista, as there was an obligatory $3 raffle I couldn't win as I wasn't a native. Also I'll forget the quality of the 90 minutes of football I was treated to. An easy feat, because there was none in a contest that didn't warrant a goal, let alone an injury time winner. But one of the benefits of travelling is it gets you thinking about your glass, and on that glorious afternoon it was definitely half-full.

A ten day gap until my next fixture allowed me time to explore some of Ecuador's spectacularly diverse geography. Baños, a peaceful mountainous spa town with thermal baths and beautiful waterfalls, was a good starting point. I spent a few relaxing days doing uncharacteristically touristy activities, such as hiking and biking. One day I cycled from Baños to Puyo, descending 1,000 metres on the 60 kilometre journey; at the same time theoretically going from Andes to Amazon. It was an awe-inspiring ride downhill on winding rocky roads, trying to appreciate the stunning waterfalls along the powerful Pastaza River, whilst avoiding cars and trucks - all of which appeared to be driven by maniacs. Halfway through I crossed paths with the ginger Gringa who'd been trying to catch footballs at the Deportivo Quito game. She was an avid soccer fan from Seattle who was very passionate about her MLS side, the Sounders.

A couple of bus stops later I arrived at the jungle town of Tena, situated at the confluence of two of Ecuador's largest rivers. I passed some time with a girl from New Hampshire, who was living in Quito and a prominent foreign voice on Ecuadorian politics. My highly sophisticated advances involved me kissing her on the cheek and saying goodnight, when she was practically inviting me to stay in her room. I was more successful the proceeding evening, but not being massively fond of brief flings, was a little disappointed when she returned to the capital the next day after we'd been white-water rafting. This typically awkward romantic liaison raised an unusual question: if you only sleep with a girl once, does it count as a one night stand if you go rafting together the following day?

Thankfully it was time to move on, as I had to head towards the coast for my next match. It was a breath-taking ride to Guayaquil; the road climbed to 4,000 metres, passing volcanic glaciers and craggy snow-covered crests, before plunging down through the clouds to sea level.

Game 29

Barcelona v Emelec – (Primera A) - 0 v 0
Saturday 30th October 2010 – 18:00
Estadio Monumental Isidro Romero Carbo, Guayaquil

At 05:06 I was woken by a telephone ringing close to my ear. This was slightly disorientating as I'd not really used phones for over a year. It startled me so much that I knocked the receiver down the back of a chest of drawers upon which it was perched, taking me a good two minutes to retrieve it. On the other end of the line was a Scottish guy I'd met in Quito. He'd taken an overnight bus especially to see el clásico and was in reception. I re-woke at a more reasonable hour to see Arsenal score a late winner against relegation-bound West Ham United.

Ecuador's largest city, situated on the bank of the Guayas River, was home to the country's biggest football club, as well as its fiercest clásico. Guayaquil didn't feature highly on most travellers' itineraries, understandable when you take into account the abundance of natural wonders elsewhere in Ecuador - a small nation in South American terms. I fell in love with Guayaquil for the lack of conventional tourist attractions and its passionate football culture.

The morning of the game was spent wandering round bustling markets and shops, in awe of the quantity of football shirts being worn by locals. I'd never seen so many people wearing colours in all my life. It wasn't just Ecuadorian sides or even the big Spanish teams as was normally the case in Latin cities. The jerseys on show ranged from Everton, to Ajax, to PSG and even Catania. After strolling across Parque Bolívar, where there were numerous iguanas and turtles lounging around waiting to be fed, we stumbled upon the renovated Malecón boasting sparkling new restaurants and spacious riverside walkways. We were then afforded good views of the city having climbed Las Peñas' quaint cobbled alleys, to a lighthouse on top of a hill.

Leaving a few hours to spare until kick-off, we caught a bus which passed as close to the venue as possible. Armed with a couple of litros for the remaining kilometre saunter down a closed highway, the atmosphere began to build. Taking into account how passionate the rivalry between these two clubs was, it was surreal to see fans in Barcelona and Emelec colours mingling peacefully by the ground. This fixture was deemed so important that a film was made about it in the mid 1970's. More recently it had been the setting for a destroyed stadium and the death of a child. But none of that was apparent in the hours leading up to kick off.

We arrived at Estadio Monumental Isidro Romero Carbo at the same time as the Emelec players' coach, which suffered a customary volley of abuse, but nothing violent. After buying an $8 ticket another cerveza was the priority. We gravitated towards a row of garages with their roller shutters raised, which doubled as watering holes. Picking the least busy one, we'd not had time to order a drink before we were surrounded by inquisitive Barca supporters. Soon the beer was flowing, girls were taking pictures on their phones with my teenage companion, and we were all having photos with various flags. They were very warm and welcoming, principally because they didn't receive too many foreign visitors.

The association was founded by a Spanish immigrant in the 1920's, and had since grown to become the country's most popular. During my time in Ecuador I was acutely aware of Barcelona, as in seemingly every town I passed through there were folk showing their loyalty by wearing one of the distinctive replica kits. This was their most prestigious game of the season – the shipyard derby. Barca's preparations hadn't been the best; they'd lost their previous home encounter by three goals against ESPOLI (Quito's police academy team). In hindsight that result might not have been as disastrous as it appeared. After all I think we have already established that you don't mess with the Ecuadorian police!

At 17:15 the roller shutters descended, and 30 of us staggered to the turnstiles. We split into two groups and headed with the barra to the south end, unfortunately the girls went in the more tranquil main stand. South America's second largest football venue (89,000 capacity) was an impressive sight, even when only a quarter full. Considering the standard of Ecuadorian football and particularly the host's lack of recent success, it seemed extravagant to be playing in such a grandiose arena. Two double-tiered ends housed the popular or general crowds, with the barra favouring the lower south terrace. Preferencial seating arced around either side and there were five rows of executive boxes above the upper tier.

We were led by our new Barca buddies straight into the heart of La Sur Oscura barra, ten meters away from the band. Despite there being over half an hour to kick-off, the atmosphere was electric. As the away contingent swelled we had no choice but to jump and sing about putos azules. By the time the players entered the cauldron of noise

139

Emelec's support had increased to over 5,000 and I was ready to go home. It had been tiring leaping around, singing along to semi-familiar songs, trying to stay on my feet whilst groups of youths barged their way up and down the stand. With the pitch covered in a blanket of blue smoke, what felt like the longest ever half of football got under way. The highlight of a terrible 45 minutes was noticing young kids holding up sheet music for the band, helping them follow songs, and not being able to watch the game. It was also nice to see the barra looking after a teenager who'd taken a nasty fall in one the many surges forward. The bouncing stopped just long enough to carry him to a Red Cross station.

We spent the second period in the calmer upper tier, having inspected an imaginative range of graffiti in the concourse. My personal favourite was a simple: concha tu madre. By this time darkness had fallen and our vantage point allowed us to witness the ebb and flow of banter between the two groups of barra. Much like the English second city derby that weekend the contest was a huge let-down, it finished 0 v 0 with minimal content of note.

Not that this dampened our spirits. After the final whistle we returned to the centre, where we went to a traditional Ecuadorian dance hall. Initially befriended by some municipal workers who fell asleep on their chairs between jaunts to the bar, it wasn't long before we were both in the middle of the dance floor, each with a local woman on our arm. I couldn't vouch for much by the end of the evening, but I'm sure it involved a taxi ride with one of the ladies to a strange area of town, discovering I had no cash and somehow finding my way back to the hotel. The Beer Fairies were working overtime that night.

We attempted to leave Guayaquil the next day but neglected to account for the fact that it was school holidays, so buses to any respectable destination were sold out. I stayed for another night while my companion opted for a sleeper service to Quito. A quiet Sunday afternoon drinking in the sun was interrupted when we were invited to a party, being held on the top floor of a block of flats opposite the bar we were sat outside. As the sun was setting, we took a rusty elevator to the fifth floor, where we were greeted by booming techno music coming from inside a darkened room. Having bought a cerveza and got settled, it dawned on me the other revellers were predominantly gay. It was a strangely funny experience and the university students who were hosting the event were really welcoming. The evening's climax was a drunken dance-off, where the two attractive young female finalists ended up in nothing but their underwear. I realised it might be time to leave, as one of the organisers asked me which of the two teenagers I wanted to take home. He didn't accept my explanation about inappropriate age gaps and called the winner over. There was an uncomfortable few minutes of small talk before I made my excuses and left.

By Monday morning things had calmed down sufficiently so I was able to get a bus to the coast. This was a mistake. The weather was lousy and the beach towns were expensive and rammed full of people. Montañita, a popular surf spot, resembled some kind of bizarre Ecuadorian Spring Break, as students wrapped up against the elements partied on a grey and miserable beach in the daytime. It didn't take long for me to decide to return to Guayaquil's welcome warmth and prepare for my last match in the country.

Game 30

Emelec v El Nacional – (Primera A) - 2 v 0
Friday 5th November 2010 – 18:00
Estadio George Capwell, Guayaquil

You know a beer is cold when the first gulp gives you a little headache. At six o'clock on my Mother's birthday and Bonfire Night (surprisingly neither of which were celebrated in Ecuador) I was trying to down an ice cold litro, purchase a replica shirt, a ticket and some food, all at the same time. Characteristically I was late for kick-off after failing to alight at the correct bus stop, meaning I had to retrace my steps for half an hour. But with a $5 shirt, a $3 ticket and a $1 burger, I'd not missed too much by the time I found a place in La Avenida Quito's vertigo-inducing upper tier. One of the reasons for staying in Guayaquil an extra week was to attend a game at Estadio George Capwell. As far as I could see, Leicester City dismantled Filbert Street in 2003 and moved it brick by brick to the south coast of Ecuador. There was a large and modern main stand opposite a tiny shed of a side, in addition to two steep double tiered ends.

Emelec was founded by a group who were employed by an electricity company. The team hadn't been as successful on the pitch as their bitter city rival, but did boast an interesting barra brava. Oddly titled Boca del Pozo (mouth of the well) was the oldest supporter group in Ecuador and always well represented at away ties. Their commitment to travelling had won La Boca many admirers from barra in other countries. The guy I was chatting to during an uneventful first half boasted that he didn't have to pay for accommodation when visiting any major city on the continent, because of his association with Emelec's loyal fans. He claimed that he'd been to several fixtures in the Libertadores and Sudamericana and the local barra had always helped him out. At the time I was sceptical as to the legitimacy of his story, but a bit of research confirmed that for some reason there was a lot of love for Emelec's barra from their rival South American firms.

The second period was an improvement on the first. Emelec scored twice to record a comfortable victory over the visitors from Quito. I was a bit underwhelmed by the tame celebrations from their legendary followers, although anything more exuberant would have been hazardous to their wellbeing. La Avenida de Quito end was set at such a sheer angle that it felt like one wrong move could result in a very big fall. I'm confident a British Health and Safety official would be less than impressed with the architecture. This win helped Emelec finish in second place, leading to a tense playoff against LDU Quito for the championship. The highlanders brought a two goal advantage to Guayaquil, which they defended even after conceding in the second half and ending the contest with nine men.

On Saturday I continued my journey south towards the Peruvian border. I spent an enjoyable month or so in Ecuador, which considering its relatively small size, offered some incredible natural charms. The football had also been fun, despite antisocial kick-offs such as ten o'clock on a Saturday morning and four o'clock on a Wednesday afternoon. It was arguably the best footballing country in South America as it was the only one where I could buy alcohol inside the stadiums.

PERU

Population – 29 million
Size – 1.28 million km²
Time Zone – GMT ⁻5
Currency – Nuevo Sol
FIFA World Ranking – #68 (2010)
Best World Cup Finish – Quarter-finals (1970)
Biggest Teams – Universitario, Alianza Lima, Sporting Cristal

You might have heard of:
Nolberto Solano, Claudio Pizarro, Jefferson Farfan, Israel Zuniga, Machu Picchu

Essential Spanish:
Voluntarios – Donation/Bribe
Litro - Litre
Trinchera – Trench
Norte - North
Campesino – Farmers/People from the country
Sendero Luminoso – Shining Path
Divertido – Fun

Game 31

Defensor San José v Unión Comercio - (Copa Peru Final 16) - 2 v 0
Sunday 7th November 2010 – 15:30
Estadio Mariscal Caceres, Tumbes

I checked out a hotel on my first morning in Peru intending on taking a bus to the touristy beach town of Máncora. Within half an hour of returning the keys, thanking and bidding farewell to the pleasant elderly owners, I was checking back into the same room. In my possession: a ticket to the big game being played in Tumbes that afternoon.
　　The previous day's travelling had taken me eight hours south from Guayaquil, through green banana growing countryside to the border. I'd read and heard a few stories about Gringos being robbed in Peru and planned to treat it with suspicion. Lo and behold, having completed Ecuadorian formalities, I was crossing a busy bridge from one country to another, chatting to a local taxi driver who was half-heartedly trying to win my business, when Peruvian immigration officers stopped me. An officious pair ushered me into their cabin where they inspected my passport and demanded a copy of my Yellow Fever certification. Fully aware that it was not a compulsory requirement, I delved into my bag and produced the documentation. Undeterred by my paperwork being in order, the two officers expected me to provide a letter from Interpol confirming I wasn't wanted for a crime in my homeland. Upon questioning what they proposed to do with this, they pointed to a non-functioning, antiquated computer saying they needed to verify my eligibility to enter Peru. As soon as I said I'd never heard of, and certainly didn't need such an item, they started discussing voluntarios. I laughed, snatched my passport back with a shake of the head and left muttering about how I'd anticipated this. Blatantly the whole operation was to extort money out of unwitting foreigners.
　　After a night's rest in the non-descript town of Tumbes, located 20 kilometres from the border, I hailed a moto-taxi to a bus terminal. During the five minute ride the usual pleasantries passed between me and the driver. The second I mentioned football, he enthusiastically informed me there was a match being played that afternoon. Once he explained the significance of the fixture, I was sold. We did a dangerous U-turn in the middle of a busy highway and headed for the stadium. There was already a buzz around tiny Estadio Mariscal

145

Caceres when we arrived, over four hours before kick-off. I bought a ticket and requested to return to where we started. All of a sudden I was sat outside the hotel I'd only just left, arguing about the fare.

My first footballing experience in the new country was the brilliant Copa Peru. This competition commenced early in the season with a regional league, which included teams registered with the area's Football Association. Each league winner progressed to a knockout tournament; the overall champions gained automatic promotion to the Premier División, and the runner-up to their second tier. The inclusive nature and to a limited degree romance of it, was similar to our FA Cup (with better weather). On that sun-baked afternoon, with lines of moto-taxis clogging the dual carriageway out of town, it felt a lot like a FA Cup third round tie. It was a good job I purchased my ticket in advance as shortly after my arrival it was declared a sell-out. The home colours were a garish combination of luminous orange and bright blue, so naturally I bought a replica shirt, the comical-looking sleeveless version.

Estadio Mariscal Caceres had two entrances accessible via either a cheap ticket (sol) or a marginally more expensive one (preferencial). Both sides were practically identical, the difference being that one was blessed with shaded cover whilst the other was exposed to the sun. I was in the less expensive one, which initially I saw as an opportunity to work on my tan, but regretted it after half an hour in the unforgiving 30 degree heat. Full with an approximate 6,000 people housed in small stands wrapped around an oval running track, there was a fairly strong barra presence even at this level. In the middle of the cheaper side a collection of drums and trumpets were giving the singing momentum. Surrounding the band was a compact section of jumping supporters, with children playing and dancing in front of them.

A kind police officer took my Zulu Army photo, while the radio commentary was supplied by two men in a tiny dugout, shouting into an ancient mobile phone. Large clouds of dust were created every time there was action in the grassless centre of the pitch. It reminded me of Folkestone Invicta FC, the team from where I'd grown up on the Kent coast. There were many comparisons to be drawn between the club from Tumbes and the one I followed in the Ryman Leagues throughout my adolescence. It wasn't only their hideous Orange shirts, the setup was noticeably semi-professional. There was a sense of community amongst the spectators; it felt like the whole town had come to watch the game.

Tumbes ran out 2 v 0 winners, scoring a goal in each half on a difficult surface. Despite a clear advantage going into the following Sunday's octavos de final second leg, the departing Defensor fans looked slightly dejected. I spoke to a handful of locals who felt that they needed a greater margin to progress. Unión Comercio, from the jungle plateau town of Moyobamba, were a much bigger club and vastly superior in terms of resources. As it turned out a 2 v 0 home victory was the score line in the second leg; Unión going on to win the tie on penalties. They eventually progressed to the final, which they won, and the next season more than held their own in the Primera División.

On the way back to my hotel I stopped for a quick beverage outside a little roadside cabin. The business was apparently closed, but the owner was keen for me to join him and a friend as they enjoyed some social drinks. The pair of them, both in their mid-40's, were absolutely plastered and sharing litre bottles of cerveza using a solitary short glass. This Latin American custom wasn't the most hygienic way to consume beer. After the first person had slugged their portion, they shook the foam out of the bottom and passed it on, repeating the process until a new bottle was required. I declined to join their rounds, instead I bought my own litro which I drank straight from the receptacle. As daylight began to fade and the duo became more incomprehensible, a three man mariachi–style band passed where we were sitting. The excitable proprietor paid a disproportionate amount of money for them to play for us. It was an amusing end to an unexpected day as we sang songs such as the legendary Guantanamera late into the night.

Game 32

Uni César Vallejo v Juan Aurich – (Primera División) - 0 v 0
Wednesday 10th November 2010 - 16:00
Estadio Mansiche, Trujillo

Tumbes had been fun. A scan of Peru's league schedule the next morning informed me there was a game on Tuesday in Trujillo, a coastal town roughly halfway between Ecuador and Lima. Discarding the idea of sunning myself in Máncora, I went chasing the footballing dragon. At this stage I was using a website called www.soccerway.com to plan my adventures. In Central America I'd been quite literally playing it by ear, in Colombia I was using their helpful FA website called Dimayor, but the Ecuadorian association's site was such a mess I had to find an alternative. I've since become a huge fan of soccerway, which contained accurate information relating to pretty much every league in the world. It listed fixtures, results, had good archives and even maps showing you the location of the stadiums. It was a shame that on this particular occasion their facts were inaccurate.

By Monday evening I'd managed to get as far as Chiclayo, home of Juan Aurich, leaving a four hour ride to Trujillo on match day. The scenery had changed drastically from lush mountainous greenery in Ecuador, to bleak rolling sand dunes as far as the eye could see. Transport in South America was a dramatic improvement from Central – gone were the chicken buses, replaced by more modern double-decker coaches. I really liked the individually customised ancient vehicles in Nicaragua and Guatemala, but at the same time appreciated the increment in luxury as I was covering far greater distances in the southern continent. What I couldn't understand was why a ticket for the lower level of these new coaches was up to twice as expensive as the upper. After all you got a better view in a more elevated position.

A taxi driver taking me from the terminal to the city centre advised me the tie was actually on Wednesday at 18:00. This proved rather confusing, as at 16:15 the following day, an Argentinian I'd befriended told me it had already kicked off. I assumed he was referring to the Manchester derby being shown live on ESPN, but after checking realised I was missing the first half of a fixture I'd trekked 13 hours to see. Fortunately it was only a five minute march to the ground, where the ticket was a merciful $1. We arrived just in time to see the players leaving for the break. It wasn't too much of a disaster as there had been no goals. A man sat next to us in Estadio Mansiche's modest 25,000 capacity bowl of an open arena, made it perfectly clear up to that point it'd been dull and we'd done ourselves a favour by turning up late.

Within ten minutes of the restart we'd witnessed a fight, three red cards, two open goal misses and a saved penalty. The rest of the half was comically terrible. In a way it was a shame there was hardly anyone in attendance as I don't think I've ever laughed so much at a football match. The players didn't exactly cover themselves in glory on that chaotic afternoon in Trujillo, it's still a mystery to me how it finished goalless. Juan Aurich's best chances were squandered by Panamanian international striker Luis Tejada, who'd been so deadly when I'd seen him in his homeland. Unsurprisingly neither team challenged for the title that season.

El clásico Peruano was later that evening between Lima rivals Alianza and Universitario. In the confusion surrounding the César Vallejo farce I'd forgotten it was being played. Strolling through Trujillo's colonial centre I was startled to see a group of 50 men crowded around a large screen outside a casino. The atmosphere looked electric and the contest was a cracker. Alianza, the home side, scored a late equaliser in front of the most populous segment of their fans, who celebrated as wildly as any I'd seen.

I woke up the next morning not feeling right, so bought some supplies from a supermarket and retired to my hotel room. I stayed there for 48 hours, unable to move owing to painful and unpredictable bowel movements. When travelling it's important to acknowledge that you will inevitably get ill and it will likely be stomach-related. I treated my two days in bed as a welcome opportunity to catch up on some trash US TV. Once recovered I headed to the coastal town of Puerto Chicama, purportedly home to the world's longest wave. Due to the bay's unique geography it was possible to ride a single wave for over two kilometres; there were pictures in the town's surf shops proving it. I attempted to negotiate the rolling swells with absolutely no success. They were definitely very long, but unlike my previous meetings with the Pacific Ocean the water was freezing cold, and I wasn't an especially accomplished surfer. I'm English after all, it's a bit like salsa dancing - it's just not in my blood.

Game 33

Universidad San Martín v Inti Gas - (Primera División) - 4 v 1
Sunday 21st November 2010 – 15:30
Estadio San Martín de Porres, Lima

Game 34

Alianza Lima v Total Chalaco - (Primera División) - 2 v 1
Sunday 21st November 2010 – 17:45
Estadio Alejandro Villanueva, Lima

Lima Super Sunday started with league leaders San Martín against mid-table Inti Gas. For some reason the fixture was being played at Sporting Cristal's Estadio San Martín de Porres, which conveniently was very close to my hotel. Crossing the Río Rímac the venue was inconspicuous without any floodlights, signs, crowds or even noise. On another glorious afternoon a $3.50 ticket saw me sitting opposite the main stand, shading my eyes from the glare. I was watching the best team in the division take their tally to 91 points from 42 games. It was a quiet opening half an hour, but suddenly San Martín slipped a couple of gears, split the Inti defence in two, allowing Pedro García to fire home. They doubled their advantage on the stroke of half time when a deflected cross fell to midfielder Quinteros, whose clever overhead kick nestled in the bottom corner.

The majority of the small crowd were fairly subdued, but there was an interesting and vocal section of barra. 100 students with drums, horns and an enormous flag (which was unfurled after each goal) were being led by their talisman and club mascot – a tooth. I couldn't work out what was going on, but on closer inspection it was clear that there was a man in a large white tooth costume conducting the singing. The tooth also had its own song: 'Que bailar la abuela' which as far as I was concerned meant 'how does the grandmother dance' although something might have been lost in translation. It musn't have been a pleasant job in the heavy outfit on such a warm day, but throughout the 90 minutes he tirelessly endeavoured to bring the crowd to life. Obviously there was only one Zulu Army photo to be had. I approached him during the second period and without saying a word he posed, shook my hand, listened to me asking what the significance of the costume was, responded by doing his trademark shuffle, before wandering off. I figured that as real teeth can't speak he was a consummate professional by remaining in character at all times. As I was later to discover, the relevance of a tooth for this university club was that their most devoted barra were dental students.

Interestingly the second half got underway with a 22 man brawl, as a result only 20 of them stayed on the pitch. This didn't go any way towards changing the outcome, by the hour mark San Martín had scored another couple of goals, triggering two more appearances for the flag and much gyration from the tooth. The match finished with Inti Gas claiming a consolation and the tooth in the corporate area trying to get bemused people to dance with him.

I didn't have time to dither as there was less than 30 minutes until kick-off in the day's second fixture. Following a little confusion I managed to get a minibus to the other side of central Lima, and strutted four intimidatingly rough blocks to Estadio Alejandro Villanueva. With three games left in the season, Alianza, although out of the title race, were battling to keep hold of their third position in order to secure a valuable place in the subsequent year's Copa Libertadores. The Lima heavyweights were rightfully deemed to be the country's second biggest club. Challenging them for a top three finish were their archenemy Universitario, Peru's largest club.

A generous crowd witnessed a captivating tie, as Total Chalaco scored in the first half and Alianza then struggled to break them down. There was an air of desperation in the home crowd, but with 20 minutes remaining the contest was turned on its head. A crazy five minutes began with Chalaco's best opportunity of the half and ended with Alianza scoring two scrappy goals, followed by a visiting Colombian defender being given his marching orders. In the last quarter of an hour the hosts wasted numerous openings to seal it, before Chalco missed their inevitable chance to equalise in injury time. This win put Alianza in pole position to qualify for the continent's most prestigious club tournament.

I spent an uneasy evening standing in the south terrace amid El Comando Sur barra brava. The area surrounding Estadio Alejandro Villanueva was clearly a poor barrio; it had a lawless feel to it which seemed to carry into the ground. From my vantage point high in the corner I was a safe distance from the bulk of the lunatics. They energetically bounced and sang throughout, their trademark appearing to be throwing navy blue and white umbrellas into the air. It was the groups of youths near to me play-fighting and messing about that was unsettling. Camouflaged in a replica Alianza shirt it was an anonymous game, the only person I spoke to for its duration was a lad who took a quick Zulu Army photo. I was probably being paranoid as I arrived at my hotel unscathed, after an hour-long walk through the dark and dangerous streets of Lima. There were many venues in the Americas I felt welcome as a foreigner, but this was certainly not one of them.

I really enjoyed my day: eight goals, three red cards, flying umbrellas and a dancing tooth, all in the space of four hours. It was interesting to see Peru's best footballing side playing in such a modest setting, whilst one of the largest clubs looked comparatively inept on the pitch despite playing in front of over 20,000 people in a nice stadium. It raised a question that I'd contemplated after my weekend in Bogotá. Does the environment change your perception of the quality of football being played?

Historically the Peruvian league was similar to the majority of its Latin American counterparts. Introduced by British expatriates in the late 19th century, the first competition was held in 1912 and the sport went professional in 1951. Until 1965 exclusively clubs from Lima or nearby Callao were allowed to participate. This was eventually expanded to the whole country. The silly league format employed whilst I was there involved the teams playing each other once, before being split into two groups. The sides in 1st, 3rd, 5th, 7th, 9th, 11th, 13th and 15th places at the halfway stage went into one group, whilst the others went into a second. They then reversed the fixtures and the two group winners had a playoff to determine who would be champion. San Martín competed against León de Huánuco from the central highlands in the final, winning the two legged tie by a solitary goal.

The decider was an unusual affair as four players had been sent off in the first leg after a mass brawl. Peru's FA made an incredibly controversial call by rescinding the dismissal of only one of the four; León's star Argentine midfielder Gustavo Rodas. This was regardless of the fact he'd tried to punch opponents, as the referee had stated in his match report. Although he was cleared for the second leg, León's manager made the honourable decision not to include Rodas in the squad, even though he was their best player. Franco Navarro acknowledged the injustice of the ruling by enforcing his own suspension, at the same time proving that occasionally there is chivalry in football.

I spent a relatively uneventful ten days in Lima hidden away in a nice hotel room, recovering from the bug I'd picked up in Trujillo and three month's hectic travelling. I was keen to see Universitario at home the following Saturday, but my primary reason for hanging around was that The Smashing Pumpkins and Stereophonics were playing a concert at Estadio San Marcos. By that time I'd established there were three things I missed about England: food, cricket and live music. In the first month of the trip I saw three fantastic bands. Also, just before Nicaragua's Revolutionary celebrations, I'd watched the excellent Calle 13 perform a free show in the middle of a rainy Carretera Masaya, to support the Sandinistas (next to the statue of their mate Alexis).

One proper gig in over a year meant that I was excited about seeing two groups that were, at that point in their careers, essentially tribute acts. I had a great time in a big football stadium on Thanksgiving, drunkenly singing along to anthems that'd been an integral part of my adolescence. But to be honest both bands sounded tired and dated. It was a shame really because there was a time when I'd have genuinely believed it was an amazing line-up. Unfortunately that time was 1997.

For all the dangerous and dodgy places I stayed in the Americas, Lima was the worst. I deliberately picked a hotel away from the tourist areas so I was afforded a bit of a disguise from potential thieves; even then I was still the victim of an elaborate scam which cost me $40. Peruvians struck me as being a little unstable in comparison to other Latinos I'd met on my merry way. I was always conscious that there seemed to be an ulterior motive to their interactions with foreigners, which generally involved money. This impression was probably unfair as I did meet some sincere and affable natives there; the difference was that they were in the minority, which was the opposite in other countries I visited.

Peru, much like Colombia, had a cocaine mafia subsidising their terrorist groups. The Shining Path was the most prominent and violent of the organisations; their objectives included attempting to bring down the government so as to redistribute property and wealth. Based in rural mountainous provinces, el Sendero Luminoso was financed by narco-trafficking and controlled vast coca growing regions, much like the Colombian guerrillas FARC. The Peruvian group, whose ideology was based on Chinese anti-capitalist Mao Zedong's teachings, enforced their rule on los campesinos by banning alcohol and outlawing private parties. Popular support was limited due to their violent actions; often publically executing people for minor offences and then refusing to bury the bodies.

In the 1980's the Shining Path's directed their violence at high profile targets. A failed governmental bid to quash the terrorists, by giving the military almost unlimited power in rural districts, led to increased violence. It's estimated that over 60,000 died in a 20 year period of conflict. Sendero Luminoso's influence slowly dwindled in the early 1990's following the capture of their founder and leader, former professor of philosophy, Abimael Guzman. During the month I spent in Peru they garnered very little media attention, although that could change as cocaine production increased, providing the terrorists with a larger revenue stream.

Game 35

Universitario v Sporting Cristal - (Primera División) - 1 v 1
Sunday 28th November 2010 – 15:00
Estadio Monumental, Lima

A Copa Libertadores place was up for grabs on the season's penultimate weekend. Universitario (La U) knew they needed to beat Lima rival Sporting Cristal, and hope Inti Gas could do them a favour at home to Alianza. It was quite an exciting prospect as I took an hour-long bus ride from majestic Plaza San Martín, looking weird bathed in summer sunshine and covered in Christmas decorations, to barrio Tupac Amaru. Estadio Monumental was flanked by large sandy cliffs and the surrounding area had been purpose-built for pedestrians, with wide colour-coded paths leading to different parts of the ground. Its scale and setup impressed me; that was until I'd hiked around the bloody great thing to find there was nowhere to buy tickets. It transpired the best place to have bought an entrada would have been a supermarket, which was completely logical. I'd initially pondered going in the Sporting Cristal end, but their gangs of bedraggled youths loitering by the entrance dissuaded me. So I paid a tout $5 (twice the face value) and joined a gigantic queue to enter the north stand, home to La U's Trinchera Norte barra brava.

Passing through the turnstiles sometime after kick-off, two policemen confronted me requesting I hand over my documents and belt. They got neither. I found a comparatively calm spot amid the cream-shirted masses and watched the remainder of a listless first half stalemate. Estadio Monumental was very similar to Barcelona's ground of the same name; the vast lower tiers sloped up to a wide band of executive boxes. The 80,000 capacity venue was half full. A reasonable amount of Sporting Cristal supporters at one end attempted to counter the noise created by a huge section of bouncing barra at the other. Even after 35 matches, the sight of such an enormous number of people singing and jumping in unison was still mesmerizing, especially considering they did it for three hours in 30 degree heat.

With 20 minutes to go in a marginally livelier second period, a U defender inexplicably passed the ball straight to Peruvian striker Andy Pando, who had the simple task of scoring past an exposed keeper. This sparked wild scenes of celebration from the visiting contingent, which antagonised the authorities. Their glee was short-lived as a line of riot police moved swiftly to brutally supress their jubilation. Once that calmed down news filtered through that Alianza (who'd been trailing 1 v 0 at half time) had scored twice. It led to a mass exodus, as la U faithful resigned themselves to playing in 2011's Copa Sudamericana. Those that stayed behind witnessed a sweetly struck half-volleyed equaliser, which was by definition, too little, too late.

The fun and games didn't stop there though as they didn't retain one set of fans after the final whistle. Consequently, as I was returning to the highway along a special pedestrian walkway, it was necessary to dodge a plethora of items being thrown from the other side of the road. A pitched battle between the two sets of barra was on the verge of getting genuinely dangerous, until a line of police on horses swept Sporting Cristal's youths back towards Estadio Monumental, leaving a line of bloodied casualties in their wake.

Alianza's afternoon ended in a draw, which was sufficient to see them into Copa Libertadores' qualifying round. In the end all the fuss surrounding third spot was totally pointless. Two months later, in their first leg qualifier at home to Jaguares (Mexico - game 2) Alianza lost 2 v 0, whimpering out of the competition 4 v 0 on aggregate before the group stage had even started.

Game 36

Cienciano v Alianza Athletico - (Primera División) - 2 v 1
Sunday 5th December 2010 – 15:00
Estadio Inca Garcilaso de la Vega, Cusco

I'd planned to watch Cienciano at home in the season's final round of matches, but had completely overlooked the fixture's importance. Blissfully unaware that there were relegation issues to be resolved, I endured a 20 hour bus journey from Lima to Cusco. The overnight ride wasn't particularly comfortable as I was woken at three in the morning by an English girl sitting next to me, to discover I was the prime suspect in the case of her missing camera. She didn't ever find out who took it (I'm with Shaggy - It Wasn't Me) but she did steal a drunken kiss from me precisely 24 hours after the incident.

This memorable contest was the highlight of my time in a place most famous for its proximity to some rubbishy old buildings, called Machu something or another. The situation was relatively simple: Cienciano had to win or they'd be relegated. Alianza Athlético required a point to secure safety, although they would stay up regardless of the result if José Galivez, from the industrial coastal city of Chimbote, lost in Lima against Sporting Cristal.

On Saturday afternoon I went to see whether it was possible to purchase a ticket. It was, but there were two queues, both at least a kilometre long, snaking around Estadio Inca Garcilaso de la Vega and into a local barrio. At first I was excited about queuing in advance to buy a football ticket, the last time I'd done that was to gain entry to Blues' playoff final victory in Cardiff. After half an hour of standing motionless in incessant rain I made an executive decision to buy one from a tout on match day. Which I did the following morning for three times face value, less than $7. I was amazed to see that with over four hours to go the doors weren't open, and the queue to enter was further than I could see or care to walk. I figured it would be best to return at kick-off when everyone was settled inside and there'd be no delays.

Great idea in theory. However I'd not anticipated that the fixture was sold out twice over. Apparently Cienciano had initially issued the correct quantity of tickets (45,000) but when they'd all been snapped up in advance thought it'd only be fair to release another batch, to capitalise on their biggest tie for seven years. Then Cusco's council saw they were missing out on a good way of making cash, so printed

157

their own set, which they sold from the town hall.

Ten minutes prior to kick-off I strutted two short uphill blocks from my hotel to Estadio Inca Garcilaso de la Vega. It was worrying to see thousands of Peruvians still queuing, as the ground had looked full on the television coverage. I headed towards the main entrance with half a litre of cerveza to finish. Rather ominously it was closed. Having double checked this was the one I should use, I stood observing the crowds. It was minutes until the whistle and a mob at the front of the line was getting restless. A vendor told me the police had closed the doors an hour beforehand, promising they'd be reopened just before the match began. Banging and shouting soon evolved into a group of 20 men trying to push their way through the gates. With a little assistance they succeeded and the doors swung open to an enormous roar from the waiting supporters. Not wanting to miss my opportunity I ran and joined a stampede trying to squeeze into the opening. It was very much like game 10 in Honduras, I took a deep breath and squirmed my way around the periphery into the entrance.

By the time I was halfway inside the crowd's forward momentum had been halted and we were all stuck. Using the frame of the gate to pull myself up and over the bodies, I burst out of the huddle into a small field, quickly checking I still had all my belongings intact (including a half-drunk litre bottle of beer). As my composure returned I saw why there was only a trickle of people moving through the doors. To my horror I realised that a group at the front had fallen over, and were being crushed by the weight of the masses trying to move forward. Discarding my beverage I went to help drag some of the unfortunate souls away from the crush, but it was a fruitless task due to the surging Peruvians behind them. Some folk whose friends and family were buried in the human avalanche were throwing rocks into the oncoming hordes, trying to drive them back in order to assist what were, disturbingly, mostly women and children on the floor.

There was no time to dawdle as riot police came charging from inside the stadium. I narrowly dodged a couple of baton blows aimed in my direction and ran at full speed to the comparative safety of the stands. I paused momentarily to see officers beating the multitude back, before climbing some steep steps into the upper tier. After catching my breath I checked the entrance and saw three pickup trucks with wounded bodies sprawled out on the rear, while a line of police secured the gates. The next day a local newspaper reported there had been an undisclosed number hospitalised, but no fatalities.

Following the harrowing introduction I found a reasonable

158

viewpoint in the overcrowded terrace and witnessed the remainder of a nervous first half. Despite there being a distinct lack of quality on the pitch, the slippery conditions and stakes contributed to an engrossing encounter. Although Alianza were in the ascendancy, Cienciano scored after half an hour. A sweeping counterattack saw a striker go clean through. With just the goalkeeper to beat, he slipped on the greasy surface, managing to knock the ball across the face of goal. It seemed as though the chance had passed with two Alianza defenders in the vicinity, though neither was able to gain control, allowing defender Renzo Reaños to hammer into an unguarded net. The celebrations were suitably wild, both on and off the field, for a comical but incredibly significant goal.

At the interval I returned to the entrance; all the casualties had been cleared and the gates were braced with several large wooden planks. An inspection of La Furia Roja barra revealed it was made up of the usual shirtless youths with crazed looks in their eyes, as well as a few locals in festive Inca costumes. It wasn't a comfortable atmosphere so I retreated to the relative sanctity of the upper tier.

Cienciano were a little anxious in the second period, and with Alianza dominating midfield it wasn't a huge shock when they equalised. Shortly after the restart a sloppy back-pass was punished with a delightfully chipped finish in front of Cusco's barra. The players celebrated whilst debris of all shapes and sizes rained down upon them. It took five minutes for staff to pacify the spectators in the main stand, as their reaction to the visiting dugout's jubilation looked like turning violent. Thankfully the tie wasn't level for long. On 57 minutes Juan Carlos Mariño wrote his name into Cienciano folklore by gaining possession 30 yards out, before dispatching a low drive into the corner of the net. The game was delayed for a further five minutes as every home player, staff and substitute celebrated deliriously.

All of a sudden the contest ceased to be a competitive spectacle. It degenerated into some kind of strange training routine, as both sides were happy to play within themselves without any real challenge from the opposition. José Galivez were losing in Lima, so the result in Cusco as it stood ensured both clubs stayed in the league. A surreal half an hour passed without incident, and everybody who had managed to get into Estadio Inca Garcilaso de la Vega went home happy that their team would once again be able to compete in the Primera División.

The final day of my third season watching football in the Americas couldn't of have ended any better. I got back to my hotel and streamed live coverage of England winning the second Ashes test against Australia in Adelaide, our first victory on Aussie soil since January 2002 in Sydney (which I attended).

After Colombia's suave, eye-opening, civilised chaos, and amiable Ecuador, with its spectacular easily accessible scenery, I thought Peru was disappointing in comparison. From the second I'd set foot in the country I found the people to be slightly more devious than other Latinos and not as warm and friendly as I was used to. Travelling is a completely subjective experience and various different factors contribute towards my appreciation of a place. For me nothing really clicked and I ended up leaving with a somewhat negative opinion of the nation. So negative in fact, that in a spate of bloody-mindedness I refused to pay a privately owned company - PeruRail - $150 to spend three hours with hundreds of other tourists at Machu Picchu. Speaking to other Gringos later in the trip they recoiled in horror that I hadn't been to an attraction which was to most the highlight of their South American tour. I was sceptical prior to arriving in Cusco, as to hike the famous Inca Trail it was necessary to book at least three months in advance and it cost an unrepresentative amount of money for the privilege. If I'd have been bothered about seeing the ancient wonder I'd have taken one of the alternative trekking routes, which were a fraction of the cost and weren't part of the Gringo Trail. But I was in Cusco for a specific reason and I enjoyed my stay. Even though I didn't relish Peru as much as other countries I spent a decent period of time in, it had one brilliant redeeming aspect: fútbol.

Bolivia was next on the agenda. With a break in football seasons for a couple of months I was determined to partake in some conventional tourist activities. I started in Copacabana, on the shore of Lake Titicaca, deemed to be the world's largest high altitude lake. At almost four kilometres above sea level it felt like the clouds were so low that you could touch them, and the lake itself - sandwiched between Peru and Bolivia - was a stunning pure blue colour, particularly at sunset. A day's hike around mystical Isla del Sol with a crowd of other Gringos was a pleasant excursion, even though at seemingly every gatepost or fallen tree you were expected to pay a toll. I'd been at altitude for over a week, but still found it a breathless march to complete the circuit in time to catch a boat back to the mainland. It actually wouldn't have been such a bad idea to have spent a peaceful night in the rustic accommodations, amongst Inca ruins where it's thought they believed the sun was born.

In a country of 'the world's highest' the approach to the capital was a dramatic reminder of how elevated I was. Twisting and turning into La Paz, houses clung to slopes, as the developed central zone's glistening modern elegance dropped away towards towering, snow-capped Mt Illamani in the distance. I had a successful shopping spree in the Black Market, which smothered the uneven meandering steep roads, containing genuinely fake merchandise and bizarre fast food offerings. The nightlife was a funky mix of backpacker strongholds and grimy local clubs, selling beer at room temperature. This was to be an unwelcome feature in Bolivia, although in fairness at that altitude and with a distinct lack of insulation, room temperature tended to be similar to that inside my fridge at home.

Many other male Gringos I met in La Paz were there to visit San Pedro prison, featured in the book 'Marching Powder'. Situated in a less than imposing, whitewashed building on an ordinary-looking street; spending time in this jail was once a daring achievement, involving arrangements with inmates. The guards had since realised the moneymaking potential. People I spoke to said that it was an interesting outing, but it was just that, a tour. A few months later I heard from other travellers who'd recently left Bolivia that San Pedro prison had been temporarily closed to tourists. Supposedly, some Australian lads had kicked-off about the quality and price of cocaine they'd bought from the convicts. Bloody bogans.

From the highest capital city in the world it was possible to ride the infamous Death Road. Dubbed by the Inter-American Development Bank as 'The World's Most Dangerous Road' the 70 kilometre track from La Cumbre to Coroico was a well-established tourist attraction. Previously the grandiose title was justified; an average of 25 vehicles per year fell to their peril. Since a paved relief road was constructed in 2007, the dirt and gravel trail was used virtually exclusively by cycling Gringos in fluorescent jackets. That's not to say the route was no longer perilous, the thin single lane snaking round the mountainside still had nothing to prevent you from falling off the sheer cliff faces. The weather was suitably treacherous on my descent, with low cloud and constant drizzle. In reality it was the freewheeling 20 kilometre stretch of tarmac before the Death Road itself which proved most hazardous. I sped through the clouds as ice formed on my goggles, reducing visibility to less than two metres.

The main event was absolutely exhilarating, despite damp conditions slowing the pace. The distractingly stunning views proved dangerous as I attempted to divide my attentions between gawping at the scenery and concentrating on the route. An array of crucifixes at regular intervals was a reminder of the many lives that had been claimed by the Death Road. Apparently the last to perish had been a French girl who was taking a photo when she stepped backwards to allow a truck past, slipping and plunging to her death. Our group made it to the bottom in one piece, but others hadn't been so fortunate. Casualties that day comprised of a broken arm and three smashed teeth.

La Paz was up there with Panama City as one of the oddest capitals I've ever visited, and it provided one entirely unique personal experience; I went to a museum that I actually enjoyed. For less than $1 I wandered around the Museum of Musical Instruments, trying out a number of weird and wonderful items along the way, such as: homemade pipe organs, giant bamboo shakers and the typically Bolivian Charango. ¡Divertido!

Oruro Police v EU Trust – (Friendly) – 4 v 4
Thursday 16ᵗʰ December 2010 – 15:00
Estadio Jesús Bermúdez – Oruro – Bolivia

Before catching a train to the Uyuni Salt Flats I had a day to kill in the bleak, dusty town of Oruro. I found myself sauntering through the streets looking for entertainment and stumbled upon the local football stadium, a modest-sized venue whose gates were wide open. I strolled into the last 25 minutes of a charity match, witnessing four goals, including two classy free kicks. There was only one European on the field of play and the organisers enthusiastically informed me I'd have got run out if I'd have turned up with my boots an hour earlier.

There was a week until Christmas, so I signed up for a standard three day tour of Salar de Uyuni. It was my favourite excursion of the trip and probably the most impressive natural wonder I've ever seen. As I have already opined: travelling is a wholly subjective pastime. For me the enjoyment of an expedition was dependent on the group of people I shared the jaunt with. A mixture of Mexicans, Brazilians and an Italian for this one worked well, and key to appreciating an arduous few days. It started well. I stepped off the train and bumped straight into the Swiss couple who I'd sailed with from Panama to Colombia. They'd completed a tour and were about to head to Argentina. During our brief conversation they outlined the location of a sizeable herbal package they'd just jettisoned, prior to crossing the border. I walked out the station with a big grin on my face, having picked up a black plastic bag from a bin on the way. An early Christmas present.

Because Salar de Uyuni was so photogenic, it's difficult to adequately describe the sparse beauty. A unique combination of altitude and geology produced a place of pure white (salt) and pure blue (sky). This was the world's largest salt flat and lithium reserve, a prehistoric saline lake over three and a half kilometres above sea level. Although it sounds dull, in reality it was a riot of colour, surrounded by vivid multi-layered red, yellow and orange mountains. There were also random 'islands' dotted around the pristine salt wilderness, remnants of ancient volcanoes. Added to the mix were thousands of pink flamingos who bred there prolifically, and jeeps full of international tourists, all constantly trying to take a perfect picture of the bizarrely isometric landscape.

The tour, much like the environment, was uncompromising. We slept in rustic accommodations and were woken at some ungodly hours when it was still dark. Watching the sun rise over steaming geysers and bubbling mud holes, followed by a pre-breakfast soak in mineral rich hot springs, was well worth overcoming the pain of an altitude-exacerbated hangover. This magnificent setting altered its appearance during rainy season, water sat on the salt surface creating a shimmering mirror which reflected the vast horizon.

In Potosí, the world's highest city, I wandered into a local club's training session. Breathlessly climbing a terrace in a venue that had hosted Libertadores fixtures, I observed Real Potosí's drills and pondered the effects of altitude on football. The Bolivian Selección's attempts to qualify for South Africa 2010 was pretty hopeless - apart from two extraordinary results which saw a victory against Brazil and a 6 v 1 mauling of Argentina. Both matches played in La Paz were accompanied by complaints about the altitude; predominantly from the FA stupid enough to appoint Diego Maradona as their head coach.

There could be no denying that being over four kilometres above sea level had a detrimental effect on an unaccustomed body. As an asthmatic I was used to feeling out of breath, but it was most noticeable in Potosí where air was especially thin and oxygen scare. I'd also found Bogotá, Quito and Cusco slightly uncomfortable. But then surely home advantage in any sport is attributable to the conditions. I'm sure the Bolivians had equally valid complaints about competing in subtropical coastal heat. Even so, I know where I'd rather play. It's definitely not the place where you desperately need to sit down after walking up a set of stairs.

Descending over a kilometre to Sucre, Bolivia's charming judicial capital, I booked myself into a Gringo hostel for Christmas. Shortly after my arrival a national strike was called, prompted by the government's threat to cut fuel subsidies, bringing the country to a standstill. This really shouldn't have surprised me in a nation that had almost 200 regime changes since it became independent in 1825. Originally called Alto Peru, it was Símon Bolívar who liberated the territory with help from General Sucre. Bolívar became the first President (the country was named after him) Sucre the second, and its history had been a story of constant upheaval. Recent developments had been encouraging following the 2005 election of former coca grower Evo Morales. His socialist collectivist policies and land reforms championed the rights of indigenous people (the majority of the population which included Morales himself) and reduced poverty levels. He recorded a massive victory at the polls in 2009 and his time in power appeared to be a rare phenomenon: a positive Latin American political success story.

Morales was a unique character and certainly not a typical South American head of state. He was single, claiming to be dedicated to Bolivia, so his sister assumed the role of first lady. Despite having close links with Hugo Chávez and Fidel Castro, his left-wing politics were much softer than his socialist peers. He was a keen footballer; prior to entering the political arena he was head of his regional association and regularly participated in provincial fixtures. After taking power he stayed true to his campesino roots by protecting the rights of coca growers. The UN had declared the plant a controlled substance, along with narcotics such as opium and heroin. In 2008 Morales famously expelled the US Drugs Enforcement Authority. Under the slogan 'coca not cocaine' Bolivia's leader campaigned for the UN to change their stance. He once chewed leaves whilst delivering a speech to delegates. Morales argued that the leaf was part of traditional Andean culture and had been an ingredient in medicines and religious ceremonies for centuries. In its natural form chewing leaves or drinking coca tea acts as a weak stimulant that reduces hunger, thirst, weariness, pain and altitude sickness. It was very much commonplace in a country where many believed burying a dead lama foetus under the entrance to their house would bring them good fortune.

Although the US government had been trying to solve its recreational drugs issues by cutting the problem off at its source, the leaf's de-cocainised extract was used in a range of industries and was a fundamental ingredient in the world's most valuable brand. Coca-Cola's main stimulant was caffeine from Kola nuts, but the original version contained coca in its pure form, meaning there were traces of cocaine in the early formulas. Whilst there was a strong argument that there were far more coca plants in Bolivia than were required for purely legal purposes, Morales continued to fight the UN, and above all the common enemy of socialism – the United States of America. That goes some way to explaining why it cost a US citizen $135 for a Bolivian visa whilst I was there. It was gratis to everybody else.

For the week between Christmas and New Year the roads were blocked so nobody could enter or leave Sucre. This wasn't a particularly irksome situation as I met a law student from Newtown, Sydney, NSW, on Christmas Eve. We spent the nights filling our accommodation with explicit noises. To be honest I was scathing towards the modern backpacker way of travelling: pre or post university students staying in chain hostels in tourist centres, meeting the same people and rarely leaving their comfortable lodgings. On this occasion I was lucky to be part of a great group for a week, and appreciated sitting around getting wasted, speaking English and acting like a Brit abroad.

This was my fourth Christmas outside the UK; much like the previous three it was thoroughly enjoyable. We took an outing to a dinosaur park set in the salubrious setting of a cement quarry. There were allegedly over 500 well preserved tracks from at least eight species of dinosaurs. The fact that you couldn't get within 400 metres of them (and they were running vertically up and down a cliff face) made this cynical Gringo rather sceptical. If prehistoric creatures are your thing I'd recommend visiting the site as soon as possible. A Bolivian mining company had a concession for the quarry and had already started work, which caused a large section of the foot-printed rock face to collapse.

It was after dark when everyone in the hostel came alive; we had some messy forays into Sucre's nightlife. One of the most outstanding performances I saw on my trip was by an 18 year old Australian guy, who was part of our band of merry men (and woman). One evening we elected to go to Mitos, the city's big nightclub. Our pre-departure drinks were too much for the teenage Aussie, he was violently sick all over the hostel kitchen. He assured us that he'd clear up the mess as the rest of us went to our destination. A loud Yorkshireman, who with Miss Newtown made up our fantastic foursome, was on form. Mr Dewsbury somehow managed to come back from the bar with a box of Corona under one arm and a Bolivian girl under the other.

Following a couple of hours cleaning and a change of clothes later, our sickly friend made it to the club and carried on partying long after we'd retired. On his way home two drunken Bolivian teenagers asked him whether he knew a place they could stay. As there were a few spare beds in his dormitory, he invited them to bunk with him, telling them that in order to get past the security guard they'd have to pretend to be French backpackers. After teaching them some basic Français, they negotiated their way past the night staff. In the morning he woke to find they'd left. This incident caused considerable confusion for the hostel owner, who challenged the pair on their departure; by which time they'd forgotten they were supposed to be French and responded in Spanish. As I was in reception settling my bill there was a heated argument between the security guard - who swore blind the duo he let in were speaking French - and the owner who'd conversed with two locals. I thought it was an intriguing concept to arrive somewhere as a French tourist and leave the next morning as a Bolivian teenager.

By the final day of 2010 Evo Morales had agreed to reinstate fuel subsidies and we were all free to move on from Sucre. New Year's Eve was the highlight of an entertaining week translating Yorkshire into English, that had seen drunken Kiwis, puking Aussies (both of them – more than once), terrible karaoke, gate-crashing a wedding, firework accidents, horrible fairground rides, an interesting new recipe and a lot of drunken outings. It capped a whole calendar year away from Britain. 2010 had begun in a gay hotel on a Mexican nudist beach, and finished under an impressive firework display in a lively city plaza. In a way it was the start of my long and convoluted journey home, though I had some serious football to watch before then.

Season 4

Game 37

Gimnasia y Tiro v Concepción FC - (Argentino B) - 1 v 0
Friday 21st January 2011 – 22:00
Estadio El Gigante del Norte, Salta, Argentina

My original plan for the new football season involved working in Argentina and perhaps Paraguay. However, I left Sucre with a companion and decided I'd have a bit of a holiday prior to worrying about earning money. Whilst England wrapped up a glorious three tests to one Ashes victory, I embarked with Miss Newtown on an enjoyable six weeks roaming around South Bolivia and the northern sections of Argentina and Chile.

We'd honed our wine-tasting skills in the Bolivian town of Tarija, where the most polite thing I could say about the produce was drinkable, although I was sold on a place that was incredibly hospitable. We then hired bicycles to blag as much free grog as possible in temperate, attractive Cafayate. Numerous wineries within a small area allowed us to hop from one to another. Upon arrival we pretended to be interested in buying a bottle, prompting staff to pour us generous tasters, before we slipped away and repeated the process. Getting drunk on amazing Argentinian wine for free was great fun. Add to the mix a crazy Reggae festival, quad biking, horse riding along the Butch Cassidy and Sundance Kid trail, spectacular waterfalls and having to pay a fine to Bolivian border guards because I'd outstayed my welcome - we'd arrived in Salta.

I'd not intended on watching football in Argentina until I reached Buenos Aires, but on a Friday morning a newspaper informed me there was a local fixture that evening. Naturally I didn't need any persuading. The concept of kick-off at ten at night wasn't too disconcerting, as I'd already attuned myself to Argentina's abnormal nocturnal lifestyle. My fourth and final season of football in the Americas started with a taxi ride across the nondescript city of Salta, to witness a fourth tier tie between the division's two best teams. It felt weird downing cans of beer surrounded by armoured police vehicles, outside a game I was half an hour late for – it'd been eight weeks since my last competitive match. It was a lower league contest and the quality reflected this. We missed the solitary goal and with it the only incident of note on the field of play.

This my first encounter with the barra brava in the country

from which they originated. Even at this relatively insignificant level they were present. Estadio El Gigante del Norte was actually fairly small and there were no more than a few thousand spectators in attendance. You wouldn't have been able to predict that entering through lines of well-armed riot police. In the middle of the home end was a tireless crowd of bouncing blue and white, supported by a skilful backing band. The first thing I noticed was the songs had changed. Gone were the regulars about the club being 'in the heart' and 'tonight we have to win' to be replaced by more intricate musical arrangements and lyrics I could barely understand. My impression was that they were well organised and experienced at what they did. It was a good little taster of what was to come.

Due to the geographical implications of operating football leagues in the world's eighth largest country, most competitions were regional. Even though the top flight was open to the whole nation, 17 of the 20 participants were from Buenos Aires province. Salta, one of Argentina's more populous cities containing over half a million people, was the centre of the north-eastern division. Gimnasia won the Zone 7 tournament, 13 points ahead of the second placed team from Tucuman who lost by a goal that Friday night. The promotion system was very intricate with a number of different groups and knockout stages. Concepción fell at the next phase, while Gimnasia y Tiro qualified and won a two legged playoff with Chaco For Ever, before emerging victorious from the final against Social Defensores de Belgrano de Villa Ramallo. Their efforts were rewarded by a place in Argentino A, one of the nation's two third tier leagues. Simple really.

CHILE

Population – 17 million
Size – 756,000 km^2
Time Zone – GMT ⁻5
Currency – Peso
FIFA World Ranking – #15 (January 2011)
Best World Cup Finish – 3rd (1962)
Biggest Teams – Colo-Colo, Universidad de Chile, Universidad Católica

You might have heard of:
Marcelo Salas, Iván Zamorano, Alexis Sánchez, Jean Beausejour, Humberto Suazo, Claudio Bravo, Gary Medel, Arturo Vidal, Eduardo Vargas, Augusto Pinochet

Essential Spanish:
Cuadras – Blocks (street)

Game 38

Deportes Iquique v Uni Católica – (Primera División) - 0 v 2
Friday 28th January 2011 – 22:00
Estadio Tierra de Campeones, Iquique

The real opener to my last Latin American season came in North Chile. We'd crossed the Andes in a single bus ride from Salta to San Pedro, situated in the middle of the Atacama Desert. Our modern coach climbed 2,500 meters of craggy Andean switchbacks, to a deserted but efficient Argentine border post. It was a two hour drive between the country's customs buildings through a bleak, high altitude military-controlled no man's land. Snow-capped peaks, hail storms and high winds were eventually replaced by a desert landscape, not too dissimilar to Salar de Uyuni. Wanting to get to the beach as soon as possible we continued to Calama, an ugly copper mining city, where it was necessary to spend an expensive night in a hotel surrounded by brothels. One of the world's driest cities was where footballing superstar Alexis Sánchez began his professional career. I got a feel for how obsessed Chileans were with the Arsenal forward, whilst watching televised highlights of an Udinese tie (who he played for at the time). It didn't feature either goal, just a montage of Alexis' every single touch of the ball, lasting three minutes.

Another day's travelling saw us descend 2,100 metres into a dazzling desert sunset to the coastal city of Iquique. We emerged from the terminal to be greeted by two local students asking whether we'd already reserved a hostel. As we hadn't, one of them said we could stay at his brother's house for $14 a night. We hopped in the back of his rusty car and ended up spending the best part of a week in the company of a Chilean family. Driving along the windy Iquiqueño seafront our conversation inevitably strayed towards football. Our hosts were delighted to inform us 2011's first Primera División fixture was being played five minutes away from their house, in three days' time.

Santiago's Católica (ranked third most successful and popular in the country) were reigning champions, meaning they opened the tournament and wore their preferred strip. This match was Iquique's first back in the top flight after promotion from the second tier. We purchased our tickets in advance, giving us time to enjoy the beautiful beachside setting with its thunderous waves and picturesque Pacific sunsets. One afternoon Blues' League Cup semi-final second leg verses

West Ham was being aired live. The family kindly allowed me to watch our extra time victory on their TV, a decision they regretted as I nervously bounced around their living room for two hours.

It was summer holidays, which would explain the presence of Católica fans in Iquique before the event. On Friday the main stretch of seafront was awash with supporters from Santiago, boozing, singing, kicking footballs and generally making a nuisance of themselves. It was all good natured, there was plenty of banter but no hint of violence. First games of the season are always strange affairs. From my experience they tend to be relaxed days with an air of a friendly about them, aided by the fact that it's normally decent weather in England. On that baking Chilean summer evening, wearing my new $10 sky-blue Iquique shirt, shorts and flip-flops, it definitely felt like the start of a new season.

Whilst strolling four cuadras from our accommodation to the stadium, I could hear the unmistakeable rising crescendo of human noise. As we got closer the sound of music coming from the stands became more audible. It soon became apparent this was no ordinary football band. We entered Estadio Tierra de Campeones without anyone caring to search us and climbed the nearest set of stairs, where a steward halted our progress. He advised me it might not be the best idea to go in the away end wearing the host's shirt; we needed to continue further round the concourse.

Crossing to the other side of the stadia it dawned on me there was no segregation. As this was the equivalent of Arsenal playing in Blackpool at 22:00 on a Friday, it seemed odd that ten minutes after kick-off both sets of fans had access to each other with very little police interference. Not that I dwelt on the matter, because within seconds of finding a spot amongst La Fiel del Norte barra the band began playing. I counted six trumpets, four tubas and a trombone, in addition to the usual array of drums, which was impressive considering the official attendance was just over 8,000. What shocked me was I didn't recognise any of the songs.

As mentioned previously; during season three similar songs had been sung from Colombia to Peru. They always had a repetitive drum beat, occasionally with a trumpet or two thrown in for good measure. Don't get me wrong, I'm not criticising this. The atmosphere in many grounds was head and shoulders above anything I'd ever seen in the British leagues. But this was different. It was like salsa or samba, with lyrics about winning the cup, living by the sea, and dancing for the boys in blue. It was almost impossible not to dance, the whole stand

173

was moving in time to the melody. I swear that a song played after half time was the Strictly Come Dancing theme tune, with lyrics about their opponent's mothers being prostitutes. As I marvelled at the musical extravaganza my Aussie companion had made friends with two local eight year old girls. They were entertaining themselves by collecting handfuls of shredded paper and throwing them in the air, covering those around us. Funnily the young girls got bored of the infantile pastime after a while, not Miss Newtown, she continued until we left.

Predictably it wasn't much of a contest. Iquique had plenty of possession but were sadly lacking in the final third. Católica were superior in every department; their first half dominance was capped with a smartly taken goal. The second period was a similar story. Iquique huffed and puffed - buoyed by their partisan dancing La Fiel del Norte barra - but with no end product. Surprisingly they were still in the running for a share of the spoils until the very end; saved on countless occasions by poor finishing and the woodwork. The visitors got the second they deserved in stoppage time, a glorious curling shot sending 2,000 travelling Los Cruzados barra into raptures. Católica (who I was to watch again in slightly more spectacular circumstances) finished top of the league. They lost the finals competition to Universidad de Chile 4 v 3 over two legs, the second of which concluded in typical Latin fashion: eight men against ten. Iquique respectably ended up in mid-table.

That balmy evening by the seaside was the only game I saw in Chile, which on reflection I was a bit dismayed about. Santiago looked an interesting place with a number of top flight football clubs in close proximity. By this stage I'd been through the majority of Latin America's countries and was startled to find that Chile was arguably the most prosperous. It weathered 2008's global financial crisis by using $20 billion of savings, mainly accrued from exporting copper, to invest in their public sector. The origins of their economic stability can be traced back to the most controversial personality in their history.

General Augusto Pinochet was a descendant of French settlers, in his early days rose up the military rankings. He befriended a young socialist senator – Salvador Allende – who was to become President in 1970. Pinochet helped Allende suppress his enemies, but in 1973, less than three weeks after the President had promoted his ally to commander-in-chief, he was the driving force behind a coup. This takeover (backed by the US) led to Allende committing suicide. Eventually Pinochet seized power, which he maintained until 1990. At the start of his rule he was instrumental in Operation Condor, a

174

collaboration between South American right-wing despots aiming to crush their left-wing opposition. Naturally the CIA was also involved in what they perceived to be 'a counterterrorism organisation' which kidnapped, tortured and murdered thousands of individuals. Pinochet's regime alone was thought to have killed 3,000 people and tortured nearly ten times as many, although that could be the tip of the iceberg.

Despite his terrible human rights record, Chileans were divided in their opinion of Augusto and whether he was responsible for their resurgent national economy. His financial advisors (known as 'the Chicago Boys' due to their US-based education) privatised key industries and enticed foreign investments. Initially this caused unemployment issues and assisted Pinochet in embezzling a massive personal wealth. The economy recovered and when I was there it was one of the strongest in Latin America. All of which is where my wonderful country comes into the equation.

Throughout this book I have been scathing towards the US and its foreign policy, particularly in Central America. Nevertheless, England doesn't exactly have the most salubrious history when it comes to colonialism. How did the US come into being in the first place? Also, by rights Belize should be part of Guatemala; but we settled there with our slaves. Much of Pinochet's wealth came from his connections with arms corporations such as British Aerospace Engineering, and in the 1980's he enjoyed a cosy relationship with our Conservative government. Some experts contend that without the help of the Chilean military Margaret Thatcher might not have won the Falklands War. It was their long-range radars which gave the British Navy vital warnings of Argentina's aerial attacks.

In 1998, when Pinochet visited London, we repaid him by refusing Spain's extradition request. They were trying to bring charges against the former dictator for murdering their citizens during Operation Condor. Instead of aiding our European alley, Britain kept him under house arrest in a comfortable Wentworth detached property, where his old chum Maggie would call round. Two years later Home Secretary Jack Straw deemed he was unfit to stand trial and sent him back to Chile, via a RAF base. He was never held accountable for his crimes and died in December 2006.

With the South American leagues underway it was time for me to cross the continent, from Pacific to Atlantic. The urban beach resort of Arica was my final stop in Chile and potentially where Miss Newtown and I went our separate ways. There was just enough time to witness one last picture-perfect Pacific sunset on a blustery summer evening. It was to be my last dip in an ocean which had been an integral part of the trip. Having battered me around on many surf and body boards, concealed a stingray so I trod on it, and accommodated more than one of my sexual experiences, it had a trick left up its sleeve. As dwindling rays of light emanated from a ball of fire sinking below the horizon, we were discussing returning to our hotel. Out of nowhere a freakishly large wave crashed on the shore. Caught unawares, we managed to rescue our cameras before salt water drenched the rest of our belongings, sending us wandering off into the twilight wearing soggy clothes. Legend.

South American Under 20 Qualifiers

Game 39 - Uruguay v Ecuador - 1 v 1
Game 40 - Chile v Argentina - 2 v 3
Game 41 - Brazil v Colombia - 2 v 0

Thursday 3rd February 2011 – 17:00 to 23:00
Estadio de la Universidad Nacional San Augustin, Arequipa, Peru

I couldn't resist. Miss Newtown and I had planned to part in Arica, but the lure of a new format and three fixtures in one evening was too strong, so I found myself back in dreaded Peru. Arequipa, the country's second largest city, boasted a lovely colonial centre but not a fantastic footballing history. One of the most important matches hosted there was in 2003. Estadio San Augustin had been the venue for Cienciano's historic Copa Sudamericana final triumph over Argentina's mighty River Plate.

Approaching the towering stadium I was met by a familiar sight: Colombians begging for their entrance money. I deliberately purchased our tickets from the window closest to where they were standing. Their pitch was remarkable: 'We've come all the way from Colombia to support our Selección and now we don't have enough money for a ticket.' I thought Cartagena fans from game 24 were idiotic travelling 50 hours to see 45 minutes of football, but this was another level. The minimum length of time it could have possibly taken them to get from the southern border of Colombia to Arequipa by bus was 60 hours. Had they really travelled across half a continent without enough money to pay for the $3 entry? I figured it must be a fake story, as nobody was that crazy or desperate.

South America's Under 20 competition involved all ten CONMEBOL member countries competing in two leagues. The top three from each group progressed to a conclusive league, where they played each other for a place at 2011's Under 20 World Cup and 2012's Olympics. Colombia was participating even though they were hosts of the 2011 tournament so had an automatic berth. Essentially their presence in the last six meant there were five qualifying places for the World Cup. But the big prize for the winners and runners-up was a ticket to London 2012.

We arrived at half time in the first match, having seen Uruguay

177

score on a monitor at a bus terminal, whilst checking our bags in for separate journeys later that night. Ecuador were dominant in the second period. They'd already missed some good chances prior to equalising via a powerful header on the hour mark. During a gorgeous fiery sunset Ecuador should have taken all three points, but in the dying moments striker Marlon de Jesús inexplicably missed an open goal from inside the six yard box.

In attendance were an interesting mix of folk; the majority were Peruvians even though their Selección hadn't made it to the final round. There didn't appear to be many Uruguayans or Ecuadorians in the sparsely populated terraces. Towards the end of the first tie, a big 'Marea Roja' banner was unfurled and a group of 40 Chilean fans began singing in the main stand. This brought a hostile reaction from the locals, whose jeering was replaced by applause when Argentina's squad came out to warm-up, making it clear who they were backing. Just before the Ecuadorian Jesús' shocking miss, a larger group of Chileans adopted a position in the end next to me, hanging flags and singing their own songs.

As a feisty little atmosphere was brewing, the teams changed over remarkably quickly and the second contest kicked off. The Chileans in the cheaper section looked like a group of holidaying students, they were enjoying their evening by singing and bouncing around passionately. After a quarter of an hour they had something to celebrate, Bryan Carrasco dummied a defender and beat Argentina's keeper at his near post. This prompted the party's male members to remove their shirts and swing them maniacally above their heads. The Peruvians responded with a round of chanting 'Chileano Putos.'

Chile carried a single goal advantage into the break, at which juncture I left the stadium briefly to escort my Australian companion to a taxi. We stood in the darkness saying our slightly emotional goodbyes, as she was catching an overnight bus to Cusco. The game turned on a half time substitution, Argentina's manager introduced 17 year old attacking midfielder Juan Manuel Iturbe to the fray. Chile were unable cope with his pace and movement. Within 20 minutes he'd won a penalty and scored a sublime solo effort, dribbling from the halfway line, beating defenders and goalkeeper with ease. His diminutive stature and immaculate close control drew immediate comparisons to other Argentine playmakers such as Maradona and Messi. Argentina scored a third to seal victory with 20 minutes to spare, before Chile claimed a consolation in stoppage time.

Once the final whistle blew the Chileans sulkily made their

way to the exits, to be replaced by the three scruffy Colombians who I'd seen begging outside. Evidently they'd obtained sufficient funds to gain entry. They stood not too far from me and began singing and jumping around. A group hug was part of Brazil's preparation for the last match of the extravaganza. Their arrival was greeted with enthusiastic cheers, signalling the locals were supporting their Portuguese-speaking neighbours. The event's big draw was Brazil's newest footballing idol, mohicaned 20 year old Neymar da Silva Santos Junior. Brazil, unbeaten in the competition, took an early lead through São Paulo defender Casimiro's downward header from a corner. On a night when Neymar struggled to exert his influence, the tournament favourites had to wait until the 90th minute to secure victory; Flamengo's Diego Mauricio scoring from an acute angle.

Typically the real entertainment was in the stands. The three crazy Colombians had spent the first half an hour supporting their Selección with an admirable vocal performance, especially considering their meagre numbers. As Brazil increasingly dominated, the yellow-shirted barra switched their attentions from the pitch to the other spectators. A group of approximately 100 Peruvians nearby had been applauding politely for Brazil, without provoking them. Maybe they were bored or just plain stupid, probably both, as the trio turned their backs to the field and sang songs about their opposition.

Initially it seemed like a bit of a joke. Those close to me chuckled at the first two renditions, but it soon turned nasty. The third chant involved swearwords directed at Brazil, which didn't go down too well. It was when the threesome's singing switched to Peru that it got heated. At first the locals shouted and jeered in response, then threw things at the northerners. The torrent of debris encouraged them to sing louder and more abusively. When a small group of middle-aged men approached them attempting to calm the situation, it turned violent. In fairness to the foreigners, the Peruvians were the first to throw a punch. Within seconds a brawl had broken out, resulting in the locals running back up the terrace to the safety of their compatriots.

It didn't take long before they returned with reinforcements to confront the mocking tourists. For some reason the sight of 30 men charging at them didn't deter the three barra, who continued gesticulating and taunting. For the first few seconds of the fight it appeared the vicious Colombians were going to hold their own (kind of like a hooligan version of the film 300). After a minute they'd each taken a couple of heavy blows and were retreating towards the pitch. They scaled a wire fence, leapt over a moat around the perimeter and landed straight in front of a line of police, who'd passively watched the entire show. To a chorus of jeers the handcuffed trio were led along the running track to an armoured vehicle, whilst the flag and bag they'd left behind were being ceremoniously burnt. My favourite part of the whole charade was the guy sat next to me shouting as they passed us: 'Go back to your tree!'

Although Neymar hadn't shown his best form that evening, he ended up as top scorer. Brazil finished top with Uruguay coming runners-up. Both qualified for the Olympics, while Argentina missed out by a solitary point. Brazil went on to win the Under 20 World Cup, recording a 3 v 2 victory against Portugal in the final, held at Bogotá's El Campín stadium. Internacional's Chelsea-bound 19 year old midfielder, Oscar, scored a hat trick in a match decided after extra time.

BOLIVIA

Population – 11 million
Size – 1.1 million km²
Time Zone – GMT ‾5
Currency - Boliviano
FIFA World Ranking – #99 (February 2011)
Best World Cup Finish – First Round (1930, 1950, 1994)
Biggest Teams – Bolívar, The Strongest, Blooming, Jorge Wilstermann, Oriente Petrolero

You might have heard of:
Marco Etcheverry, Jamie Moreno, Evo Morales

Essential Spanish:
Collectivo – Local bus service
Vamos – Let's go
Dalé – Come on

Game 42

Blooming v Oriente Petrolero – (Liga Professional) - 0 v 2
Sunday 6th February 2011 – 18:00
Estadio Ramón Aguilera Costas, Santa Cruz de la Sierra

At 03:30 on my only Bolivian match day I was jolted awake as my latest bus entered Santa Cruz's main transport terminal. I'd spent two intense days travelling 900 kilometres from Arequipa. Shortly after Brazil v Colombia I caught an overnight service to Lake Titicaca. As a damp dawn broke a combination of local bus and moto-taxi got me as far as a deserted Bolivian border. Once the formalities were complete I was informed there were demonstrations along the road to the nearest town. This resulted in me hiking three of the five kilometres to Copacabana in incessant drizzle with my heavy bag on my back. Around me people in traditional dress had covered the road with boulders and were letting off fireworks. Having been trapped in Sucre for over a week, I was pleasantly surprised that it was possible to pass this blockade. It was necessary to take three separate collectivos to La Paz, where I hailed a bus to Cochabamba from Terminal Alta.

I arrived at my interim destination 23 hours after leaving Arequipa, following nine transport changes. A brief sleep later and I had the seemingly easy task of negotiating a ten hour direct coach to Santa Cruz. Stupidly I didn't check the ticket I'd bought. When I came to board my intended bus I realised they'd sold me a seat on the early morning service, which had left half an hour before I'd paid for it. This was the last departure of the day and it was sold out, meaning I'd have to stay an extra night and miss the game. In an uncharacteristic display of bloody-mindedness I created such a scene that they allowed me on board, as long as I sat on a little wooden stool next to the driver and paid my fare a second time.

Of the hundreds of buses I rode on this trip, the 2,200 metre descent to Santa Cruz was the most memorable. It didn't take long to strike up a conversation with the driver and his co-pilot, who took great pleasure in explaining we were driving the most dangerous route in Bolivia. This I seriously doubted in a country famous for its Death Road. I was soon convinced when they revealed that the previous night ten people had died in an accident, taking the total fatalities for the year into triple figures. It was only the start of February. Further evidence appeared in the form of a double-decker coach with the whole of its

182

front caved in being towed in the opposite direction.

A couple of hours into the journey, on a winding jungle road, we ground to a halt. Inevitably there'd been a crash. We sat waiting for four hours, during which time I discovered the service I had a valid ticket for was a ten minute walk ahead of us, along a stationary line of traffic. Eventually a procession of ambulances, police cars and a smashed bus passed us. In all honesty it was rather morbid. As the wreck went by the portly driver and his undernourished assistant (a boy of 15) were discussing whether there were any visible blood marks in the cockpit. It was chilling that they were regularly reminded of their own mortality - there was no way the driver of either of the two destroyed vehicles I saw that day could have survived. Statistically there must have been an unhealthily high chance the pair I was talking to would end up as red stains, on a bus being towed from a crash scene.

Any sympathy I had for their precarious position evaporated within a quarter of an hour of moving again. In an attempt to make up some of the lost time, they were aggressively over and undertaking any vehicle which wasn't going at 80 kilometres per hour. I could understand why they were doing it once we got to the main road; but on a treacherous mountain pass around blind bends? The driver's insurance policy against our potential demise was his young colleague hanging out a window shouting 'Dalé' whenever he thought it safe to pass the next obstacle. There's an argument that being involved in lethal accidents was an occupational hazard for a Bolivian bus driver. Yet on that leg of the journey, in the pouring rain, fully aware of the fate of two other buses over the last 12 hours, driving like a maniac to try and save a little bit of time was suicidal. But it was fascinating to witness, especially as I'd been a passenger on Latin American public transport for over a year and had been blissfully ignorant of the perils the drivers faced.

The precious 15 minutes we'd saved playing Russian Roulette was completely pointless, as we sat stationary for another three hours further down the road. This time it wasn't an accident but locals partaking in their favourite pastime: protesting. Interestingly Bolivians were the most restless of passengers, if a bus left five minutes later than scheduled they all shouted Vamos at the driver. However, if someone was protesting they were remarkably patient. I discussed this subject with my new friends as we were waiting. They didn't really have an explanation, the best incite I could garner was a shrug of the shoulders followed by: 'This is Bolivia.'

In the chaos of being at a standstill for seven hours, with people getting on and off the bus, it appeared we left a passenger behind, which I was grateful for as it meant I had a comfortable seat for the final leg of the expedition. Waking at 03:30 I spent the rest of the night in a hotel by the terminal. Suitably refreshed, I caught a collectivo into Santa Cruz's city centre, found a hostel occupied by Colombian hippies and staff who were more interested in their game of Pro Evo than the guests, and made my way in the gathering dusk to Bolivia's biggest and best clásico.

What alarmed me first was the volume of people wearing football shirts streaming away from the venue. I thought I'd got the kick-off time wrong, but a quick circuit of Estadio Ramón Aguilera Costas made me realise I'd wholly underestimated the ticketing situation. It was irrelevant that there were none for sale, official or otherwise, as all the gates were closed and the only way in was through a VIP entrance in the main stand. It had been such a monumental effort to get to the fixture I clearly wasn't going to give up easily.

My first tactic was to try and bribe a steward 100 Bob ($15) to let me in. He wasn't able to because his superior was watching, so I spoke to the manager and explained my story. He couldn't help, but pointed me in the direction of another supervisor. I recounted my tale a third time and got referred to..... another manager. I'd worked in complaints most my professional life so had a reasonable grasp of how the process operated. I repeated my story to five different employees, by which time they ran out of managers to refer me to. Eventually they decided it was far easier to let me in for free than having to listen to nonsense about writing a book.

It had all been worth it, this was pure footballing gold. The arena was packed. I don't mean busy or even full, it was overflowing with people. In the second half I found a few inches of room on a stairway, but it was a tight squeeze. Obviously the atmosphere was amazing. Neither Los Chiflados barra (Blooming) nor La Pesada Verde barra (Oriente) had a prominent band, they were singing incredibly loudly with very little assistance. Blooming had the more active support although they were outnumbered by their deadly rivals. It was a pleasant change to be in the posh main stand surrounded by spectators from both sides. They were mixed in together behaving in a civilised fashion, much like the Merseyside derbies of a bygone age.

Characteristically events on the pitch were of no real interest, but it was captivating observing a mass of luminous green at one end and royal blue at the other, bouncing, dancing and setting off fireworks. It was already 1 v 0 to Oriente by the time I'd blagged my way in. Santa

184

Cruz's most successful club wrapped up the points with ten minutes to spare following a defensive howler. By then Blooming's barra had left the stadium as they'd lost an epic fight with the police. At one stage it looked like the Old Bill were going to be overwhelmed by the weight of numbers against them. They rallied and hit back hard, using riot shields and large wooden sticks to sweep the terrace, violently quelling the disturbance. The trouble didn't spill outside the ground as I'd expected. I waited for a bit but everyone made their way home in a peaceful manner.

My Sunday ended watching the Super Bowl for only the second time ever. Before embarking on my trip I'd not really understood the appeal of American Football, particularly the laborious way contests stopped and started. On my Mexican nudist beach I'd viewed an intriguingly fluid encounter in which Drew Brees' New Orleans Saints overcame Payton Manning's Indianapolis Colts, 31 v 17. Latin American television coverage of the NFL, much like our EPL, was fairly comprehensive. After 15 months exposure to the sport I'd got to grips with the rules and had even learned to tolerate the unnecessary breaks in play. Once I began to comprehend the separate workings of attack and defence I really appreciated the intricacies involved - like a game of human chess.

2011's final was as enthralling as the previous year's. Green Bay Packers led 21 v 3 in the second quarter. Pittsburgh Steelers pulled it back and just needed a touchdown with two minutes remaining to claim victory. They failed to do so, and I was happy that a team from Wisconsin could win one of the planet's biggest sporting prizes.

PARAGUAY

Population – 6.5 million
Size – 406,000 km²
Time Zone – GMT ⁻4
Currency - Guaraní
FIFA World Ranking – #24 (February 2011)
Best World Cup Finish – Quarter-finals (2010)
Biggest Teams – Olimpia, Cerro Porteño, Libertad

You might have heard of:
José Luis Chilavert, Carlos Gamarra, Roque Santa Cruz, Roberto
Acuña, Christian Riveros, Salvador Cabañas

Essential Spanish:
Taxista – Taxi Driver
Hace calor – It's hot
Fascismo – Fashism

Game 43

Nacional Asunción v Independiente – (División Profesional) - 1 v 0
Saturday 12th February 2011 – 16:00
Estadio Arsenio Erico, Asunción

Game 44

Olimpia v General Caballero - (División Profesional) - 3 v 1
Saturday 12th February 2011 – 18:30
Estadio Defensores del Chaco, Asunción

Game 43 proved to be a little bit problematic. Originally I'd wanted to attend five or six fixtures in Paraguay, starting with Libertad on Thursday after the Santa Cruz clásico. I took an overnight bus bound for Asunción, Paraguay's capital and only major city, expecting to arrive on match day with plenty of time to spare before a 20:00 kick-off. It certainly wasn't the most comfortable nights of my life, but by then I was used to sleeping on buses. We crossed the border at first light going through a very slow exit stamping rigmarole. It wasn't until lunchtime that we arrived at customs. The hours had been spent driving across the Chaco, a vast, sparsely populated area of semiarid forests, which had been the setting for a bitter war between Paraguay and Bolivia in the 1930's.

I'd been cursing that we'd been the last of a small convoy of buses to be processed in Bolivia, as it turned out this worked to my advantage. Parked at Paraguayan customs it rapidly dawned on me that this was going to be the most thorough border control of the trip thus far. My issue was that I had two sizeable bags of cannabis hidden in the toes of my spare pair of trainers, situated at the bottom of my backpack. Now reading this you probably think I was an idiot for entering remote countries carrying drugs. Clearly I was. But in my defence up to that point the crossings had been routine affairs. For example, Lonely Planet stated that at the Colombia/Ecuador border there were exhaustive drugs and weapon searches. When I was there an officer peeked through the window of our minibus and waved us past without even looking at our bags.

By the time I was sat in the intense midday heat of a desolate Paraguayan desert I'd already negotiated 20 frontiers without any difficulties; and without anyone being particularly concerned what I was carrying. There was no warning or reason why this one should be any different. Yet with a sniffer dog and meticulous individual searches of every bag, all of a sudden I had a massive problem. We were the last of three buses, the first was being examined when we arrived. I sat for three hours waiting for officers to finish inspecting the other two vehicles, attempting to fathom how I was going avoid sleeping in a cell that night. With an apology letter written to my parents (for them having to rescue me from my third world prison hell) I dragged my bag into the search station, lined up with my fellow passengers and prepared for the worst.

My first slice of luck was the scrawny sniffer dog had almost completed his shift. He was more interested in lying in the shade than finding my stash. I knew even though I survived that part of the nightmare, my casual hiding place would be discovered during the systematic luggage search. I had a plan which revolved around trying to get the least officious-looking guard to search my backpack and hope he liked football. I figured my best bet would be the youngest of them. Making eye contact with the most junior officer at the vital moment, he chose to search me. Straight away I struck up a conversation about football and was relieved to learn he was a big Olimpia fan who also loved Manchester United. Although we were having a good chat, he was still going through my belongings, methodically scrutinising every item. My collection of Latin American replica football shirts was my diversion tactic. Each time he pulled a different one out we had a brief chat about the club and how fierce their barra were. Towards the end of the inspection I passed him my Emelec jersey. Whilst he was admiring it, I quickly hid the plastic bag containing my shoes behind the pile of stuff he'd already checked. The whole ordeal was over in half an hour. To me it seemed like a lifetime before my new friend was wishing me a safe journey and to enjoy the weekend's fixtures.

There are no words to describe the relief I felt sat back in my seat, with my passport stamped and my bag securely stowed in the hold. The feeling was short-lived. Two officers boarded our bus; we drove for two minutes in the wrong direction and sat outside a hospital for a further three hours. I'd been concentrating so intently on surviving customs I hadn't noticed that a passenger was taken ill during the tortuous search process. He'd been rushed to hospital where doctors x-rayed the Bolivian, to discover 91 wraps of cocaine in his stomach, one of which had split whilst he was being interrogated. We were all brought off the bus again and I feared there was going to be another bag search. Fortunately the officers found his smuggling companion swiftly (the man's wife also had a stomach full of cocaine) and we were allowed to return to our seats. Unfortunately for the Bolivian couple the man died before we resumed our journey.

I arrived in Asunción 30 hours after leaving Santa Cruz. Consequently I missed domestic champions Libertad. On Friday a helpful tourist office directed me to the Paraguayan Football Association, located under the national arena called Defensores del Chaco. After negotiating a large queue of amateur players registering with the FA, a nice lady gave me a glossy magazine containing a comprehensive review of the previous season. She also wrote a list of the weekend's footballing schedule, including start times and stadium addresses.

I set out in the evening to watch game 43, opting to take a taxi to Guaraní's ground as I was late for kick-off. I knew it was close and had a rough idea which part of the city it was in, so didn't think it was too important when the rotund driver failed to turn his meter on. It was ten minutes into the ride, after we'd initially appeared to have gone around in circles and were heading in the wrong direction; that I began to worry. Express kidnapping - where unsuspecting tourists get driven to an ATM and forced to empty their accounts - was fairly rife in South America. I was keen for it not to be part of my experiences so asked the taxi driver to go to the address I'd been given, persisting when he argued the match was in a different location.

We eventually arrived at an unlit, deserted field which Guaraní used for training. At that point I abandoned the idea of going to the game as I was happy to view the rest of it on TV at a nearby bar. The perspiring driver, who wasn't impressed I'd contradicted him and had been wrong, demanded $16 for the journey, but after a bit of negotiation was willing to accept $10. The fare was more like $5, so my highest offer was $8. As I didn't have the correct change I advised him that I'd go to the petrol station at the end of the road to obtain it. He didn't like that idea one little bit and attempted to grab me with one hand whilst clumsily trying to punch me with the other. I wriggled free and jogged to the safety of the garage, whilst my wheezing associate followed me in his car, cursing at the top of his voice. I got the currency I needed and tried to pay him. At that stage he was so infuriated he'd only accept the original quote of $16, with the threat that if I didn't pay, he would call the police.

Having been ripped off on numerous occasions by taxistas over the previous 16 months, and unhappy I'd been attacked; I decided to

189

stand my ground. Plus there was cold beer for sale in the petrol station's shop and the whole charade was quite comical. Once I'd cracked open my fourth can (and following the third phone call) the police turned up. They weren't particularly impressed as I imagine they had better things to do on a Friday night, other than resolve a dispute between a taxi driver and some cocky foreigner. After 20 minutes of discussion the very serious-looking officers told me I had to pay him $12, or the matter would be resolved at the station. I graciously handed over the money, and as he was getting into his cab to leave cheekily asked how much it'd cost for a lift back to the centre. 'Not in a million years' was his response, which I thought was rather funny. The three surly policemen didn't see the humorous side.

Although I ended up paying more than he was willing to accept at one point, I feel that I scored a moral victory. We were sat at a petrol station for over two hours on a Friday evening, whilst he was losing potential business and I was getting drunk. Granted the incident was an exercise in pettiness, but I believed it was justified revenge for all the times I'd been overcharged and couldn't do anything about it. Also, as I'd missed the match, I had to find alternative ways of amusing myself. At the time I couldn't imagine anything better than winding-up a South American taxi driver.

Overzealous customs officers and an ill-informed Paraguayan Football Association had denied me getting to game 43; so on Saturday I was determined to watch some football. Obviously not that determined, because I didn't manage to arrive until after the interval. It wasn't too bad as they let me in for free. The 4,500 capacity Estadio Arsenio Erico was roughly half full for this meeting between two of Asunción's smaller clubs. The two sided venue had a smattering of away fans in a miniature end. Next to me in the side terrace a 20 strong Garra Alba barra following Nacional were trying their best to generate some kind of atmosphere. Their lone drummer tirelessly kept a beat, whilst others divided their time between singing, trying to distract a cameraman (who was broadcasting the fixture) and abusing Independiente's substitutes. Quite why a visiting team dugout would be situated in front of the popular terrace, with just a wire mesh separating the barra and their opponent's staff, is beyond me. Towards the end an Independiente substitute responded to the taunts he'd been receiving. The barra went wild, kicking the fence, spitting and attempting to climb over the barbed wire, as the police gazed on with an air of indifference, probably because that kind of thing happened every week.

Nacional had taken a goal advantage into the break. It was

apparent there was no danger of there being any additions to the score sheet, as all the shots I witnessed landed on the roof of a neighbouring supermarket. The highlight came with two minutes remaining when the home keeper brought down an Independiente striker in the penalty area, earning himself a red card. With all three permitted substitutes already used, the gloves were passed to Nacional's tallest defender, who stood like a statue as the spot kick was blasted wide. An incredibly nervous four minutes of stoppage time was endured by the hosts, who at the final whistle were relieved to register their first victory of the season.

Strangely enough, considering their relatively small fan base, Nacional had won la Clausura in 2009. Formed in 1904 by one of the oldest public schools in the country, their famous academy had raised Paraguay's greatest ever player in the 1930's. Arsenio Erico went on to represent Argentine giants Independiente 325 times, scoring a staggering 293 goals and winning numerous championships.

As the sun set I had enough time to stroll to my next fixture, situated a couple of kilometres away in the national stadium. Asunción was a pleasant-looking city of greenery and neat, orderly dwellings. There was an efficiency and organisation about the place which hadn't been evident in any other major Latin municipality. Also there was a strong booze culture; it was possible to buy a cold cerveza from virtually every street vendor, no matter what their primary business was. This suited me just fine. As kick-off approached I found a shop with a TV and settled in for the first half of Olimpia's match, accompanied by a litre of Paraguay's finest - Pilsen. The nation's oldest and most successful club boasted 38 league titles, three Libertadores and were ranked as one of the top five South American clubs of the 20th century. Despite their proud history the current squad looked pretty poor. They seized the initiative through a dodgy penalty, only for Caballero to equalise via a glancing header.

Taking advantage of the free entry after the break, I took my place in the side seating for a captivating half. Predictably Olimpia ran out winners via another penalty and a breakaway goal, both converted by former Cruz Azul forward Pablo Zeballos, who I'd seen score in Mexico City 15 months earlier. The real entertainment wasn't the constant misplacing of passes, petty fouls or wayward shooting, it was in the stands. For logistic reasons all Olimpia and Cerro Porteño away fixtures against teams from the capital were played in Estadio Defensores del Chaco. This was because the division's other participants had such few fans their homes generally resembled something you would find in the Ryman League South.

191

I know I've said it before and I'll say it again (but it was true) the atmosphere was genuinely awesome. La Barra de la O crammed into one end didn't stop bouncing and singing, admirably supported by the spectators in the main stand. Normally people in the more expensive seats looked to the barra to lead the singing and occasionally joined in. This group of white and black shirted Paraguayans started songs, danced up and down the aisles and generated as much noise as those without shirts in the packed end. At one stage the main stand seemed to goad their own fanatics, as they reacted aggressively to a specific chant. However it could easily have been part of a call and response song I was too mesmerised to pick up on.

Walking out Estadio Defensores del Chaco I spared a thought for my friend from customs some 400 kilometres away. Whilst he was busy catching Bolivian drug smugglers, I was gratefully watching his beloved football team.

Game 45

Rubio Ñú v Cerro Porteño - (División Profesional) - 2 v 2
Sunday 13th February 2011 – 16:00
Estadio Defensores del Chaco, Asunción

On Sunday I went to see the country's other significant club, Cerro Porteño. Named after a famous 19th century military victory over Argentina; Cerro was supposed to represent the working-classes and claimed to have a larger following than their bourgeois rival. The side who had brought my new idol through their youth ranks, Juan Manuel Iturbe, boasted a plethora of famous former managers, including Ossie Ardiles and Hungarian legend Ferenc Puskas. Not that I was interested in any of these facts on my way to the venue, as I was hanging from the six litres I'd drank on Saturday, which wasn't aided by the blazing afternoon heat. After purchasing a $5 ticket from a tout I attempted to enter the stadium.

Initially I was thwarted by the police who weren't happy that I was wearing a belt. Despite encountering this problem on numerous previous occasions and overcoming it, Paraguayan officials weren't to be messed with. My arguments fell on deaf ears as I was directed to a nearby shop that would apparently be able to help. Upon arrival a blue-eyed eight year old girl sat at a wooden desk efficiently tagged my belt, put it on a shelf with dozens others just like it, and handed me a ticket, in exchange for 50 cents. Before my hazy brain could process what was going on an officer nodded acknowledgement to allow me past the check point. I traversed an automatic revolving barrier and found myself standing dazed and confused in glaring sunshine amongst La Barra 1912.

My experience entering Defensores del Chaco that day reinforced what I'd been thinking about Paraguay since my first interaction with the natives at customs. Quite simply they were as German, if not more German than the people of Germany (at this juncture I'd like to clarify it's a country I've visited on many occasions and whose efficiency, football league, women and beer I am an enormous admirer of). Even forgetting the distinctly Aryan features on the supposedly Latin population, it was impossible to ignore the uncharacteristic efficiency in a continent famous for its laidback attitude. Added to that was an abundance of immaculately brewed cerveza and the fact I'd eaten oven baked schnitzel and dumplings for lunch that day.

Having said that a cursory look at Paraguay's history indicated in its early days it had a French influence. After declaring independence from Spain (the first Latin nation to do so) the old aristocracy was replaced by state socialism under José de Francia. He was inspired by the French Revolution and became so paranoid he refused to ever sleep in the same bed on consecutive nights for fear of being assassinated. Two wars damaged the new republic. First was a disastrously savage War of the Triple Alliance against Brazil, Argentina and Uruguay, during which approximately 60,000 Paraguayans died. Second was the Chaco War from 1932 to 1935, when their numerically inferior forces, assisted by a British railway system, overcame a Bolivian invasion aided by hired German officers.

In 1931 South America's first Nazi party was formed in Asunción. For the best part of the Second World War the media were pro-Hitler, but similar to its fascist-influenced neighbours, Paraguay lent its support to the Allies in 1944. This appeared to be a token gesture, as rural German-speaking communities such as the Mennonites continued to flourish. A chaotic decade saw a short civil war and the right-wing Colorado party come to power. The organisation was divided due to its weak leadership, until General Alfredo Strossner staged a coup d'état and took the reins in 1954.

The son of an immigrant German brewer and a hero of the Chaco War; Strossner suspended constitutional freedoms, successfully divided his opposition, and created a one-party state where human rights weren't exactly high on the agenda. His rule lasted 35 years (only Fidel Castro had served a longer term in Latin America) which was a stable and prosperous period in Paraguayan history. He was virtually a dictator who brutally supressed any adversaries. Even though elections were held during his incumbency it was widely believed that these were rigged. In one of his seven 'victories' he was the sole candidate standing. Strossner was eventually ousted by a coup in 1989, although the Colorado party maintained their grip on power until 2008, despite internationally recognised fair and free elections from 1993 onwards. They held the record for the world's longest serving political party.

But why were there were so many natives roaming around with blonde hair and blues eyes? After Germany was defeated in the Second World War, it was a well-established fact that a number of Nazis escaped Europe to South America through what were called 'ratlines'. The majority of the high-profile war criminals had since been tracked down, most of whom were found in Argentina or Brazil. None to my knowledge were ever located in Paraguay, but it's generally accepted that Josef Mengle 'the angel of death' lived there for some time without ever being captured.

Surely Paraguay, with its vast desolate expanses, German communities, right-wing government and leader of Germanic descent, would be the ideal place for Nazis to hide. After all this was the place where Nicaragua's fascist dictator Anastasio Somoza fled after Daniel Ortega seized power in 1979. He didn't last too long though. In September 1980, whilst being chauffeured across Asunción, Sandinista assassins fired a rocket at his car, killing him instantly. I feel ignorant saying it, but for the duration of my stay in Paraguay I got the overwhelming feeling that I was in a country that potentially represented what the Fourth Reich would have been like, in the sun.

It was certainly sunny at Defensores del Chaco on that Sunday afternoon; temperatures at pitch level were recorded at a high of 37 degrees Celsius. I found standing in the powerful rays unbearable, so hid in a shady corner of the stand. Cerro had taken the lead whilst I was negotiating the strange entrance process, and soon added to their tally via a neat glancing header from giant Argentine striker Roberto Nanni. Even without Iturbe in their squad it looked like the hosts were going to canter to victory, as they had a clear physical superiority over their Asunción-based opposition. However, out of the blue, diminutive Rubio striker Sergio Samuel out-jumped two defenders who were at least a foot taller than him, to pull one back. Minutes later they'd equalised, Paraguayan legend Roberto Acuña dropped his shoulder and curled an exquisite shot into the top corner from 30 yards. Just when I thought I could be witnessing a real clásico, Rubio midfielder Eric Ramos was dismissed for a petulant second yellow card, meaning his teammates had to play with ten men for over 50 minutes in scorching conditions.

The second period didn't come close to the first in terms of incident, but it was still captivating, which wasn't something I'd been saying often. I really couldn't praise Rubio enough for their effort under testing circumstances. They were enterprising, passed the ball well and for most the second half looked the more likely winners. Plaudits should be heaped upon Acuña, who merely months away from his 39th birthday, controlled the game from midfield and somehow didn't stop running on a day when I struggled to spend a couple of minutes in direct sunlight.

As I have touched on before, climatic conditions were an important factor on football in the Americas. Complaints generally came from those unused to competing in oxygen-starved, high altitude venues. On that Sunday I couldn't see how the intensely dry heat was any less disadvantageous to an unaccustomed player. The timing of the two fixtures I attended at Defensores del Chaco clearly influenced events on and off the field. By the time Olimpia kicked off at half past six when the sun was almost set, it was a warm but pleasant evening. La Barra de la O put on a brilliant display, energetically bouncing and singing. The contest itself, although not as enthralling as the Cerro game, was played at a higher tempo. At four on a cloudless afternoon as the sun beat down, the football was understandably much more lethargic, and La Barra 1912's showing at the opposite end was unfavourable in comparison to their rival.

Paraguay's Football Association had sensibly introduced two minute drinks breaks, which the referee could call at any time. During Cerro's tie it was necessary to halt proceedings on three occasions in each half, so players could rehydrate themselves. If they kicked off three hours later I have no doubt that out of the glare of the sun, the whole spectacle would have been far better.

Weather hadn't been a major influence on Nacional's victory over Independiente, at the start of what turned out to be a very productive tournament. Despite losing on the opening day, they drastically improved after their first triumph, which was the catalyst for them to go on an 11 match unbeaten streak. On the last day of the season they were top, two points clear of Olimpia. La Clausura's final round saw both sides playing away. Crucially, Nacional were hosted by Cerro Porteño, and with an inferior goal difference needed a win to ensure they claimed the title. Things weren't looking too good at the break, Olimpia were winning and Nacional were floundering against a tough Cerro team. The O's conceded early in the second period to give Nacional the advantage, only for Cerro to score a 35 yard screamer a couple of minutes later. The goal was barely celebrated by the home fans, and scorer Francisco García didn't acknowledge his absolute peach of a strike. Instead he turned and jogged back to his half with a vaguely embarrassed look on his face.

Nacional took control of their fate three minutes later. Victor Aquino evaded a few spectacularly lackadaisical challenges to equalise. Shortly afterwards Silvio Torales wrote his name in Nacional's history books by thumping the ball past Cerro's keeper, who made no real effort to save the shot. The goals were celebrated wildly by the massed ranks of visiting Garra Alba barra (who were notable in their absence at the Independiente game) and also La Barra 1912. In the end it didn't matter as Olimpia lost their fixture, meaning Nacional's result was irrelevant to the outcome of the championship.

Conspiracy theories were very popular in Latin America. Seeing the Cerro Porteño faithful enthusiastically celebrating conceding two goals (and the manner in which they were scored) did make me wonder. Was it possible that a rivalry was so strong that Cerro threw the tie, just to ensure their deadly foe didn't add to their title collection, which at the time was ten greater than their own?

As Argentina's Primera División had kicked off that weekend I was keen to cross the border as soon as possible. Yet I couldn't leave Paraguay without calling into CONMEBOL, the headquarters of South American football. It required three buses, a lot of faffing around and some accurate directions from a Cub Scout leader, to find my way to Luque on the outskirts of Asunción. Surrounded by a huge grassed area with an array of flag poles dotted about, the ultramodern administrative building sat opposite the gleaming white concrete and reflective glass of South America's Football Museum. I'd called the office earlier that day to be told facilities were only open to the public on Saturday mornings. Undeterred by such a trivial obstacle I strutted into reception. The offices didn't appear to receive too many visitors, especially not ones wearing Birmingham City shirts and flip-flops. It wasn't until I'd garbled an explanation for my presence and was waiting to be seen by someone, I realised that I was wholly unprepared for an interview.

A tanned, lean man in his late thirties, whose name I criminally didn't take note of, greeted me. He told me that he was a representative of CONMEBOL; he'd competed in Mexico for Monterrey and had played for Paraguay's U-20 Selección at Old Trafford. We made small talk, I outlined my ridiculous quest and he told me he'd be happy to answer the questions I had prepared. The problem was the ones I'd hastily scribbled down were in English, and I was trying to recover from a weekend of excessive boozing, so my Spanish wasn't at its most eloquent. I struggled through, using my best Spanglish to try and communicate words I'd not really used before. To be fair to him he was very empathetic.

He explained CONMEBOL organised South America's international football tournaments and regulated each national league, with observers at every top flight fixture. The head office was based in Paraguay because this was the home of the confederation's President, Nicolás Leoz. He was celebrating 25 years at the helm and the administrative centre would remain there even after Leoz retires. I personally felt this was probably for the best. Although Paraguay was statistically the continent's most corrupt nation, it seemed the most orderly. Also if the base was in Brazil or Argentina, the other would cry foul play.

We also discussed their objectives, which were principally to try and bring the lesser member's standard of football up to that of the more successful ones. Neither of us believed this would ever be achieved in our lifetime. We were both proven wrong five months later when Peru and Venezuela progressed further in 2011's Copa América than Brazil and Argentina.

At the end of our conversation he reluctantly agreed to take me to have a quick look at the museum. Inside the spacious halls there were legions of school children attending a conference addressing the sport's future. After less than an hour I left CONMEBOL's head office and returned to my hotel with a huge grin on my face. Despite showing myself up as an amateur journalist, I'd achieved my objective: a Zulu Army photo with the original Copa Libertadores trophy.

ARGENTINA

Population – 40 million
Size – 2.7 million Km²
Time Zone – GMT ⁻3
Currency – Peso
FIFA World Ranking – #5 (February 2011)
Best World Cup Finish – Winners (1978, 1986)
Biggest Teams – River Plate, Boca Juniors, Independiente, San Lorenzo, Vélez Sársfield, Racing, Estudiantes

You might have heard of:
Ossie Ardiles, Diego Maradona, Gabriel Batistuta, Javier Zanetti, Lionel Messi, Juan Sebastián Verón, Pablo Zabaleta, Carlos Tévez, Sergio Agüero, Juan Manuel Iturbe, Evita, Islas Malvinas

Essential Spanish:
La Albiceleste – Sky blue and whites
Pecho - Chest
Los Cebollitas – Little Onions
Trequartista – Three quarters
Vino – Wine
Fútbol para todo – Football for everyone
Fecha – Date/Round of games
Torneo – Tournament
Banda – Band
Bandera – Flag
Sin – Without
Hijo de puta – Son of a bitch
Borracho – Drunk
Tablón – Terrace
Jugador – Player
Corazón – Heart
Tenemos que ganar – We have to win
Loco – Crazy
Cervecero – Brewer

Game 46

Argentinos Juniors v Independiente – (Torneo Néstor Kirchner Clausura 2011, Copa Islas Malvinas – TNKC, CIM) - 0 v 0
Saturday 19th February 2011 – 18:10
Estadio Diego Armando Maradona, La Paternal

Buenos Aires was always the Promised Land. Sat on my Mexican beach 14 months earlier, I formed the idea that my trip would be a success if I could make it all the way to Argentina. Since then I'd refined the way I travelled around football, but the ultimate destination remained. I arrived in Capital Federal (cee-efay) with a club to support, and ideas about working in what is generally considered to be one of the world's greatest cities. I knew whatever happened I intended on watching a lot of football.

I'd left Paraguay in a hurry, missing Cerro Porteño's big Libertadores tie against Santiago giants Colo-Colo, which saw the introduction of Juan Manuel Iturbe at half time to devastating effect. The Argentine youngster scored twice in a resounding 5 v 2 victory over Chile's most decorated team. The reason for my hurry was that I'd set my sights on attending my new side's first home fixture of the season.

Selecting a club had been a slightly traumatic process. As a child I'd flirted with the idea of being a Tottenham fan and regularly saw 'local' teams like Gillingham, Charlton and Wimbledon. My Dad took me to Blues v West Brom over Christmas 1993 and there has been no turning back. My footballing monogamy was such that I didn't really care for the English Selección. I've never understood how Leeds fans could burn effigies of David Beckham one week and applaud him representing England the next. Personally I thought it was all a little hypocritical. But I wanted to follow an Argentinian side for the duration of my stay in Buenos Aires (BA) and therefore needed to choose one.

My conditions were fairly specific. Firstly, I wasn't interested in the two big boys – Boca Juniors or River Plate – and secondly I wanted to watch Libertadores football. My choice was between Vélez Sársfield, Independiente and Argentinos Juniors. Whilst conducting my research in advance it became very clear which one I should go for. Originally named 'The Martyrs of Chicago' after the conviction of eight anarchists involved in the 19th century Black Market Riots in

Chicago (game 1) their first Libertadores home tie for 20 years was against América de Mexico (game 2). Argentinos or Bichos (Bee-chos – the bugs) as they were more commonly known, were a small team from a residential neighbourhood. They were most famous for nurturing a precocious talent called Diego Armando Maradona.

Reunited with Miss Newtown for a few days prior to her flight back to Sydney, we'd spent a lovely sunny afternoon in Palermo's suburban greenery, before taking a short train journey to barrio La Paternal. Ambling to the stadium with half an hour to spare, I questioned whether I'd chosen my new club wisely - there didn't seem to be the usual flocks of people wearing replica kits heading in the same direction. Within a couple of blocks of Estadio Maradona it got busier. Having purchased our tickets ($12.50 men, $7.50 women) I was keen to soak up the atmosphere with a cold litre of beer. Much to my dismay a barman informed me that all Argentinian Primera División venues had an alcohol exclusion zone on match days. The equivalent of drinking in the build-up to a game was eating a Choripán with your mates. The road leading to the main entrance was lined with massive barbecues and large groups milling around, discussing the contents of a football newspaper, whilst munching on what was essentially a chorizo hotdog. Not overly impressed with my introduction to their football culture, I decided to break the mould and enter a ground prior to kick-off.

As it was my first fixture and I had a lady in tow, I opted against going in with Los Ninjas 82 barra and headed towards the quiet end. It transpired that Estadio Maradona's quiet end was really sedate; it didn't have a stand, just a line of trees. Attempting to get to an area that didn't exist prompted some head shaking from the stewards, who ushered us into the main stand. Emerging from the concourse the first thing that struck me was a smoky mass of 6,000 bodies on the opposite side, although it didn't take long to work out they were the Independiente fans. Bichos' barra were housed in the lone end. It was a modest affair, holding no more than 3,000 people and generating a rather understated atmosphere.

The main stand had three tiers, with popular tickets in the first, executive in the second and preferencial located on top. The other side was comparatively large and simple. It was divided between a sparsely populated seating section and a packed terrace, where the visitors were making an almighty racket. With a 24,000 capacity it wasn't a bad little ground, but the fact that it only had three stands and the away contingent almost outnumbered the locals gave it the feel of a League Two venue like Oxford United's Kassam Stadium.

At the midway point in the first half, with minimal incident on the field of play and the late summer sun fading, it was time for a Zulu Army snap. This was Miss Newtown's fifth match so our flag photo routine was pretty efficient; the whole thing was over in less than two minutes. As we retook our position, a curly haired guy in the executive boxes shouted in broken English 'where you from?' He was visibly shocked when I responded in Spanish stating my nationality. I thought nothing of the exchange and continued to watch both teams struggle to establish a grip on the contest. Five minutes later the same man leaned over from the tier above and enthusiastically asked: 'Hey Zulu, a foto?' Slightly embarrassed but ultimately willing, I stood near Los Ninjas 82 with my bandera whilst he took some shots on a large, expensive-looking camera. As I was folding my piece of cloth a Bichos official approached me asking in perfect English whether we'd like a complimentary tour of the club museum at the break. I gratefully accepted and as the 45 minute mark rapidly approached we stood chatting. Soon it was time for us to wear a laminate, and be escorted out the popular entrance and up a set of carpeted steps.

It turned out the gentleman who'd been shouting at me was the museum's curator. He shook my hand and invited us to take a look around. It predominantly focused on Maradona's exploits, but also featured plenty of historical Argentinos-related artefacts and trophies, all in a long low-ceilinged room. The curator and his assistant spoke enthusiastically about Bichos, its unique structure and proud history, whilst small groups of Spanish speakers perused the exhibits. Once the interval drew to a close we were ushered into the executive tier, where we were allocated a pair of posh seats and told to return to the museum at full time.

I sat there in bewilderment, as Independiente's barra bounced and the teams squandered the limited chances on offer. Every time a substitution was made a journalist in front of me shouted the details into a walkie-talkie, keeping a national radio station up-to-date with the changes. Once it was over (with nothing to note from a dour goalless draw) we returned to the museum, where there were two couples speaking in US accents. Before I could strike up a conversation we were rounded up, led to the back of the room, down a staircase, along a corridor and out into an open space surrounded by glaring lights.

It took a few seconds to sink in that we were stood on the touchline by the dugouts, facing the Independiente followers making their way out of the stadium. I was stunned, my first game at my new club and I was already walking on the playing surface. Not wanting to waste the opportunity I touched the pitch, made the sign of the cross - as was customary in Latin America - and jogged towards the centre circle, shouting instructions to my camera-lady. Oblivious to what was going on around me, I excitedly adopted a position in front of the small end and pulled out my St. George's cross, posing with a satisfied grin on my face.

Although I was aware there were still people in the stands, I completely failed to appreciate that in Argentina, much like El Campín, Bogotá - the home supporters were held behind after the final whistle whilst police shepherded the visitors out. The match had finished less than ten minutes earlier, meaning the Bichos faithful were waiting with nothing to do. After witnessing an uninspiring opening to their season, and with the prospect of a minimum 30 minute delay to go home, they were already quite restless. This was explicably compounded when a Gringo stood in the middle of their beloved turf waving a piece of cloth, which on closer inspection was the national flag of one of their deadliest footballing rivals.

It started with shouting and then turned into jeers, which were swiftly drowned out by whistling that got louder and louder. Realising the terraces were still populated and the locals were unhappy about something, I looked around expecting to see a stray Independiente player or coach in the vicinity. However it quickly dawned on me that I was the subject of their derision. All of a sudden feeling very self-conscious I marched back to the group, trying to retain as much dignity as possible. At the halfway point of what seemed like a marathon trek, the whistling died down to be replaced by Los Ninjas 82 singing a song and bouncing. By the time I'd got to the dugouts the main stand had joined in with a rendition of (to the tune of Go West by the Pet Shop Boys) 'El que no salta es un Inglés'.

Hugely embarrassed, as red as the cross on my flag and with an Aussie shaking her head at me, I re-joined the party feeling like a pantomime villain. As I was going to apologise to the museum curator and other officials, one of the four US speakers approached me chuckling. He asked a couple of introductory questions before explaining what the crowd were singing: 'Jump around if you're not English.'

Game 47

Bichos v Club América – (Copa Libertadores) - 3 v 1
Thursday 24th February 2011 – 21:30
Estadio Diego Armando Maradona, La Paternal

True to form I was late to meet my new friend, and had to sprint six blocks from the bus stop to the ground so we weren't late for kick-off. Five days earlier the staff had allowed me to complete the tour in spite of my exploits on the pitch. Whilst visiting a press room and watching various players being interviewed, I continued my conversation with the guy who'd translated the song. Appropriately from Illinois and having lived in Chicago for some time, he was married to an Argentinian and had been working in BA for a decade. Much of that time had been spent following Bichos, so he was a great source of information about my new club.

Copa Libertadores was into its second round of matches. Earlier in the evening BA residents Independiente had hosted Uruguayan heavyweights Peñarol, beating them convincingly. I'd been out in the city during the day fruitlessly searching for teaching jobs, and had been astounded by the masses of gold and black shirted Barra Amsterdam, congregating around el Obelisco. Rising out the middle of BA's central thoroughfare, Avenida 9 Julio, the enormous German-built, phallic concrete structure dominated its surroundings. There was a party atmosphere that afternoon with an estimated 7,000 Uruguayans drinking, singing, dancing and waving banners at the passing traffic.

América weren't quite so well represented at Estadio Maradona; I counted 76 that had potentially made the ten hour flight from DF. Bearing in mind the distance involved it was fair to assume most of them were like my new amigo, expatriates living in BA. I couldn't envisage any of them making the journey by land as it had taken me over a year. Having said that if they'd been Colombians...

The meagre Mexican representation was rightly housed in the small end. This gave Los Ninjas 82 the opportunity to fill the large side Independiente had occupied so impressively. The spectators' location in Estadio Maradona had been a bit of a sticking point for the home fanatics, because in their own stadium they were situated in the worst of the three stands. Furthermore, when they played a lesser club the open side terrace tended to be pretty much vacant. As the TV cameras were in the main stand, on live broadcasts it looked as if the venue was almost empty. There was some vanity to this method of thinking, although anyone who'd spent any time amongst porteños (inhabitants of Buenos Aires) would know that being proud was part of their way of life.

Los Ninjas 82 didn't squander their big chance to show South America – and Mexico – how they supported their team. The side was full to the rafters and the atmosphere was as good as any I was to witness in Estadio Maradona. I was peeved we were in the main stand, as opposite us was a sea of jumping bodies. When I mentioned this Mr Illinois pointed out we had the option to change ends at the break. Much like I'd done in my teenage years watching Folkestone Invicta (where the whole of Cheriton Road was open) we stood at the end towards which Argentinos were shooting in the first half, and switched at the interval. In a way the Bichos experience was more Folkestone Invicta than Birmingham City, which I say in the most endearing way possible. The difference is that Folkestone never have and undoubtedly never will participate in an international club tournament. Birmingham's last venture was in the 1960's.

Argentinos had returned from Rio de Janeiro with a credible draw against a star-studded Fluminese in the first fecha, and a victory would give them control of Group 3. Much like in the Champions League group stages, home victories were of vital importance due to the vast distances away teams were required to travel. Unfortunately with the spine of the midfield missing, manager Pedro Troglio's experimental 5-2-3 formation allowed América to dominate.

With 27 minutes gone, journeyman striker Daniel Montenegro stooped unchallenged to head a free kick into an unguarded net, right in front of the handful of Mexicans. It was sweet revenge for the Argentina international who'd recently represented la Albiceleste against Scotland; the Bichos fans had directed the lion's share of their abuse at him. The former River and Boca forward had been subject to shouts of 'pecho frío' signifying the individual plays without passion. As the half petered out Bichos were awarded a soft penalty following a seemingly innocuous push by an América defender. Recently signed Paraguayan, Santiago Salcedo, calmly sent the keeper the wrong way to register his first goal for the club.

At the break former Argentine Selección manager Troglio switched to 4-4-2. The contest had far more ebb and flow to it in the second period, Bichos attacked intently and América countered dangerously. A set piece paid dividends for the hosts as Salcedo met a corner at the front post with a sweetly struck volley. Argentinos wrapped it up in stoppage time when injured Mexican international Pavel Pardo surrendered possession. A neat one-two resulted in the ball being laid invitingly to substitute Sánchez Prette, who fired into the top corner from distance. ¡Que Golazo!

It was during the build-up to my second Bichos fixture I researched the mercurial talent and flawed legend that was Diego Maradona. Born into a poor family, his unique ability was spotted at an early age when Argentinos signed him to their Los Cebollitas academy. A league debut aged 15 was the youngest ever until his future son-in-law Sergio Agüero broke the record in 2003. He helped the minnows from La Paternal to their highest ever finish, which encouraged Boca Juniors to acquire him for £1 million, an extravagant sum in 1981. This money enabled Argentinos to rebuild their squad and eventually win Copa Libertadores in 1985.

Maradona represented Boca for just over a year before Barcelona paid £5 million for his services. His stay in Catalonia was equally brief. The playmaker was transferred to Napoli following a serious bout of hepatitis and gaining a reputation for being a problematic character. His greatest achievement came in 1986 when he captained Argentina to World Cup triumph in Mexico. In doing so he scored two of the most famous goals in the competition's history, both against England in the quarter-final.

Back in Naples he was instrumental in the Azzurri winning their first Scudetto and European Cup. Diego was expected to produce prodigious things in 1990 when his world champions were defending their crown on his adopted home's soil. Even though la Albiceleste reached the final and only lost to a dodgy German penalty, Maradona flattered to deceive. His star was waning. In March 1991 he failed a random drugs test, was banned for 15 months and never turned out for Napoli again. Unsuccessful stints at Sevilla, Newells and Boca prompted retirement on his 37th birthday, days after featuring in a 2 v 1 Superclásico (Boca v River) victory. After retiring the former number ten battled addictions, hosted his own chat show (interviewing a range of guests from Pelé to Fidel Castro) and had a few failed forays into management.

In 2008 Maradona stated his intent to apply for the vacant Argentine Selección managerial position. Although he had hardly any experience and was running against some well-qualified candidates, he was awarded the role. After a stuttering start (including the nation's biggest ever losing margin in Bolivia) he oversaw qualification to the World Cup in South Africa. They crashed out in the quarter-final to his old adversary Germany and his contract was not renewed after the tournament. Despite his chequered past and none too accomplished present, the man was well and truly an Argentine hero. He held a particularly special place in the hearts of Bichos and Boca Juniors fans.

After a week in Buenos Aires my plans to live and work there had hit a couple of stumbling blocks. Accommodation was expensive and difficult to come by. Finding employment had also proved tricky. There were teaching roles available, but the hours were sporadic and the pay wouldn't have sustained the type of financial self-sufficiency I achieved in Mexico and Nicaragua. By the end of February 2010 I'd been on the road for over 16 months, and the prospect of trying to establish myself in one of the world's largest cities wasn't enticing. With all my possessions showing signs of wear and tear, my finances looking distinctly fragile and with one eye on a return home prior to Easter, I decided it wasn't going to happen. It was a real shame considering the monumental effort it had taken to get from Mexico to BA, that once I got there, I was too mentally and physically drained to be able to assimilate myself properly into porteño society. So I checked myself into the cheapest hostel available, with a view to watching as much football as possible in the month or so I could spin out the remainder of my travelling budget.

Game 48

Lanús v Quilmes – (TNKC - CIM) - 2 v 1
Saturday 26th February 2011 – 17:00
Estadio Cuidad de Lanús Néstor Diaz Perez, Lanús

My first jaunt out of central BA took me to the pleasant city of Lanús, situated south of the metropolitan district. I was planning to attend two fixtures that day with Boca Juniors kicking off at nine o'clock. Late as ever, a man selling flowers in Lanús train station told his wife to shut up before directing me ten blocks to the ground. Whilst negotiating a ticket, Choripán and long line to enter the stadium, Diego Valeri chipped the hosts into an early lead.

Estadio Néstor Diaz Perez could hold up to 46,000 people and had a sizeable end full with a passionate La Barra 14. I was surprised how good the view was. The main stand curved around the field into an uncovered away end (which for this clásico del sur was packed) and back to a respectable side. Emblazoned across the bare sections of concrete on the outside and inside were signs enthusiastically promoting their recent triumphs in la Apertura (2007) and Sudamericana (1996).

Shaded from glorious late afternoon sunshine I observed an honest game of football, as the home favourites dominated their recently promoted neighbours. Even though they were under the cosh for long periods, Quilmes equalised ten minutes prior to the break right in front of their delirious fans. Parity was short-lived, three minutes later Valeri scored again, beating the keeper at his near post with a sweetly struck low drive. The tall Lanús striker was back at the club he'd represented since 2003, following unproductive loan spells in Europe at Porto and Almería.

Pulling the strings in Lanús' midfield that afternoon was none other than Italian World Cup winner, Mauro Camoranesi. The Juventus legend won Serie A three times with la Bianconeri, although two of those were later rescinded due to 2006's match fixing scandal. As one of the high profile players that stayed with them during their subsequent relegation, he was instrumental in Juve's return to the top flight, and went on to represent them 224 times over eight seasons. In 2010 he left Italy for an unsuccessful Bundesliga stint with Stuttgart, before returning to his homeland to play for Lanús with a view to becoming a coach when he retired.

At full time, whilst we were waiting for Quilmes to vacate their end, two skinny bare-chested youths struck up a conversation. They'd seen me posing with my flag earlier, and as big admirers of English-style hooliganism were keen to discuss the barra brava. When I asked about their club and why they were proud to be Lanús supporters, they didn't mention winning their first ever championship and Sudamericana, but an incident from the previous season. To cut a long story short; after crashing out the Copa Libertadores to Universitario at Estadio Néstor Diaz Perez, La Barra 14 scaled the perimeter fences, ran the length of the pitch and attacked the Peruvians. Their punishment was playing a handful of fixtures behind closed doors. At the end of the explanation they both looked at me intently, as if searching for acknowledgment that this was a glorious achievement in their history. I smiled and changed the subject.

I thoroughly enjoyed my only time seeing Lanús, and was pleased when they went on an 11 game unbeaten streak to be involved in the title race. Newly promoted Quilmes were rock bottom following a terrible Apertura and losing all their Clausura ties up to that point. Initially I'd found Argentina's Promedios relegation system quite complicated, but concluded it was an interesting way of deciding who goes down. It was calculated on the average points per game over three full years (six tournaments). This meant that every match counted, no matter where you were in the table. Bichos had performed outstandingly in 2010 when they won la Clausura, meaning they were comfortably placed towards the top of the table. A couple of poor years for River Plate and Independiente saw them languishing in the relegation zone.

Newly promoted clubs were at an immediate disadvantage (particularly if they had a slow start) although a patch of good form allowed them to get out of trouble quickly, as the variant of their percentage was a lot steeper. At the end of la Apertura and Clausura the lowest two sides were relegated automatically, whilst third and fourth bottom contested a playoff against third and fourth from the Primera B Nacional. There could be no doubt this system was in place to protect the big teams from being demoted, therefore maximising television revenue. But 2011's Clausura was to prove the system didn't always function as it was intended to.

Two hours later I was stood outside the home of Boca Juniors, excited by the prospect of seeing arguably the continent's most famous sporting club. Towering Estadio Alberto Armando (Bombonera – chocolate box) looked imposing in the dark. Even though I had some preconceived negative ideas regarding the hype surrounding Boca, I was keen to see what all the fuss was about. Not having a ticket wasn't going to be a problem as I knew for a fact that the low-key fixture against newly promoted All Boys wasn't close to being sold out.

It wasn't until I'd completed a full circuit of the venue and had asked an array of stewards and police where to purchase a ticket, I realised there could be an issue. The officials had provided conflicting advice, so I resorted to asking a senior steward monitoring proceedings at the member's entrance. He informed me in no uncertain terms they didn't sell tickets to non-members, and the only way tourists could attend a tie was if they came as part of an organised group. My explanation of a footballing mission was met with disinterest, as was highlighting the numerous vacant seats on the live coverage being shown on a nearby television. As he appeared to be getting agitated by my questioning I conceded that for the first time on the trip, despite being outside a ground whilst a match was in progress, I wasn't going to enter. Frustrated, I asked whether they would rather play to a half empty stadium than sell tickets to the general public. His response was an expletive-heavy tirade about how Boca Juniors was the biggest club and they didn't have to sell tickets if they didn't want to.

Latin football clubs were structured differently to those in Britain as generally they were owned by the supporters. The equivalent of buying a season ticket was to become a Socio (member of the club). By paying their monthly dues they were permitted entry on match day, in addition to access to the associations' sporting facilities. I discovered in Medellín that these could be extensive; in BA it was on an even larger scale. In a way it was a democratic setup, as membership gave fans the right to vote on key issues such as the club's presidency. There was a lot more emphasis on being a part of the team they followed, which was one of the reasons they were so passionate about the game. This sense of community was most evident in the sides that were closely connected to a particular barrio.

To be a Socio genuinely defined a person, the bigger organisations even had their own educational establishments, from preschool to university. This level of involvement may sound more attractive than the British system of just turning up and not having any real say on how your club is run. Nonetheless, with a populous vote controlling the hierarchy, it was the barra brava that generally had the strongest influence. Being in possession of that type of power inevitably led to corruption, something I'd found was rife throughout Latin America.

For me Argentina's footballing mandate was summarised by their television coverage of Torneo Néstor Kirchner (a former President). Under the banner of 'fútbol para todo' all domestic fixtures were shown on public terrestrial television. Some of the friends I made in BA were disappointed they weren't aired on Fox Sports or ESPN. Coverage on the dedicated sporting channels was clearly superior, primarily because there were less in-game advertisements.

Since Mexico I'd become accustomed to cartoon trucks driving across the screen every five minutes to promote a specific product. I saw a Colombian league game where both goals were obscured by different popup ads that appeared at inappropriate moments. It wouldn't have been so bad if publicity was limited to periods when play was stopped, but to interrupt tournament finals to promote mobile telephones seemed to devalue the importance of the competitions. By allowing everybody to watch each game their chosen team was involved in, it increased the popularity of the local leagues. Football for everyone – a semi-socialist doctrine which helped explain why there was a greater devotion to the sport in Latin America than Europe.

Game 49

Bichos v Vélez Sársfield - (TNKC - CIM) - 1 v 1
Sunday 27ᵗʰ February 2011 – 18:00
Estadio Diego Armando Maradona, La Paternal

'Obafemi Martins… goooooooooooooooooooooollllllll, gol, gol, gol, gol, goooooooooooooooooooooooooooooooooooollll.'

I was stood in a Palermo bar, hands on head, motionless, staring at a screen. It didn't feel real. It still doesn't. A momentarily lapse of concentration by Messrs Koscielny and Szczesny gave Blues the opportunity to win their first major trophy for 48 years, and arguably ever. It had been one of the most exciting matches I'd seen us play in, especially considering it was against a big team like Arsenal. Rarely have we performed with such verve and character when the odds aren't in our favour, normally reverting to a containing, defensive strategy. But we created chances, were denied a stonewall penalty, took the lead, were pressed back and hit them on the break.

I bounced around a deserted bar when Zigic scored, swore loudly when Van Persie deservedly equalised, and was ready for extra time before that surreal winner. McLeish made an uncharacteristic attacking substitution with ten minutes remaining and it somehow paid off. Although Martins grabbed the headlines, the lion's share of credit should go to Ben Foster and Roger Johnson for keeping us in the contest for 90 minutes, constructing a platform from which to win the League Cup. Victory meant we would be playing in a serious European tournament for the first time in my life (the Anglo-Italian cup blatantly doesn't count).

Stumbling out into a bright sunny Sunday, slightly tipsy and very confused, I was accompanied by the Yorkshireman who'd been part of the gang I'd spent Christmas with in Bolivia. He was staying in BA for a few weeks with his Guatemalan girlfriend, so we spent the rest of the afternoon catching up prior to taking a train to La Paternal. By the time our tickets had been purchased we'd consumed seven litres between us and Vélez had scored. To be completely honest the game was a bit of a blur. I spent most the time sat in a Birmingham City shirt trying to fathom how on earth Blues beat Arsenal.

During the second half we bumped into Mr Illinois. He was there with Martín, an Argentinian guy who spoke better English than the lad from Dewsbury accompanying me. Through the haze I can remember a Zulu Army photo being taken by a random backpacker who was also a Blues fan (but not really as he didn't even know we'd won the final) Bichos having a player sent off, and then finding the net. I have a vague recollection of Franco Neill, the second smallest person on the pitch, scoring a front post header to rescue a credible point for Argentinos against their near neighbours.

Throughout proceedings I'd spent a large amount of time staring at the shortest individual on display, wondering in my drunken daze why a schoolboy was allowed to play professional football. Vélez's Maxi Morales - at a commanding five foot three - was the archetypal Argentine number ten; a playmaker or trequartista. Employed to operate just behind the forwards, the lack of defensive responsibilities enabled them to get into dangerous positions. Like numerous Argentinian traits, the concept originated in Italy. Examples of players who have succeeded in this role included Totti and Baggio, as well as other Europeans such as Zidane and Figo. Generally the Argentines who were best at this position tended to be slight characters like Riquelme, Ayala, Messi, and the greatest of all, Maradona. Many locals mourned the demise of Riquelme as probably the best trequartista of his generation, but when I was there the future was bright should their Selección wish to fill that specialist slot.

All in all it had been a cracking day of football, and not a bad day's cricket either. Before leaving in the morning I'd streamed England's incredible 338 apiece tie in the World Cup, against hosts India. Unfortunately we were eliminated under embarrassing circumstances to Sri Lanka in the quarter-final, following an inconsistent tournament. We beat South Africa and the West Indies, but lost to Bangladesh and the titans of cricket that were Ireland.

Game 50

Huracán v Arsenal - (TNKC - CIM) - 1 v 1
Monday 28th February 2011 – 19:10
Estadio Tomás Adolfo Duco, Parque Patricios

My half century of games was brought up the day after Blues'
Wembley success, appropriately witnessing Arsenal's visit to Huracán.
I was getting into the swing of watching football in Capital Federal,
aided by the abundance of big teams in a relatively small area, and the
cheap, efficient public transport. At the time Buenos Aires was home to
more professional football clubs than any other city in the world. My
journey to Huracán consisted of a four block walk from my hostel and a
20 minute Subte ride, BA's version of the London Underground. This
was built by the British, so naturally trains ran on the left side of the
track. A return combined with a ticket at the average Primera División
price totalled less than £7.00. In England you'd have struggled to see a
respectable non-league fixture for that amount.

Another brilliant thing about top flight matches in Argentina
was the stadiums. Estadio Tomás Adolfo Duco was an absolute beauty.
As it was built on a former rubbish burning site the locals were known
as Los Quemeros (the burners). The 48,000 capacity open dome felt
almost Coliseum like. Its bare brick exterior had a retro 1960's look to it
and reminded me of Highbury. Entering through automatic turnstiles
and climbing a steep set of stairs, I found myself in a concourse
confronted by a procession of chanting fans. It was a spontaneous thing
to stumble onto and a little bit intimidating. There was a large
concentration of highly charged barra in a claustrophobic enclosed area.
Trying to blend in as best as possible, I bounced in time to the singing
and headed towards the group's periphery, eventually managing to
squeeze into the arena.

Inside the scene was enhanced by the sun setting into a
cloudless pale blue sky behind me. This cast dramatic shadows across
the terraces, and bathed half the playing surface in a dark orange hue.
The setting was complimented by an active crowd of animated Huracán
supporters to my left, and a fairly spectacular (though pointless
looking) tower rising 50 meters out of the side to my right. There was a
small, quiet group representing Arsenal at the opposite end, shading
their eyes from the glare. I assumed this could be attributable to the
antisocial kick-off time (although seven o'clock on a Monday evening

was bliss in comparison to early on a Saturday morning in Quito). La Banda de la Quema barra made up for the visitor's lack of atmosphere. Their renditions of some original songs, sung at good volume and a high tempo got a lot of the people in the peripheral sections moving, including yours truly. The raucous locals also compensated for what could politely be described as a subdued performance from both teams.

On the 30 minute mark there was a stirring in the away end. A group of ten lads appeared from the concourse. They scurried about the stand, tying flags to fences and securing giant banners against metal posts. Soon they vanished back from where they came, whilst there was a distinct sound of music, which was getting louder and louder. Then with an air of drama, led by their band, the Arsenal barra entered the fray. Their presence encouraged the home faithful to be even more animated. For five minutes the noise around the quarter full venue was deafening. By the time La Mafia barra had got through the entrance, their band had settled and everybody had taken their place, the referee blew for half time. That's my definition of fashionably late.

Thankfully things picked up on the pitch after the interval. The relegation threatened hosts forced the pace in their new manager's first game in charge. Self-confessed Huracán fan, Roberto Pompei, had taken the helm only two weeks into the new torneo. He sent his charges out with intent and was rewarded with an early goal, Javier Cámpora sliding home. It was then down to Arsenal's manager, Gustavo Alfaro, to make his mark on proceedings. The introduction of substitute Leguizamón immediately changed things. It was his well won challenge and deep cross that setup Mauro Obolo's equaliser, a fine header from the striker that had previously been prolific for AIK of Sweden. Huracán had already noticeably dropped a gear after they scored, and the Arsenal goal appeared to make them self-destruct.

For a quarter of an hour the contest threatened to be a competitive spectacle, but rapidly descended into comedy of error mode. Huracán were the more culpable, spraying wild passes in dangerous parts of their own half, regularly giving the ball away and practically inviting Arsenal to score. Once the clock had reached 90 minutes I'd counted four one-on-ones and two open goals, but no addition to the score line. Although I've unfairly criticised the quality of football at some matches, I have to confess that the last half an hour of this charade was pure entertainment. This sentiment wasn't shared by the majority of the spectators. Many of those around me spent the final third of the game with their hands over their eyes or their backs to the field. I can empathise with them having spent more than a few

215

embarrassing afternoons at St. Andrews. A 3 v 1 loss to Bury in the late 1990's springs readily to mind.

Whilst waiting to leave a group who'd seen my St. George's cross approached me, interested in why a Gringo would be watching one of BA's less glamorous clubs. I was very complimentary about how a smaller association had such a passionate following, regardless of events on the pitch. I'd read varying accounts as to who were Huracán's traditional rival and was intrigued to find out what they considered their biggest derby. I got a different answer from each person; my favourite was 'el clásico sin banderas' which evolved as Huracán fanatics regularly stole flags and banners from their San Lorenzo counterparts. La Banda Quema displayed the stolen items at encounters between the two, provoking strong reactions from the victims and resulting in violent scenes during and after matches. Antagonism reached such a level that Argentina's Football Authority (AFA) banned all flags from stadiums at that specific fixture. I have to admit to enjoying the immaturity of grown men stealing one another's toys and then showing them off, yet for these guys it was totally serious.

Perennial championship runners-up, Huracán were to play a pivotal role in 2011's Clausura at both ends of the table. Despite performing averagely whilst I was in BA, the ship started sinking halfway through the tournament. They claimed a solitary point from nine games and were heading for relegation. It all got a bit too much for La Banda de la Quema. After conceding two goals in the first five minutes at home to Estudiantes, they shouted insults and threw pieces of wood at the visiting barra, forcing the tie to be abandoned. The trapdoor loomed on the last day of the season, but Gimnasia de la Plata were pulled into the fight following Boca Juniors' injury time equaliser against them. This left the two clubs on an identical 1.096 Promedios percentage. Consequently Huracán and Gimnasia competed in a playoff to see who would be relegated automatically and who would go on to a decider against San Martín. Gimnasia won the contest (staged at the Bombonera) but lost to the side from San Juan.

By the beginning of March I was settled into the cheap accommodation located during my first week in the Argentine capital. I turned up at an establishment called The Tango Hostel, enticed by $7 beds and free onsite dance lessons. What I found was a large building housing a student community who were attending a nearby university. The monthly rent was affordable and its location close to some transport hubs was perfect. Even though my plan to work in BA had collapsed, I was determined to stretch my budget to its limit and cover as much football as was humanly possible. It was my last big assignment of the trip: I was playing at being a football journalist in the birthplace of the barra brava.

Game 51

Vélez Sársfield v Universidad Católica - (Copa Libertadores) - 3 v 4
Thursday 3rd March 2011 – 19:15
Estadio José Amalfitani, Liniers

Why take a train which gets you there in 25 minutes when you can catch a bus that costs twice the price and takes 80 minutes? It's funny how a split-second decision can alter your perception of an entire evening. In my defence I was excited about this fixture and had allowed plenty of time to make kick-off. That was until I hopped onto a bus (because the stop was marginally closer than the train station) which I cursed for over an hour standing in a cramped aisle, as we somehow hit every red traffic light in BA. By the time a nice couple had pointed out where to alight the contest was already a few minutes old, so I sprinted the remaining six blocks in the growing darkness.

I'd planned to go in with Vélez's La Pandilla barra but changed my mind when a steward informed me the home entrance was a further 20 minutes' walk, whereas the away end was behind us. I swiftly negotiated two lines of riot police, unlike a poor guy who'd just got off a bus from Santiago and was having his large backpack meticulously searched. Taking my place amongst Los Cruzados barra for Copa Libertadores second group match, I was grateful that on this occasion I wasn't wearing the opposition's shirt (like at game 38). I was roughly ten minutes late, but was happy to learn from a man next to me that there'd been no goals.

Several people had told me Vélez's El Fortín (Little Fort) was one of the best stadiums in Argentina, but I wasn't that impressed. The atmosphere generated from all corners was excellent, although after 17 months I was becoming blasé about it all. Undoubtedly two side stands towering over smaller ends gave a good view of the pitch, and the singing and jumping carried on all the way around the venue. It just seemed to lack the character of Lanús or Huracán which were also approximately 50,000 capacity. I should be grateful I wasn't at Estadio Maradona - I got a decent view of a cracking game.

From the moment I arrived Vélez dominated while Católica adopted a far more cautious approach. After 20 minutes the hosts took the lead, central defender Fernando Ortiz scoring an unchallenged glancing header from a free kick. A minute later the Católica defenders went AWOL again, giving Augusto Fernández time to control a cross, ponder the meaning of life, before firing into the roof of the net. Vélez added a third in stoppage time when impressive left back Emiliano Papa was given too much space to head a precise cross past the stranded keeper.

At the break I was surprised how upbeat the Católica fans were, considering they'd travelled such a distance and their team were taking a pasting. Two of the more tattooed and diseased looking barra (one with a comical ginger afro) were going about persuading folk to donate money to pay for the band's journey home. I was shocked how willing they were to hand over substantial sums to the two bedraggled-looking youths, and felt particularly sorry for one family whose group photo was invaded until they coughed up. Fair play to the Chilean supporters, they knew their way around a musical instrument or two. Los Cruzados' band, much like the one I witnessed in Iquique, was brilliant. I really appreciated the prominence of the Tuba, which in my opinion was criminally underused by Latin American football bands.

Católica began the second half with a flourish both on and off the pitch. They created a handful of good opportunities while their barra sang with renewed energy. After squandering their early chances I couldn't see a way back for the Catholic students, but the contest was turned on its head when Fernando Ortiz picked up a needless second booking. Vélez's manager substituted tiny Maxi Morales – presumably so he could finish his homework and get to bed before his mum told him off – replacing him with Uruguayan Santiago Silva. Shortly after midfielder Tomás Costo fired an unstoppable 35 yard screamer which flew in off the far post. Having watched 75 minutes of Católica ineptness it was bizarre to see a strike of such quality. Even as Vélez looked increasingly ragged, the Chileans still didn't look capable of generating enough openings to score the two goals they needed for a share of the spoils. But that's why I, and millions of others all over the world, love football.

With two minutes of normal time left striker Lucas Pratto received a pass inside the home penalty area, controlled neatly and volleyed clinically past a despairing dive. Chaos ensued. Despite my best efforts to avoid the most enthusiastic celebrations I had to pick myself off the floor ten rows down from where I'd started. I returned to a vertical position just in time to see Vélez have a guilt edged chance to secure all three points, but poor control and good defending by substitute Francisco Pizarro denied them. Once he'd won the ball Pizarro ran the length of the pitch, exchanged passes with two players and gleefully chipped the advancing keeper, sparking delirious scenes on the visiting bench.

There was barely time to kick-off before the final whistle sounded, prompting the Católica squad to run over to celebrate with the travelling faithful. It all seemed a little exuberant to me. Granted an away draw was a respectable result, but they were acting as if they'd won. I discovered the next day they actually had. Lucas Pratto scored for Católica after 40 seconds (whilst I was still on a bus) meaning they'd claimed an 88th minute equaliser and a 90th minute winner to make it 3 v 4.

This was the most dramatic game I saw in the Americas and rather comical due to my perception of it at the time. I was perturbed that the man I asked upon arrival wasn't aware of his side's early advantage, but not quite as annoyed as I was with Vélez's Estadio José Amalfitani. Rising high above the home end was a giant electronic scoreboard, which considering its location should have displayed information relating the match taking place. Not once was anything relevant to the evening's events posted for spectators to see. Instead there were endless advertisements for a local restaurant chain and Pedro's Bookstore. But such is life.

The night was in keeping with what turned out to be a very eventful season for Vélez. They recovered from the trauma of losing on their own turf and progressed to Copa Libertadores' knockout stages along with their Chilean conquerors (with whom they played out a goalless draw in Santiago a few weeks later). Both made it to the quarter-finals where Católica lost to Peñarol and Vélez hammered Libertad. The two sides would have met in the semi's, instead Vélez faced los Aurinegros and trailed 1v 0 from the first leg in Montevideo. They conceded early in the decisive tie at El Fortin before scoring twice to restore parity. Down to ten men and needing to find the net once more to avoid elimination on away goals, they were awarded a penalty in the last quarter of an hour. Santiago Silva blazed over, booking Peñarol's place in the final.

At El Fortín I'd observed the Católica barra conducting the singing. From their precarious perch on top of metal barriers dotted around the stand, the way various members took their turn to lead the chanting indicated there was a carefully planned order to their behaviour. Many were wearing t-shirts with the slogan: 'Barra Brava – always supporting the team, never promoting violence'. Each shirt had an Argentine flag printed on it and made reference to the original barra brava.

After some research it transpired there was a barra shop in BA

220

which sold memorabilia celebrating football fanatics. There was an anti-violence message on the merchandise they sold. I thought it strange that Chileans would proudly wear an item of clothing with a rival nation's flag emblazoned across the front. I'd started to gain an impression as to what the barra brava represented in Buenos Aires, although the more I read and spoke to people about it, the more it intrigued me.

From what I could discern the barra had adapted a business model to suit the Socio system. This enabled them to control the clubs they followed and earn a healthy living at the same time. In a structure where the majority ruled, it was the individuals who had sway over the masses that wielded the real power. The senior barra had such a strong influence over their legions that they could apparently dictate their voting patterns. It was therefore within the interests of an organisation's hierarchy to have the barra on their side. This was achieved by allowing them to manage much of their revenue stream. Consequently almost every element of the match day experience was governed by the barra, from car parking and food stalls outside the stadium, to distribution and touting complimentary tickets. Each association President was well aware that a successful tenure was only guaranteed if he had the backing of the team's most prominent fans. To a Gringo it seemed fanciful hearing how the system operated, but this state of affairs wasn't just limited to football. In national politics it was said the party who garners the Boca Juniors vote (estimated to be up to half Argentina's overall population) would more than likely come to power.

Game 52

All Boys v San Lorenzo - (TNKC - CIM) - 0 v 3
Friday 4th March 2011 – 19:10
Estadio Islas Malvinas, Floresta

Back in western Buenos Aires 24 hours later I learnt from the previous day's mistake and caught a train. The peaceful, leafy barrio of Floresta was a close neighbour of Liniers (home of Vélez Sársfield) as both were built along the same busy railway line. Porteño commuters were unforgiving at five o'clock on a Friday evening. The second the doors opened people flooded into the carriage without permitting anyone to alight first. Notwithstanding the crush, the train was another cheap and efficient method of transport in this great city.

Newly promoted All Boys had struggled in la Apertura, leaving them with an uphill task in la Clausura to stay in the division. Going into their fixture against San Lorenzo (one of the country's 'big five') they were buoyed by a historic 2 v1 win at Vélez in the last fecha. All Boys had been the visitors for my failed excursion to Boca Juniors six days earlier, and during an infuriating circuit of La Bombonera I stumbled upon the arrival of their La Peste Blanca barra (White Plague). As they made their way to the entrance, surrounded by a heavy police escort, I followed the procession and had been stunned at how openly aggressive the fans from Floresta were. Uncharacteristically the female members of the group were equally as animated as the men. During my brief accompaniment I saw two 'ladies' approach a group of darker skinned men wearing Boca shirts, making monkey signs at them.

Arriving at the same time as a convoy of decrepit buses with La Gloriosa Butteler barra hanging out of the windows, I observed their rituals whilst finishing my can of beer. In less than ten minutes the coaches had been parked and everyone was inside. It was surreal to witness the efficiency with which the gangs of youths organised themselves, distributing instruments and flags, parking vehicles and marching two blocks to the entrance en mass. In a way it was similar to the controlled rabble at Nicaragua's socialist Revolution Day celebrations.

By the time I'd bought an overpriced ticket and negotiated the entrance their banners were all in place and San Lorenzo's band was in full swing, generating an electric atmosphere in a compact end. The focal section of home support inside the 18,000 strong stadia was situated on the side opposite the main stand, as the other end was miniscule. I have issues with open side terraces as the sound doesn't travel well, so the continuity of singing suffers. This was the case at Estadio Islas Malvinas, as from the far corner I could barely hear the enthusiastic La Peste Blanca stood in line with the centre circle.

Before finding somewhere to watch proceedings I asked someone to take a quick snap. My routine was pretty well honed at that stage. Ordinarily the whole process was over and done with in less than two minutes, and unless I was in the middle of the pitch, without the majority of the crowd noticing. All Boys' faithful didn't take kindly to my flag. In the minute it was on show I was subject to a torrent of abuse from three different directions. Slightly confused I retrieved my camera, thanked the photographer and slipped away to another area of the stand. It wasn't until the second half got under way I realised why it received such a hostile reception - I was at the Falkland Islands stadium.

Politics in Argentina like so many Latin countries was dominated by the military throughout much of the 20ᵗʰ century. Even the celebrated Perón era was characterised by fascist tendencies. In the early 1980's, with their economy in decline, presiding General Leopoldo Galtieri sought to bolster his popular support by invading las Islas Malvinas. Although geographically much closer to South America than Europe; Britain had governed these three tiny windswept islands for over a century and a half. On April 2ⁿᵈ 1982 Argentine forces occupied the home of a couple of thousand British subjects, most of whom were sheep farmers. Margaret Thatcher (who was encountering her own political difficulties at the time) responded by deploying the Navy to reclaim the territory. A 74 day war ensued, leading to the loss of approximately 900 lives, mostly young, badly trained and poorly equipped Argentine servicemen.

Argentina's surrender led to the end of military control, Raúl Alfonsin was given the presidency in 1983. This improved the Iron Lady's approval ratings and she was re-elected the following year. Official relations were restored in 1989, but there was no doubt that Argentines claimed Islas Malvinas were rightfully theirs (much like the Galápagos and Easter Islands belonged to Ecuador and Chile respectively). Over two decades later there was still a lot of animosity towards us. When I asked Martín, Mr Illinois' friend from BA, about the song the Bichos fans had been chanting to me at my first fixture, he explained Argentinians had been singing it about the British for 20 years. He added that we were thieving people who had sexual relations with our mothers.

The contest only really came alive in the last 30 minutes. For an hour All Boys dominated possession, but like so many of the smaller clubs I'd seen, lacked a goal threat. San Lorenzo had looked tidy but low on confidence after losing at home against Racing the previous week. For the second night in a row a red card changed proceedings, and if I described Vélez's as needless, then this one was nothing short of pure idiocy. On 64 minutes All Boys defender Hugo Barrientos conceded a questionable foul on the edge of his penalty area. Met with the usual overdramatic protests from the hosts, the referee appeared to want to assert his authority, so he booked the perpetrator. This brought the crowd to life and a variety of objects were thrown at the officials. All Boys organised themselves for the resultant free kick, apart from Barrientos, who was so incensed he continued to argue with the referee. The set-piece was taken and wasted by San Lorenzo, but play was immediately called back so the ref could issue a second yellow card to Barrientos.

Predictably there was two minutes of chaos as lads tried to scale fences to get at the officials, while loud chants of 'hijo de puta' rang around the terraces. All Boys' players reacted just as favourably to the decision. The wall used their feet to rub out the temporary white free kick line and advanced five paces. It was reapplied on three separate occasions before play could be resumed. From there on in the contest was over. San Lorenzo missed some prime opportunities prior to scoring three easy goals in the last 20 minutes. It was the second time in consecutive days I'd seen a side collapse after having a player dismissed.

As the final whistle approached the entire crowd stood in unison to give substituted All Boys midfielder Ariel Ortega a warm ovation. The former Argentine international hadn't been as influential on the game as I'd hoped. Throughout the first half I sensed the frustration of a man in the twilight of his distinguished career, unable to pull the same strings as he could in his prime. In the 1990's he was seen as the successor to Maradona's crown, and the coveted Selección number 10 role. His most productive spells came in Serie A with Parma and Sampdoria. Back in his homeland for his second stint at River Plate, he went on loan to prove his fitness. Whilst I applauded the 37 year old for his desire to carry on playing regularly, I couldn't help but feel sorry for him competing alongside players of a lesser calibre. The man who arguably caused Argentina's exit from France '98 (when he was sent off in the quarter-final for a head butt on Holland's Edwin Van de Sar) graciously clapped his appreciation as he exited the field.

Much of the second half entertainment was supplied by a chubby San Lorenzo supporter. He had scaled the wall at the back of the away stand and was directing the singing from his vantage point. Estadio Islas Malvinas staff were not happy with this move so made regular requests over the public announcement system to get him to come down. As the messages switched from pleading to threatening; the police made half-hearted attempts to remove him. Although I couldn't hear what was being said, it was clear through his gesticulations that he would descend once he'd untied the row of banners attached to the wall on which he was sitting. The red-faced youth carried on coordinating a flamboyant call and response chant between the right side, left side and middle of the fans, whilst removing one corner of each piece of cloth. He then continued orchestrating whilst reattaching the flag's corners back to the wall, before producing a comically exaggerated display of indignation when the officers chastised him. Clearly not wanting to provoke any violence the police allowed the pantomime to continue. It was only halted when the idiot almost fell whilst celebrating San Lorenzo's second goal, and gingerly climbed down from his perch.

My good humour towards the visiting contingent was short-lived as we waited an hour to leave. With relegation starring them in the face it was all too much for some people. The following day a newspaper reported that an 'important' group of barra waited after the game to abuse the referee for his performance. Quite what that achieved I don't know, although a late season flourish ensured All Boys survived fairly comfortably.

Game 53

Atlanta v Defensores de Belgrano – (Metro B) - 1 v 2
Saturday 5ᵗʰ March 2011 – 16:00
Estadio Don León Kolovski, Villa Crespo

The build-up to this Metro B fixture was all about champions elect Atlanta being unbeaten at home for 357 days. They needed one more victory to make it over the year mark. It was a feat Blues managed between September 2009 and October 2010, eventually losing to Everton 371 days after the prologue. More enticing for me at the time was that the stadium was a two minute stroll from Dorego Subte station, which in turn was four stops away from my local station, named after legendary Tango singer Carlos Gardel.

On a cloudless 33 degree afternoon I ambled up to buy a ticket which disgracefully cost only $1.25 less than the country's top clubs. Lying in fifth place, the visitors had claimed 45 points from their 27 games, in comparison to Atlanta's 57. Crucially, the league leaders had been beaten 3 v 0 the previous weekend. Could their title charge be halted? In all honesty who really cared? After all I was watching third tier football.

Atlanta were nicknamed los Bohemios due to the fact that they didn't have their own home for over 60 years. Bunking down in various borrowed grounds - including Argentinos Juniors' - they settled at Estadio Don León Kolovski in the 1960's. They were forced to improve their facilities following crowd trouble when All Boys visited in 2008. La Peste Blanca tore up the old wooden stands, using them as ammunition after a pre-match fight continued inside the stadium. The AFA once again had to confiscate the barra's toys, rightly decreeing all wood should be replaced. The reconstructed venue was functional but exposed to the elements, which on that Saturday in March was the searing heat. I got so sunburnt whilst I was there that I was unable to make it to my second fixture of the day, Racing v Olimpo. This proved to be irksome as it was a seven goal thriller.

Commendably the teams on display played football that belied their lower league status. Defensores, as their name suggested, were suitably sound at the back and very much fighting for a playoff place. On the quarter hour mark Atlanta took the lead their early dominance warranted, a thumping header from a corner, courtesy of defender Juan Segovia. Although they didn't replicate the finesse of their hosts, the away side were combative and forced an equaliser from the penalty spot with half an hour gone. For the third time in as many days, a silly red card after the interval turned the contest in the visitor's favour. The surprising thing about this one was that it was shown to a Defensores player. Six minutes later Diego Caria converted a low cross to put them in front. The goal was celebrated wildly by the players and substitutes, whilst their 30 fans situated in the top tier of the main stand applauded ecstatically. Shortly after, following a double elbow (that's one player elbowing two opponents at the same time) Atlanta had squandered their numerical advantage. In the afternoon heat with ten men a piece the game opened up. Admirably both sides attacked right until the whistle, but there was no addition to the score line.

Atlanta were unable to sustain their proud home record but won the league at canter, setting up a reunion with their opponent from that scorching Saturday in the second tier. Defensores de Belgrano built on their encouraging victory in Villa Crespo, finishing third. They ran out winners of the postseason finals by beating Nueva Chicago on away goals.

Game 54

River Plate v Bichos - (TNKC - CIM) - 0 v 0
Sunday 6th March 2011 – 19:10
Estadio Monumental Antonio Vespucto Liberti, Belgrano

Of all the games I attended, the most highly anticipated was watching my adopted team in one of the world's most iconic football stadiums. On Saturday morning before heading off to Atlanta I'd taken a bus to La Paternal and bought five tickets for the away end at El Monumental. Just having them in my possession increased the excitement levels significantly. My roommate in the Tango Hostel was a big River enthusiast and was keen to join me, as was the Yorkshireman who'd been to Bichos the previous week. The other two tickets were for Mr Illinois and Martín.

We all met in the swanky Belgrano neighbourhood, near to BA's token China Town district. This consisted of a couple of feebly decorated streets and some shops with roast ducks hanging in the windows. Even though there was over an hour until kick-off the three Americans were keen to get to the venue, whereas the Europeans were desperate to stay in a bar until the last possible minute. Later we learnt that it was fortunate the majority ruled. Whilst sharing a litre bottle of cerveza, Mr Dewsbury and I followed the locals.

Argentina's largest ground overlooked a highway on one side and an exclusive neighbourhood on the other. The houses surrounded El Monumental so closely that in order to curtail potential confrontations between rival fans, streets were shut on match day. Unless you had a valid ticket or proof of residency you weren't able to enter the 16 square blocks closest to the visiting entrance. As there were a minimum 19 home fixtures a year, I imagined this devalued the area's hefty property prices somewhat. Discarding our bottle at a police cordon we sauntered for ten minutes down a tree-lined avenue, to come across a very odd sight. It was so strange that both my fellow Englishman and I barged straight past it, speaking our native tongue as loudly as possible, ignoring requests from the police and stewards to join a line to be tested. Once we were a relatively safe distance away we stood starring at the most bizarre and wrong thing I've ever seen at a football match.

The officials were breathalysing supporters. If they exceeded the drink driving limit they weren't permitted to pass. At this stage I don't want to get too indignant as I appreciate alcohol and hooliganism go hand in hand, and particularly against the Argentine barra the police were fighting a losing battle. However, I am of the opinion that just because a person has had a cerveza, it doesn't mean they are going to cause trouble. Having said that I fully understand the minority spoil it for everyone else. Ultimately it's a subjective debate; I enjoy a peaceful beer (or three litres in this instance) before a game. On the other hand many families would praise authorities for trying to rid the sport of its unpleasant side. As a football fan I believe this touches on the complicated subject as to who has more right to follow their team. It's something I have no desire to explore as there isn't a correct answer.

This attempt to discourage booze consumption gave me some good ammunition for my discussions with Argentinians, the overwhelming majority of whom thought theirs was the best footballing culture in Latin America, if not the world. They had a strong case, but the fact remained: when I walked into Mexico's national stadium they gave me a cup containing two bottles of Corona. When I approached Argentina's they tried to breathalyse me. You can judge which was preferable.

Anyway, the English contingent negotiated the entrance without problems, but the others weren't so successful. It took three tests and a lot of pleading for them to allow my roommate past (who'd only drunk a litre). Reunited, we climbed up, up, up towards the rafters and out into the away end to behold a stunningly beautiful view. My initial impressions were enhanced by a massive rainbow arcing from one side of the arena to the other, and a Boeing 747 circling to land at a nearby airport. El Monumental was pure Coliseum. Its 65,000 capacity and huge, curvaceous red and white upper tiers made it monumental in every way.

We arrived as the game reached 60 minutes, which I didn't think was too much of a novelty. That was until I realised it was a reserve fixture preceding the main event. I was aware that one of the reasons people turned up so early was to watch the second string, but had never been punctual enough to observe it with my own eyes. As far as I was concerned (backed by Mr Dewsbury) this was a waste of valuable drinking time, especially as we were sobering up before the real contest had even started. But enough about alcohol for one chapter, the matinee proved to be a rather entertaining 3 v 2 home win.

By the time the final whistle had blown El Monumental was almost full. There were some vacant seats along the sides and a noticeably large empty space in the middle of the end opposite us. This wasn't unoccupied for long, as with ten minutes until kick-off Los Borrachos del Tablón barra appeared. Drummers led the procession with their instruments held above their head, followed by the rest of the band. They were proceeded by a group of what I imagine was the most senior barra, and then a mass of flag-wielding youths. Much like San Lorenzo's fanatics two days earlier, the precision and order in which they moved indicated that this was a well-oiled machine. Once everyone was in place a signal went up and the whole upper tier - containing approximately 15,000 bodies - erupted in unison. There are not enough superlatives to adequately describe that moment.

River's players didn't mirror the passion generated by their partisan support, and looked bereft of ideas prior to the match's turning point. In the moments leading up to the interval I witnessed my fifth and sixth red cards of the past four days. Paulo Ferrari and Miguel Torrén were given their marching orders. Replays were inconclusive as why they were both dismissed, there was definitely contact, but it seemed an extreme call. At full time it was fair to say that Bichos had the better of a poor contest.

River Plate was one of the most respected names in world football, with two Libertadores and an Intercontinental Cup to their name. Their anglicised name reflected Argentina's footballing heritage. English expatriates Thomas and James Hogg introduced fútbol in the 1860's, before Scottish teacher Alexander Hutton created the first league outside the UK in the 1880's. River was founded in 1901 and was soon known as Los Millonarios after some heavy spending in the 1930's. This established them as representing the wealthy in contrast to Boca's working-class following. Named after the waterway dividing Argentina and Uruguay, they were country's most decorated club and their barra were arguably the fiercest on the continent. Despite their glorious history and wealthy backing, the team I saw that Sunday were embroiled in a relegation battle. It was an inconceivable prospect as in their 110 years of existence River Plate had never been demoted.

Life in the Tango Hostel wasn't dull. There was an endless turnover of residents from all corners of Latin America, including Chileans, Brazilians and a guy from El Salvador. As the only European inhabitant my presence was a bit of a novelty, chiefly for those who'd lived there for a substantial period of time. It wasn't until a couple of days after the River match that I really made a name for myself.

There was a little Colombian mafia who'd formed a football squad and challenged the 'rest of the world' to beat them in a weekly five-aside game. Apparently the contests had been quite rough, as the boys from Bogotá were keen on intimidating their opponents. One evening whilst I was drunkenly trying to write my diary I was called upon to make the numbers up for the other side. I had no boots, but in my inebriated state wasn't going to let that be an obstacle. After my old trainers collapsed a few minutes into proceedings I opted to continue playing in my bare feet.

Ideally I should have realised after my first 50/50 tackle it wasn't a good idea, but I'd enough cerveza and red wine inside me to not really feel the pain. AstroTurf was unforgiving to exposed skin; it wasn't long before my feet were a bloody mess of torn flesh and blisters. But I was determined to show Colombians that the English would not be bullied on the field of play, so threw myself aggressively into challenges whilst goading them in their own language. Perhaps they felt sorry for my painful situation or didn't want to get a stranger's blood all over their pristine white boots, because as the game wore on they increasingly shied away from my tackles. I ended up on the losing team but like to think that I made my point. I certainly made an impression – for the remainder of my stay in BA I was known as el loco Rooney.

Game 55

San Lorenzo v Boca Juniors - (TNKC - CIM) - 1 v 0
Saturday 12th March 2011 – 19:10
Estadio Pedro Bidegaín, Flores

San Lorenzo defender Aureliano Torres picked up a loose ball just inside his own half and ran down the left hand side of the pitch. He took five touches unchallenged by the Boca midfield or defence, and from 35 yards fired a rocket of a shot that was drifting wide of the far post. At the very last moment the ball bent back towards goal and nestled in the side netting. For a split-second nobody moved because it came from nowhere. The keeper stood still as Torres wheeled away in celebration, at which point the crowd suddenly gathered he'd scored and started going crazy. There was an obvious comparison between the Paraguayan left back's strike that evening and Brazilian Roberto Carlos' trademark thumpers. It was an absolute screamer, with the type of late bend that gives stoppers across the world nightmares. It was also one of the reasons why football is so universally popular: 90 minutes of mediocrity punctuated by a single moment of pure genius, which sent the majority of the spectators home with a smile on their face.

The day had begun with Blues playing their second FA Cup quarter-final in two seasons. It was another early kick-off, so I was sat watching the hostel reception's TV at half past nine, far less painful than the previous year's fixture which I'd endured at 06:30 in Guatemala. Our home tie was poised at 2 v 1 in Bolton's favour before there was a weird repetition of the prologue. Good old Kevin Phillips chipped Jaaskelainen to equalise with ten minutes to go, only for Chung-Yong Lee, the South Korean match winner from September 2009, to score a decisive goal in injury time.

It was the first cold day since I'd arrived in BA; early rain was replaced by a biting wind and cloudy skies. Sitting in an antique Subte train, I was surprised how empty the service was considering it ran from the city centre to the outlying suburbs. In London at six o'clock on a Saturday afternoon, with a game between two big clubs at the end of the line, the tube would be a chaotic mixture of shoppers and beer-swilling football fans. Argentinian culture was far different to our own as the 25 minute underground ride had a lazy, peaceful air to it and I had the majority of a carriage to myself. I tried my best to represent our lager-fuelled football traditions by swigging cans of Quilmes and singing Blues songs.

There really wasn't enough time for a cheeky litro by Varela station, but I managed to squeeze one in whilst an inquisitive Paraguayan rambled on in decent English about German immigration. Shortly after kick-off I negotiated five blocks to the ground, limping painfully from the injuries sustained in the hostel football match. Within a matter of minutes the surroundings changed from tree-lined residential streets to a rundown slum with people scavenging around in large roadside piles of rubbish. It looked an interesting if slightly rough barrio, and one which a British journalist was later to recount his experiences in with a mixture of fondness and fear. I didn't have time to go exploring it as I was too busy being sent to the wrong side of the stadium by a policeman.

Not wanting to repeat my exploits at Boca, and mindful this was my last opportunity to visit San Lorenzo, I'd purchased a ticket in advance at their plush downtown club shop. It was irritating to be stood in line behind a tourist speaking loud cockney, who was being instructed by the staff not to take public transport to Flores as it was too dangerous. Outside the shop I attempted to do a good deed and explain the cheapest way of getting there. His response to pointing out the nearest Subte station to Estadio Pedro Bidegaín was: 'Its alwight mate, arrrl take a bloody taxi, there awl so bloody cheap ahht ere.'

Thankfully it wasn't a Londoner on the gates but a kind porteño steward. The silver-haired official ushered me into the main stand irrespective that I had a ticket for the far cheaper opposite side. After I was securely through the turnstiles I expressed my appreciation and asked why I'd been given special treatment. He responded by saying it was safer for foreigners to sit in the more expensive seats. I thought it was commendable that San Lorenzo were aware there was a tourist presence at their games and did their best to try and protect them.

Even after my experiences at El Monumental a week before, the terraces were a sight to behold. Although not quite on the same scale, La Gloriosa Butteler barra section at one end was approximately 10,000 strong and moved inexhaustibly. The other end was populated by Boca Juniors' Jugador N° 12 barra with their iconic 'Nunca Hicimos Amistades' banner on display (we never make friends). Despite singing tirelessly their array of songs was abysmal. It was like being back in Peru. I was sat close to them so can testify that in the second period there was a 20 minute rendition of the 'dalé' song, followed by a ten minute version of 'corazón', proceeded by 'tenemos que ganar' for the remainder. This might seem a petty criticism, but one of the things that impressed me most in BA was each club had a range of original songs. I hadn't recognised one being repeated during my time in the capital, so was disappointed a flagship Argentine barra were singing generic and repetitive songs at a high profile away tie.

Both teams were pretty one-dimensional, overpassing to eventually craft a chance for a delivery from the flanks, only for the service to be poor or non-existent. It was endemic in the Argentine league to overplay the ball, much like Italy. Still, when all was said and done, people will remember that hour and a half for Torres' ten seconds of brilliance. You probably think I'm being overly negative when documenting my time watching Latin American football, though I can honestly say every match was a positive experience in its own way, and this was no exception.

With time to kill at the interval I decided to explore Estadio Pedro Bidegaín. Ambling across a car park I noticed workers entering and exiting a gate which allowed direct access to the pitch, manned by an elderly steward. Always on the hunt for interesting openings with my flag, I hobbled over and described my mission, asking politely whether I could have a quick photo by the playing surface. The tall gentleman was kind enough and called a policeman over, who was receptive to my story but suitably surly. I'd not explained myself properly because the officer grabbed my camera and tried to take a picture of me. Fortunately a group of catering staff were going through the gate at the time, so seized my opportunity to barge past. I pointed out to the officer where I was going to pose and assured both concerned parties it'd take a matter of seconds.

By this time the second half had just kicked off. I was stood three meters from the touchline with my St. George's cross in hand, right in front of hordes of La Gloriosa Butteler barra. The policeman took the snap before he identified what I was holding. Keen to get me out of sight in case anyone else saw what happened; he handed my camera back and angrily ushered me towards the gate. Passing and thanking the previously amicable steward, I was given a sharp retort along the lines of: 'I wouldn't have let you through if I'd have known you were going to do that!'

At that stage I'd been in BA for over three weeks and was starting to adapt to porteño lifestyle. In comparison to other Latin countries there was a greater European influence, evident in their café culture, the prominence of social smoking and obligatory use of 'ciao'. The city had a peculiar Italian flavour, reflected in the local population's classic

234

Roman profile. Most had angular faces and long, slightly hooked noses, in contrast to the rest of the continent's softer, Indian or African features. Many people had warned me about porteño snobbishness. I did detect a little condescension in my interactions, but generally found them warm and accommodating. On the surface it seemed like a civilised society that was welcoming, but not overtly friendly.

My diet was unhealthy but really tasty. For long periods on the trip I'd been consigned to a staple of rice, beans and meat. BA was all about steak, the cuts I sampled were some of the best I'd ever tasted and the value for money was second to none. But they didn't offer a lot of options as the meat was always accompanied by chips and there was a distinct lack of vegetables or anything healthy. Alcohol was readily available and I saw folks sipping cerveza and vino at all hours, but few were getting drunk. There was a very nocturnal social scene which I struggled to embrace. An ordinary night would begin with a meal around ten, followed by drinks in a bar approaching midnight. Usually porteños didn't even contemplate going to a nightclub until two in the morning, and it was common to return home at sunrise.

The city itself was enormous; an estimated 13 million lived in a metropolitan area stretching along the western bank of Río de la Plata. Part of the attraction of going to watch football in preceding countries was that it took me off the Gringo Trail to some of the less salubrious barrios. Generally stadiums were in poorer zones, but in BA the majority of the districts I visited were really respectable. I didn't even find the notoriously dodgy La Boca neighbourhood intimidating. In a way Buenos Aires was like Colombia - it was an effortlessly cool place and the residents were aware of it.

Game 56

Estudiantes v Godoy Cruz - (TNKC - CIM) - 0 v 1
Sunday 13th March 2011 – 17:00
Estadio Unico Cuidad de La Plata, La Plata

I'd become acclimatised to being a football tourist and relying on the
kindness of strangers to help me through the experience. It was
therefore surreal when I arrived at game 56 for people to start asking
me directions and how to buy tickets. A $2, hour-long bus ride south of
the city centre took me to watch reigning champions Estudiantes de la
Plata play Godoy Cruz. The anticipation had been building during the
journey, as the highway between BA and La Plata was adorned with
large signs promoting Estadio Unico Cuidad de La Plata. Construction
commenced in 1997 and following various stages of development it
was deemed to have been finished in 2011.

Opened in time for Estudiantes' first home Libertadores tie that
year, it had hosted a total of five fixtures prior to my visit. This might
explain why nobody had a bloody clue what was going on. For some
reason there were only two ticket windows, which created an
unnecessarily long wait to make the purchase, before joining an even
bigger queue at the turnstiles. I counted four separate occasions when
someone asked me how or where to buy tickets. Once I'd worked out
what was going on, it was nice to give something back to the
footballing community I'd been relying on for so long.

Rising out of a field like an oversized, space-aged oval tent,
Estadio Unico looked very modern. U2's 360 tour was one of the next
visitors. Inside I got the sense of it being a 360 degree venue - the view
was good from every position. In comparison to its peers in Buenos
Aires the 36,000 capacity was relatively humble, but unlike San
Lorenzo and Vélez, it was neat, compact and contemporary. As one of
the nominated hosts for 2011's Copa America there could be no
denying it was proper football ground. Yet with world-famous rock
bands like Aerosmith and Pearl Jam signed up to play there, it was
blatantly designed to be multifunctional. Unfortunately the interior
didn't receive much natural sunlight so the pitch was uneven and had a
noticeable amount of sand on it. Brazil's Copa America quarter-final
was held in La Plata and following a goalless 120 minutes against
Paraguay, the Samba Boys were eliminated after missing all four of
their penalties. They argued that the surface was attributable for the

failures as large chunks of turf gave way at critical times.

The chaos outside meant I just made kick-off, despite being in line for tickets over an hour beforehand. La Barra de los Pincharratas sang consistently throughout, compensating for the lack of noise from a small section of Godoy Cruz fans situated directly next to me. I'd not expected too many supporters to have made the 1,200 km trek east, but had hoped there'd be at least some La Banda del Expreso barra there. After half hour a faint sound of drums from behind the away seating got louder and louder. In a sudden blur of movement a handful of youths darted up and down the terrace, arranging flags and attaching banners, much like Arsenal's fanatics at game 50.

Once everything was in place a 200 strong barra entered the fray and tried in vain to out sing Estudiantes' faithful. I would never criticise anyone for turning up to a football match late, but as it was a 30 hour return journey, it did seem pointless to miss most of the first half. People said the timing of the barra brava's entrance could be significant. Sometimes it was a protest against a member of the association's hierarchy or a player they wanted to oust. Apparently in this case there had been transport problems.

For me this fixture was all about Juan man, Señor Verón. He was commonly referred to as La Brujita (little witch) as his father had played and was called witch. Like Chicharito he was known by the diminutive form. The former international and European club football star was a class above the rest of the players on show that afternoon. His every touch was purposeful and accurate, and in spite of his advancing years he glided around the pitch spraying the ball to all corners. Some of the cross field passes to feet were absolutely exquisite. It was a shame the rest of the team were mere mortals who appeared to be playing a different sport to him.

We didn't see the best of Juan Sebastián Verón in England, neither his spells at Chelsea or Manchester United were adjudged to have been successful. He thrived in Serie A but didn't ever really settle in the faster-paced Premier League. Sir Alex Ferguson was vexed by the bald maestro's limited impact at Old Trafford and once told a group of reporters questioning the Argentine's ability that he was a great player, and they didn't know what they were f**king talking about.

Godoy Cruz claimed the afternoon's only goal, theatrical blonde-haired midfielder Israel Damonte scored a glancing header with 25 minutes remaining. Verón ran out of steam in the closing stages and cut a frustrated figure trying to rally his colleagues. The other players were all too happy to fall into the characteristic trap of passing the ball wide and failing to deliver any quality when it counted. Godoy Cruz arrived with a plan and stuck to it, which saw them return home with three points.

The club from Mendoza province had been title contenders for long periods in la Apertura and were also in la Clausura running going into the third to last game of the season, away at Vélez Sársfield. Had Godoy won in Liniers they would have leapfrogged the hosts into pole position, but a 2 v 0 loss eliminated them from the race. Finishing third should be deemed as something of an achievement for an organisation with limited resources based outside Buenos Aires, the traditional nucleus of power.

Argentina's capital was undoubtedly the heart of la Primera División, with the majority of top flight competitors from BA province. Godoy Cruz from the central region was a rarity – a countryside team genuinely challenging for honours. Estudiantes, Newell's Old Boys and Rosario Central were the only ones to have ever taken honours away from the porteños, and that was a rare occurrence. The area around Godoy was most famous for its vineyards, from which over 70 per cent of Argentina's vino was produced, and their fans were aptly named the winemakers. There had been lots of provincial sides who'd unsuccessfully endeavoured to break the capital's stronghold. Due to the country's vast size, I was sceptical as to whether Argentine football would ever be decentralised. We Brits love an underdog, and one day I hope they'll be raising a glass of Malbec in Mendoza to celebrate winning the championship.

Game 57

Independiente v Newells - (TNKC - CIM) - 4 v 0
Monday 14th March 2011 – 20:15
Estadio Libertadores de América, Avellaneda

Next day the emphasis switched from title to relegation matters as Independiente were in real danger of dropping out of la Primera División. The self-proclaimed 'king of the cups' had concentrated their efforts on winning Copa Sudamericana in la Apertura and their league form had suffered as a result. A recent loss to fellow strugglers River Plate combined with a wobbling Libertadores campaign meant there was an air of anxiety about those feasting on Choripán waiting for kick-off.

I'd watched la Copa Sudamericana final in a Bolivian hotel room three months prior to visiting Avellaneda. Trailing by two goals from the first leg in central Brazil, Independiente scored early, only for Goiás to equalise. A combination of good luck and instinctive finishing brought the tie level. As the contest approached 180 minutes I noticed something strange. Throughout the match the television cameras had panned around Estadio Libertadores de América, focusing on nervous fans chewing their fingernails, anxiously hoping to end their 15 year international trophy drought. Just before the end of regulation time Fox Sports showed a group of Independiente followers crying. Then in extra time there were two shots of different groups of barra, also in tears. During a tense penalty shootout there was more coverage of spectators sobbing. When their outstanding defender Eduardo Tuzzio dispatched the winning spot kick, the scenes weren't of jubilant celebration, but of grown men reduced to balling their eyes out. I couldn't comprehend it. Do these fearsome porteño barra brava cry like little girls every time they win an important trophy?

My excursion to Avellaneda had disorientated me slightly. In Plaza Miserere next to my local train station, a 30 minute bus ride away, La Barra del Rojo were present. They were milling about drinking, singing and harassing pedestrians, without appearing too interested in getting to the game, which started in less than an hour. At each stop more people wearing red got on the bus which was odd as I'd hardly seen anyone going to matches on public transport in BA up to that point. The associations I'd visited all had a sense of their fans living close to the ground (even River Plate). This was the first time I'd seen supporters travel en mass to a home fixture.

The peculiarity wasn't over. I followed the red shirts off the bus and down a road, past a gigantic dark stadium. I was going to question why nobody had turned the floodlights on yet, when a second venue suddenly emerged from behind a row of houses, bathed in artificial light. In the gloom it was disorientating that two huge football clubs were situated within 200 meters of each other. Tickets in the main barra end had sold out, so I was grateful to observe proceedings from what I figured would be the calmer, south end of Estadio Libertadores. I took a position at the back of the stand, nursed my wounded feet and prepared for a nervous evening.

Three quarters of an hour later I couldn't help but wonder what all the fuss was about. Independiente had stormed into a 2 v 0 lead within ten minutes. Both goals, scored by Nicholas Cabrera, had an element of fortune to them. Firstly a speculative strike bounced kindly off the keeper, gifting the striker a tap into an empty net. Then his shot from the edge of the area diverted off a defender's trailing leg, wrong-footing Newells' number one. The visitors played their part in an engrossing half, attacking with flair and intelligence, but were denied a deserved goal by some last-ditch defending and wasteful shooting. In the 23rd minute the contest was essentially over, a good run and cut-back was converted with ease by Andrés Silvera, much to the Independiente faithful's relief. Having witnessed some pretty one-dimensional football over the weekend, it was refreshing to see two sides playing with such ingenuity, pace and directness.

At the interval I explored the venue that a few months earlier had hosted Copa Sudamericana's dramatic finale. It wasn't as spectacular in reality as the TV cameras were situated on a vacant side which was undergoing extensive construction. A sizeable main stand was flanked by two cylindrical masses of concrete rising from the ground. These iconic corners afforded grandstand views of the pitch to all manner of journalists, executives and dignitaries. What baffled me was there didn't seem to be any Newells La Hinchada Más Popular barra in attendance.

Shortly after the restart it began raining. It was light at first and then got heavier and heavier, until large sections of the crowd in front of me had to run for shelter. Water was coming down from the sky in plastic bottles. I discovered the Newells fans were above me in the south end's upper tier, caged in by two lines of tall mesh fencing. The sheets of wire were covered in barbs to prevent anyone from climbing them, and were spaced approximately a meter apart so it was impossible to drop anything into the home end.

La Hinchada Más Popular had devised a way of countering this by collecting two litre plastic bottles, cutting the tops off, filling them with a liquid (which I assumed to be water but had no desire to test my theory) and launching them into the air. They propelled their missiles high enough and with correct trajectory so the bottles just about cleared both fences and descended onto the supporters below.

Obviously a wet and bloodied La Barra del Rojo weren't going to take this attack inside their stadium lying down, and formed a committee away from the bombardment. Once their plan had been devised they braved the arsenal of bottles to adopt a position towards the bottom of the terrace. Employing the type of tactical brilliance not seen since the Somme, they launched a volley of fireworks into the upper tier in an attempt to force La Hinchada Más Popular away from the fences. Under the watchful eye of a long line of apathetic riot police a pitched battle ensued, the outcome of which was impossible to discern. After five minutes it got a little tedious so I turned my attentions back to the football. Independiente scored a fourth with ten minutes remaining, Colombian Jairo Castillo elegantly lobbing the keeper. The war between the tiers ran until the final whistle, by which time La Barra del Rojo had acquired some elastic. They were using it to catapult lit fireworks over the fences, getting the timing just right so they exploded as they fell, scattering the people stupid enough to have started the fight in the first place.

By the time I'd witnessed my twelfth match in Buenos Aires, I was of the firm opinion that the Italian influence extended from the city's culture and residents' genetic build to the football field. Games tended to be slow-paced and attacks was indirect and convoluted. They were generally low scoring, tight affairs with the emphasis on defending and not committing men forward. The player's theatrical reactions to challenges mirrored the histrionics which characterised Serie A. I was impressed with the standard of refereeing in the Argentine leagues. At every available opportunity the participants tried to deceive officials, throwing themselves to the floor clutching their faces at the slightest hint of contact. From what I saw the men in black applied common sense and made a valiant effort to keep the play flowing. I was beginning to agree with the locals that BA's football culture was superior to any other city in the world, but felt the amateur dramatics and negative tactics undermined the spectacle.

The main reason for the league's deterioration in quality was a constant exodus of local talent. A study by Euroamericas Sports Marketing estimated that in 2010 Argentina overtook Brazil as the most prolific exporter of footballers. Their clubs were not financially as strong as their northern neighbours, and relied on transfer fees to support the associations. It is thought that over 2,000 were exported in the year prior to my arrival in CF. As the talent pool drained their domestic competition was inevitably impacted.

Game 58

Bichos v Nacional - (Copa Libertadores) - 0 v 1
Tuesday 15th March 2011 – 21:10
Estadio Diego Armando Maradona, La Paternal

Bichos' fourth Copa Libertadores fixture was against Uruguay's most successful club, Nacional. They held the most domestic honours, three Libertadores titles and a record three Inter Continental Cups. This feat was only equalled by international heavyweights AC Milan, Real Madrid, Boca Juniors and the 'other' side from Montevideo, Peñarol. As there were merely two teams of any real note in a country with such a proud footballing heritage, the rivalry was epic and el clásico del fútbol Uruguayo was as fierce as any.

In 2011 both had been drawn in a Libertadores group with opposition from Buenos Aires. I'd observed Peñarol's chaotic visit to Capital Federal prior to Bichos' first home match in the tournament. Their fiercest rival was also well represented. Again the focus was on el Obelisco, as fans covered the surrounding area with an array of flags and banners. A couple of weeks earlier Bichos had come away from Uruguay with a victory. Reports coming back from those who'd crossed Río de la Plata were that whilst watching proceedings, hordes of Nacional barra had swept the streets of Montevideo, vandalising any vehicle with Argentinian registration plates. The rumour circulating La Paternal was that retribution was going to be merciless. Added to this tension was the fact that anything less than a win for Nacional would see them eliminated, whilst a draw might be enough for Bichos to qualify for the knockout round. It was therefore a rather dull 90 minutes of football, settled after half an hour by a smart finish from an acute angle.

Once again it was the fans which illuminated an otherwise forgettable evening. I'd already seen some spectacular performances from groups of supporters along the side at Estadio Maradona, but the visiting hinchas seemed the most passionate. Perhaps it was because this was their biggest away fixture of the season, heightened by skirmishes around the stadium prior to kick-off. Clearly the result assisted matters, and I know I have waxed lyrical on this subject throughout the book, but a mass of white shirted La Banda del Parque moved and sung as though their lives depended on it.

The wait to leave the ground at full time ran over an hour. On our way to Mr Dewsbury's temporary accommodation we saw why. At La Paternal train station one platform was full of Uruguayans sat on the floor with their arms tied in plastic binding. The next day newspaper reports claimed police had rounded up groups of barra who'd wanted to fight after the game, and shipped them straight back to Montevideo, leaving an assortment of abandoned vehicles with Uruguayan licence plates. At that point it didn't even cross my mind this was a coincidence. I had no doubt the police had been in collusion with Los Ninjas 82, so they could attend the match and still exact their revenge. From a distance it might sound like a farfetched conclusion, but in reality this was only the tip of the iceberg.

Worse was to come in both team's Libertadores campaign. Group 3 was decided in the final round, with Bichos at home to Fluminese and América hosting Nacional. All four still had a chance of reaching the next stage. The contest in DF finished goalless, in contrast to an electrifying evening at Estadio Maradona. Argentinos went behind on two occasions, but pulled it back before conceding a third with less than a quarter of an hour to go. If scores remained the same Nacional would have qualified with a single goal-difference advantage over Fluminese, although Bichos would progress if they found an equaliser. Fred's stoppage time penalty secured a last 16 place for the Brazilians on goals scored.

Game 59

Quilmes v Independiente - (TNKC - CIM) - 1 v 1
Saturday 19th March 2011 – 14:00
Estadio Centenario Dr José Luis Meiszner, Quilmes

My flight home was booked and only three weeks away, so I was determined to finish my stint in BA with a flourish. The intense summer heat had been fading over the past month, and with autumn slowly setting in, it signalled the beginning of earlier starts for weekend fixtures. I watched the first of these lunchtime kick-offs, taking an hour-long bus ride south to the home of Argentina's national cerveza, Quilmes. Hopelessly rooted to the bottom of the table and without a point to their name, there was no doubt the hosts would be playing in Nacional B come August. Independiente still had lingering relegation fears despite their emphatic victory over Newells five days earlier.

I hopped off the bus halfway through the journey. As we were passing Racing's stadium I thought it wise to purchase my ticket for the following day's game in advance. By the time I'd returned to the bus stop, traffic on the previously fluid-moving, five lane, one-way street had almost come to a halt. Taking up four lanes of the carriageway was a collection of dilapidated vehicles, emitting loud banging noises and large plumes of cannabis smoke, all crammed full of Independiente barra. The police were on hand lethargically observing the motoring chaos caused by the group waiting to depart for Quilmes. I made my way past lines of scooters and rusting school buses, gasping for air as the pungent aroma of weed smoke mixed with stifling exhaust fumes. Thankfully a regular bus attempting to negotiate the mayhem paused briefly to allow me aboard.

Once clear of the jam the ride was uneventful, until La Barra del Rojo delayed our progress for a second time. At a major intersection police motorbikes had blocked all but one road, causing a substantial amount of traffic to come to a halt. The family sitting in front of me got increasingly animated, anticipating that a presidential motorcade or other such VIP's would pass us. It turned out they were clearing the way for arguably the most important people in the country. A procession of red-shirted, singing, hand-flicking Independiente fans were being given an escort to their destination. Clearly the police didn't want the dignitaries to have to concern themselves with traffic lights or other motorists.

245

My arrival at the stadium coincided with that of Los Indios Kilmes barra, who were making a grand entrance. The drummers raised their instruments skywards between beats and were accompanied by an array of navy blue and white flags. Sources stated Estadio José Meiszner had a 30,200 capacity, which I was dubious about. It was a lovely little venue with double-tiered ends and a smart main stand, but certainly not the same size as St. Andrews. As Los Indios were taking their places I got my Zulu Army shot in early and found a secluded, shaded position on the periphery of the singing section. Although the shadows cast across the field indicated it was no longer summer, in the direct sunlight it definitely felt like it. Fair play to La Barra del Rojo who must have been sweltering in the full glare of the powerful rays, but continued to bounce and sing regardless.

Both sides displayed good enterprise in coming forward, which made for a compelling contest. Quilmes should have taken an early lead but were denied on two occasions by athletic, track-suited keeper Hilario Navarro. They were punished shortly afterwards as Facundo Parra applied the simple finish to a slick passing move. This didn't deter Quilmes' players or followers, who valiantly plugged away throughout. Their reward came in the second half when Juan Morales' neatly flicked header beat Navarro's outstretched arm.

As the afternoon wore on and the likelihood of obtaining their first point of the season increased; the fans started getting visibly nervous. This was particularly evident in a family stood next to me. The father spent much of the closing stages facing away from the pitch, while his six year old daughter, who'd been shouting 'puto' at appropriate moments, was screaming the insult any time an Independiente player touched the ball. Agonisingly in the dying embers they could have claimed the win, but a striker and midfielder lacked composure at the crucial moment.

This was my only visit to Quilmes and I have to admit to being quite fond of the little club. With its neat compact terraces and large inflatable beer cans dotted around (reminding you it would be really good to drink a cerveza whilst watching the game) it looked more like a second tier organisation than most of the others I visited in BA. A giant, German-founded brewery dominated both the town and its football association. Originally Quilmes Rovers and then Quilmes Athletic, reflecting its English roots, the supporters were fittingly nicknamed los cerveceros.

Game 60

Arsenal v River Plate - (TNKC - CIM) - 1 v 1
Saturday 19th March 2011 – 19:10
Estadio Julio Humboto Grondona, Sarandí

At the end of Quilmes v Independiente I took a brief train ride through the leafy outer suburbs, back towards the centre. I arrived in Sarandí with ample time to enjoy a beer and Choripán, whilst watching Godoy Cruz beat Lanús and a couple of drunken River barra trying to fight a middle-aged woman. The away fan's presence was really evident before this fixture. There were hordes of red and white shirted lads swigging cerveza from clear plastic bottles, urinating and abusing passing motorists. Inside the stadium they were even more ubiquitous, filling one end, a whole side and a third of the main stand. This was the only occasion on the trip the visitors outnumbered the locals. Arsenal's terraces weren't close to being full, whilst Los Borrachos del Tablón had sold the entirety of their allocation. In spite of their meagre following the hosts were sitting pretty in the Promedios table, so all the talk prior to kick-off was of River Plate flirting dangerously with the unthinkable 'r' word.

On a balmy evening against the backdrop of a gorgeous, milky-white full moon rising over the away end, we were treated to two early goals. River took the lead via a powerful header from a corner, only for Arsenal to respond within minutes. A lull in proceedings gave me time to wander around the home end and observe their La Mafia barra in action. A small group surrounding a moderate band were trying to generate an atmosphere, but must have been disheartened they were being out-sung on their own turf. The crowd was an unusual mix of old men and breastfeeding women, next to the bare-chested, joint-smoking male youths. Quilmes had felt like a real local's club, but this was a different level. It was as if the residents of Sarandí had left their houses and travelled no more than a block or two to support their team. Walking out after the game (having waited for River's contingent to depart) I found this was probably an accurate perception. Once I'd reached the highway merely four blocks from the ground, there was no football traffic at all. The most incomprehensible aspect of it all was that while massive organisations like River and Independiente were scrapping for their lives, this miniscule neighbourhood side was in no real danger of being relegated for at least two years.

247

Formed in 1957 and named after 2010's League Cup runners-up; Arsenal de Sarandí played in sky blue and red, the colours having been copied from the two biggest local clubs, Racing and Independiente. Their humble 16,000 capacity stadium nicknamed El Viaducto (The Viaduct, due to its proximity to one) was a far cry from the Emirates, or even Highbury. At this juncture I'd liked to have made a disparaging comment about the quality of football also being unlike Arsene Wenger's brand of flowing passing, but it's not fitting when such a small association had achieved so much. Remarkably they won la Copa Sudamericana less than four years prior to my visit, claiming superb away victories along the way at Goiás, Chivas, and in the first leg of the final, against América in DF. The second leg, held at Racing's Estadio Juan Perón for logistical reasons, began disastrously as the Mexicans scored twice. Arsenal lifted the trophy after netting late on, which saw them triumph on away goals.

The evening's entertainment didn't really pick up again until second half injury time when the hosts forced an acrobatic save from River's number one. Los Millonarios counterattacked and in a moment of controversy nearly snatched all three points. Arsenal had committed players forward, so the defence were grateful to pick up a loose pass and blast the ball over the stands, allowing them time to regroup. Unaware of this blatant piece of gamesmanship, a young ball boy threw a spare football straight to a River Plate midfielder. He took a quick throw, which presented star youngster Erik Lamela with a clear shot on target. A fingertip save prompted an almighty scramble in Arsenal's area. After another fine stop from the keeper and a saving tackle on the line from a defender, the ball returned to Lamela, who spooned it wide of the target. The pause in proceedings gave the home players and fans time to berate the ball boy, whilst the fourth official physically restrained Arsenal's seething manager from smacking the poor kid.

This draw in Sarandí inspired River's best run of the tournament, which saw them collect 13 points from their next six ties. Although the Argentine relegation system was designed to protect clubs like River Plate from the dreaded drop, unfortunately those around them in the Promedios table were also doing well. Consequently, a loss at home to All Boys and a defeat in el Superclásico left them needing a positive result in their final fixture to avoid a relegation playoff.

Game 61

Racing Club v Estudiantes - (TNKC - CIM) - 0 v 1
Sunday 20ᵗʰ March 2011 – 18:10
Estadio Presidente Juan Domingo Perón, Avellaneda

Super Sunday started at Racing's impressive goldfish bowl of a stadium. I spent much of the build-up to the game asking various club 'officials' whether I could be given special dispensation to leave when the full time whistle blew. My reasoning was that I had 20 minutes between the end of the match in Avellaneda and kick-off at La Bombonera, five kilometres away. If I was to wait with the rest of the home supporters for Estudiantes' contingent to make their way out before departing, then I'd arrive at Boca during the second half. The best any security guard offered me was to leave with 15 minutes to go and hope the police hadn't closed the exits. They were more concerned about selling tickets through the fences at a knocked-down price than my predicament.

The weekend fixture with top billing pitted league leaders, Racing, against current titleholders, Estudiantes. From my vantage point in the posh seats I had a perfect outlook over a spectacular oval, which if the moat and running track was covered in grass, could quite easily be used as a cricket pitch. Coventry City-esque sky blue and white seating covered the upper tier, while down below in the terracing La Guardia Imperial barra were afforded a fairly dismal view of the playing surface. From the back of the upper tier it was possible to see vast expanses of Avellaneda's urban landscape, a spectacular scene, especially as the fiery orange sun was setting. My elevated position gave a good perspective as to how close Racing and Independiente's homes were to each other. Separated by a training and swimming pool complex, the proximity of these two rivals made Anfield and Goodison look like they were on opposite sides of England.

On the field of play an all too familiar pattern of overpassing was adopted, with Racing being most culpable. Verón was orchestrating proceedings, trying to raise a team that on neither of the consecutive Sunday's I saw them looked anything like champions. Unsurprisingly it was 0 v 0 at the break. In the second half the football once again wasn't worthy of writing about, leaving it to the barra to keep me amused.

Both the compact section of fans from La Plata and the home

faithful had been going through the motions during the first period. Sensing that entertainment on the pitch was in short supply, La Guardia Imperial moved up a couple of gears, whipping themselves into a frenzied blur of movement. This had an astonishing effect on the rest of the stadium. Large portions of the crowd joined in with a song which encouraged the participant to leap into the air, whilst waving their shirt above their head. As the song gained momentum so did the surroundings. Initially it felt like a minor tremor, which developed into a situation where it was possible to see the concrete physically moving. The only way to counter the weird sensation? Bounce in time with the rest of them.

Not content with getting their ground to vibrate, some of the bare-chested masses below me had abandoned the jumping and formed a type of mosh pit that belonged at a heavy metal concert. Clearing a circle at the bottom of the stand, they took it in turns to run into the middle of the space and bounce off each other, with their fists and elbows flying. As more and more lunatics joined in it was difficult to discern the individuals, it just looked like a mass of writhing bodies. It was probably the first time I'd properly considered the homoerotic aspect of the barra: semi-naked men bumping against and jumping on one another.

I wasn't the only person leaving early, a sizeable quantity of supporters (chiefly the elderly and those with young families) were also trotting towards the exits before the police closed the gates. It was a shame as although I was able to catch a bus with relative ease and arrived at La Bombonera in time for kick-off; I missed the contest's most notable moment. In the final ten minutes Uruguayan Hernán López picked up a loose ball on the edge of Racing's penalty box, took a touch and chipped a delightful shot from 20 yards over a stranded keeper. Despite their early promise neither side were in contention for the championship at the end of la Clausura.

Game 62

Boca Juniors v Olimpo - (TNKC - CIM) - 0 v 2
Sunday 20th March 2011 – 20:20
Estadio Alberto Jacinto Armando, La Boca

So this was it. The climax of my footballing odyssey, and for most visitors to this part of the world, the essential South American sporting experience. I knew that I wouldn't be the only Gringo in attendance, but was confident I'd be the only tourist who'd bought a face value ticket.

This game required a significant amount of preparation. After having been denied entry three weeks earlier I was determined to purchase an entrada prior to match day. I conducted extensive internet research and couldn't find anything other than commercial packages, which involved being collected from a hotel more than two hours before kick-off. I asked people at other clubs, my friends from Bichos and the Boca fans that ran the local bar/restaurant – their answer was the same: I could only get a ticket if I was a Socio. The Tango Hostel owner was a Boca supporter and party to group emails sent to proprietors promoting tourist excursions. He was willing to forego his commission and get me the cheapest package available for $100. I couldn't believe it. I knew for a fact tickets cost $10, and la Bombonera wouldn't be full for a fixture against a lesser side like Olimpo. On the Friday leading up to the event I made my way to La Boca with the stubborn desire to purchase a ticket at cost price. It took me almost three hours, but I paid 40 pesos in return for a small piece of paper that permitted me to enter the general terraces.

I began in the press office, explaining and pleading my case. In the end they got sick of my boring story so made two phone calls and directed me to an administrative office. There I had to stand for an hour in a line to be allowed inside the stadium. As I waited outside the offices next to a club shop/museum, three tourist buses arrived and departed in the space of an hour. These were the type of transport you see happy snapping Japanese sightseers riding in central London; open-topped double-decker affairs with headphones providing a guide to the city in numerous languages. For $25 a day you could hop on and off the vehicle when you liked, and upon arrival at Estadio Alberto Jacinto Armando, most passengers were hopping off.

Once inside the ground I had to queue for a second time in a

251

high ceiling waiting room. This doubled as some kind of art gallery; the walls were covered with strange oil paintings celebrating the association's origins. There was also a plethora of commemorative plaques from other league clubs, congratulating the organisation on winning a trophy or reaching an anniversary. The room served as a thoroughfare for staff and other officials, of which there were a ridiculous number milling around on a Friday afternoon. Spying an opportunity to pass security, I left the line, mingled with a group of employees and wandered into the servicing area underneath the stands. It baffled me that two days prior to a game there would be so many people working in the venue. What were they all doing? I passed dozens of little offices housing all kinds of administrators and climbed a set of stairs into the arena.

The chocolate box was unlike any stadium I'd ever seen. Both ends were large and basic, while the upper two tiers of the all seated main stand had a miniature table for each spectator, as if designed to accommodate journalists. The thin, detached side, whose size was restricted by the residential dwellings behind it, was just odd. Fittingly I had to hurriedly return to the waiting room as a group of tourists led by a guide were heading in my direction. I didn't want to be mistaken for one of them and miss my chance to make my purchase.

Half an hour later I was granted a brief glimpse of the ticket office, before being told to re-join the queue and I'd be summoned when they were ready for me. The minute I spent inside that room revealed a great deal about the supply of Boca Juniors tickets. It looked like a normal Latin American ticket office; I'd been to enough to say that with some conviction. Amongst the staff reviewing lists, sorting money and printing Subte-style stubs, were a couple of obese, sweaty men talking purposefully into mobile phones. They looked kind of like Latino versions of Del Boy. I'd be lying if I said they were handling wads of cash and were being passed suspicious-looking envelopes, I didn't view proceedings for long enough. However, I'd spent sufficient time watching these types of people over the past 17 months to recognise senior members of the barra brava hierarchy when I saw them. I'm not an investigative journalist and I have never hacked anybody's mobile telephone, but... how did these tourist 'companies' get their hands on tickets when it was virtually impossible for anyone else to buy one? Not that I cared when I exchanged 40 Pesos for a white envelope and left grinning smugly.

The same smirk was wiped off my face two days later when a steward (I'm sure it was the same one I argued with on my first visit)

252

informed me the entrance I required was on the other side of La Bombonera. Even though I jogged all the way it still took 15 minutes to negotiate the various cordons and diversions. By the time I'd arrived at the second line of police searches I was pouring with sweat, out of breath and not in the mood for an interrogation. In all honesty the rigmarole that ensued was partly attributable to my own lack of preparation.

Entering football grounds had naturally become a bit of a routine, especially when I was carrying a rucksack. Mistakenly my St. George's cross, fresh from a photo at Racing, was screwed up in the top of my bag. A surly sergeant inspecting my belongings passed it to a colleague, instructing him to throw it in the bin. He was taken aback when I told him in near fluent Spanish that the flag had been to more football matches than he could imagine, and the last place it was going was with the rubbish. He then tried to convince me they would take care of it while I was watching the game. I responded that if the flag wasn't entering then neither was I, and snatched it off the perplexed policeman, who stared at me irritably.

Next he found my packed lunch which he shook his head at, slowly scrutinising each item. Frustrated I was missing an event that I'd invested so much time and effort in getting to, I asked what was wrong with my picnic. His simple reply was to pick out an apple and bounce it off my forehead onto the floor. He officiously told me weapons were not allowed inside. I disposed of the food, and grateful I hadn't bought the Coventry boys Racings shirts, argued for a while that my flag couldn't incite a riot. I realised that no matter how much I enjoyed winding up officials, I wasn't entering the venue with my piece of cloth, so left it with a kind lady in a nearby shop. I was fully searched again, lectured on the folly of tourists entering such a dangerous environment, before climbing urine-soaked stairs and out into the arena.

So finally, this was it, an opportunity to see what the fuss was all about. Racing v Estudiantes was the most important fixture of the day, but the big story was all about Román. Señor Riquelme, a regular in the Argentine Selección for over a decade and the architect of Villareal's admirable rise to the upper reaches of La Liga. Originally on loan from the Yellow Submarine, Boca had taken a gamble on buying the number ten outright, despite his advancing years and proneness to injury. Experienced Julio Falconi had been installed as Boca's new manager in preseason; he wasn't an advocate of the trequartista role for which Riquelme was famous. Since my arrival in BA the daily football newspaper, Olé, had published regular articles on the playmaker's absence from Boca's starting line-up. Fallouts between player and coach were meticulously documented, clearly looking to interest the majority of their readership, who statistically were Boca fans. Having been on the side-lines for the entirety of my stay in capital federal, in my final game I was to see his glorious return. The mood around the stadium, and indeed much of the country, was that with their hero back in action Boca were going to rediscover their glorious form of yesteryear.

The only problem was Olimpo hadn't read the script. Defending valiantly throughout, the club from Bahia Blanca, in the far south of Buenos Aires province, proved they weren't overawed by the occasion. What impressed me about the visitors was their pace on the break. Following a poor Apertura campaign the newly promoted side had opened their second season with a flourish. Sitting towards the top of the table they were giving themselves a genuine chance of survival. Although Boca dominated possession and had the lion's share of openings, it wasn't an enormous shock when Olimpo seized the initiative prior to the interval. Martín Rolle was another classic Argentine trequartista in that he looked like a little boy; the kit he was wearing drowned him. But credit to the kid, he had a perfectly legitimate goal ruled out for offside before somehow out-muscling two defenders and neatly slotting past an advancing keeper.

At the break everybody sat down. Well, approximately half the spectators were already seated, but those of us in the general sections including La Jugador N° 12 barra found somewhere to sit and rest for 15 minutes. The atmosphere had been good in the first period as the Socios end sang consistently and other supporters joined in every now and again. My area was an odd mix of foreigners and locals unfamiliar to each other. At other football clubs I'd visited there was a kind of camaraderie among the onlookers, a sense that everyone knew, or knew of everyone else. In most cases it was because they'd stood in the same spot watching their team for a substantial amount of time. The people in my terrace all looked like strangers. A small clique at the front intermittently got a song underway, which others unenthusiastically joined in with until it petered out. Commendably the atmosphere was noticeably lifted after Olimpo scored. Nevertheless the only real singing came from the 8,000 fans in the middle tier at the other end.

This was supposed to be an organisation representing the masses; the working-class populous in contrast to River Plate's bourgeois riches. Yet half La Bombonera was corporate-style seating. All the general zones were full to the rafters, but there were a conspicuous quantity of empty seats in the large side. Of the two cheap sectors, mine appeared to be populated by lots of day-trippers. The atmosphere was decent, but not in the same league as at the country's other big venues. Two hours beforehand Racing's Estadio Juan Perón was shaking so much I was almost getting motion sickness. Everything about travelling is subjective, and I found that the overall experience at one of the world's most iconic stadiums didn't compare favourably to its rivals, although I must admit the hype and ticketing situation meant that I'd arrived with some animosity towards the club.

During the interval I got chatting to the two individuals stood directly in front of me. Appropriately they were both ladies from Wisconsin in their early thirties. They'd paid over $50 for their tickets from a scalper, which they thought was quite cheap in comparison to the hundreds of bucks they usually spent going to major US sporting events. Wearing Boca kits and speaking really good Spanish, I was eager to learn why they chose this specific match. The attractive duo told me that they'd no real interest in soccer, but their guidebooks had recommended going to a fixture in BA and internet reviews indicated Boca was best. This conversation reminded me that Miss Newtown (who also wasn't a football aficionado) had been to a game at La Bombonera in the first week of her trip. She'd gone on a tour with a group from her hostel because everybody had told her it was brilliant. As an introduction to Latin American football I acknowledge that it was, but there were better, cheaper, more welcoming and enjoyable experiences to be had in Buenos Aires. I think Boca Juniors had marketed their product better than anyone else.

The second half was similar to the first, Boca pressed increasingly desperately and Olimpo countered with intent. Riquelme was the creative hub, but much like Verón at Estudiantes, his teammates weren't on the same level as him. The difference between the two masterful midfielders was that Verón patiently went about his business, whilst Riquelme pointed, pouted and remonstrated with those around him. On two occasions he had mini temper tantrums; the first he took out on a perimeter advertisement hoarding, and the second he beat the ground repeatedly with his fists. Much of his annoyance was aimed at Martín Palermo, a former Argentine Selección teammate, and a Boca legend. Well past his best and in painfully poor goal scoring form for a striker, his touches were laboured and shooting inaccurate. Despite not being the biggest Boca admirer even I was slightly sad to see the two formerly world-class players struggling with their own fading ability, labouring under the weight of half a nation on their shoulders.

On the 90 minute mark, as jeers and whistles rang around the stadium, Olimpo gained possession in their own half and ran in the direction of the corner flag. Miraculously their midfielder didn't hold the ball on the by-line to see out time, but sent a deep cross towards the onrushing Julio Furch. The reward for their enterprise was a second goal scored by the freshly introduced substitute. As the players left the pitch fans in the posh side seating by the exit made their feelings perfectly clear. They pelted their heroes with plastic bottles, sprayed them with water and subjected them to passionate abuse. Photos in Olé showed one red-faced man in tears as he pulled at his replica shirt, straining to express his dissatisfaction to Martín and Román two meters away, separated by a Perspex fence.

It turned out the day's big story was about Ramón and not Román. A 36 year old Post Office worker called Ramón Aramayo had died on his way to Vélez Sársfield v San Lorenzo. Initial reports cited the cause of death as either: a heart attack, being beaten by the police or by Vélez's La Pandilla barra. This fixture had been played behind closed doors for the previous year due to intense violence after 2010's corresponding match in Flores. Also, in 2008, a Vélez fan was shot dead on the way to a game at San Lorenzo, although reports stated the fatality was unrelated to football. The public were only allowed to attend on this particular Sunday after the Presidents of both clubs appealed to the AFA. International coverage of the event was limited, while the national media bleated about the dark days of football returning, but didn't elaborate on events leading up to the tragedy. On the other hand Olé provided a detailed insight into the incident.

Policing in Argentina's Primera División was possibly some of the tightest in the world, including alcohol restrictions, numerous body searches and the efficient way visiting contingents were escorted into and out of the stadiums. At 15:20 on Sunday 20th March 2011, 40 minutes prior to a derby with a history of fatalities kicked-off, one of the main streets accessing the away supporter's turnstiles – Fragueiro – didn't have a police presence. Apparently Vélez's barra had colluded with officers to create a 'free zone' between the local and visitor entrances. The idea was that the home fanatics could exact revenge on their enemy by ambushing La Gloriosa Butteler's coaches as they arrived in Liniers.

Interestingly Ramón Aramayo died three blocks from the planned ambush under a pile of orange vested police officers. The likely cause of death was a heart attack induced by the forceful way in which he was detained. Crucially the police left him handcuffed, face down on the pavement for some time without medical attention. Olé printed pictures of the detention. Background scenes were of people calmly observing without any indication of it being a violent or threatening situation.

I followed the story for the rest of the week until it petered out when another big scandal came along. Eventually the consensus was that San Lorenzo Socio #30525 had died because the police had handled the matter negligently. What astounded me was how the newspaper was on hand to take shots of officers on top of the dying man. There were no images in any newspapers of Fragueiro street where the free zone was located, either before, during or after the ambush.

Unsurprisingly San Lorenzo's fans weren't in the best of moods as kick-off approached. In a bid to try and ease tensions, the two teams entered the cauldron of noise carrying the other club's flag. However it was immediately obvious that it was never going to last 90 minutes. The sides opted to shoot towards the end where their respective support was situated. Vélez's keeper took his position only to be pelted by a volley of missiles from the visitors. Play started and stopped within seconds as it was impossible for the home number one to stand in his own penalty area. The match was suspended after seven minutes as La Gloriosa Butteler had torn holes in the wire fences separating them from the field. Police had to use a powerful water cannon mounted on an armoured vehicle to stop them getting onto the turf, as players ran to the safety of the dressing room.

In a way I could kind of empathise with the La Gloriosa Butteler. They'd been subjected to an ambush upon arrival, and having survived it were told the police had killed one of their Socios. I'm not condoning the behaviour of the bloodied and bandaged legions with t-shirts covering their faces, but in my view the authorities had to take the majority of the blame. Two photos printed in the national press of enraged barra inside the away end at El Fortín made me angry. The first was brandishing a metal frying pan at a line of riot police and the second was attempting to throw a large black television over a barbed wire fence. How the hell were they allowed into the ground with those items when my piece of red and white cloth was deemed capable of inciting unrest at Boca?

URUGUAY

Population – 3.5 million
Size – 176,000 km²
Time Zone – GMT ⁻3
Currency – Peso
FIFA World Ranking – #7 (March 2011)
Best World Cup Finish – Winners (1930, 1950)
Biggest Teams – Peñarol, Nacional

You might have heard of:
Álvaro Recoba, Gus Poyet, Diego Forlán, Edinson Cavani, Luis Suárez

Essential Spanish:
Hincha - A 'normal' fan, which was coined by a loyal Nacional
(Uruguay) supporter in the 1920's
Aurinegros - Gold and blacks
Mundial – Worldwide/World Cup

One of my biggest regrets on the trip was not seeing football in Uruguay. I was keen to see how such a small country could produce two internationally decorated teams in Peñarol and Nacional. Unfortunately Uruguay's FA suspended the weekend's fixture list just days before I'd organised to take a catamaran over Río de la Plata. When visiting Uruguay five weeks earlier with Miss Newtown I missed the opportunity to watch a game due to a delayed bus connection. We passed a few pleasant days in Montevideo, which they said was the most 'liveable' city in Latin America. Clearly 'they' hadn't had the pleasure of living in Managua! Surrounded by nice riverside beaches, it seemed like a glamorous place to reside, even though the communist-style tower block accommodations didn't have balconies or even a good view of the beautiful waterfront.

I'd spent 17 months discussing with locals who was the best Selección in the Americas. The general consensus was either Brazil or Argentina. Nevertheless at South Africa 2010 it was Uruguay that made it further than anyone else, losing to the odd goal in five against a classy Dutch side. Their forward line of Forlán, Cavani and Suárez was undoubtedly one of the tournament's most prolific, and it was no real shock when they reached the Copa America final a year later. Argentina and Brazil both bowed out in the quarters on penalties, allowing Uruguay to ease past Paraguay in the competition's showpiece occasion at El Monumental, scoring three goals without reply.

There was an English influence over their football and other aspects of the country. Similar to Argentina it was British school teachers who formed their first clubs. Uruguay's success on the international stage could be partly attributed their manager 'El Maestro' Oscar Tabárez. He took a nation of less than four million people into the top five of FIFA's global rankings, above their more glamorous continental rivals. His intelligent formation and blend of youth and experience was the reason for a dramatic improvement after they'd failed to qualify for three of the four previous World Cups. There was no doubt that Uruguay had history on its side. They hosted and won the first ever Mundial in 1930 and were crowned champions again 20 years later in Brazil. Much like my fleeting stint in Chile, I was disappointed not to have devoted more time exploring this fascinating place, investigating how a country with the same size population as Wales could be so accomplished at the world game.

Game 63

Bichos v Quilmes - (TNKC - CIM) - 0 v 0
Friday 25th March 2011 – 19:10
Estadio Diego Armando Maradona, La Paternal

My irritation at missing out on Uruguayan football was tempered by the fact that it gave me a chance to watch Bichos play one last time. My departure for Estadio Maradona had been postponed after a farewell litre of beer with the guys who ran the corner steak joint (which I'd frequented daily) turned into three. I was excited about the fixture as I stood on a bus, elegantly drinking red wine from a plastic bag-covered bottle. Star midfielder Jan Mercier had returned from injury and Ciro Rius was breaking into the starting 11 with great impact. Bichos could claim top spot for a couple of hours before Vélez's inevitable victory later that night. All they needed to do was beat helpless Quilmes at home. The most notable thing about the evening's events was Los Indios Kilmes turning up in their numbers, filling the side stand and out-singing Bichos' faithful. The only match I'd seen when Argentinos were louder than the visitors was the América Libertadores tie - there were 76 away fans in attendance. So maybe it wasn't that notable after all.

I didn't really care to be honest, it's a great football club and I was happy to have a real second team. I loved the fact that an organisation which played in an English fourth division-style ground, who had to sell its best players and whose followers were regularly out-sung on their own turf, could compete (and succeed) against some of international football's most famous names. For anybody planning to visit Buenos Aires I urge you to go and watch an association that really needs your support. The view from the general section was pretty awful, tickets were $2.50 more than most other stadiums in the top flight, and when I was there the quality of football was fairly poor. I want to avoid sentiment, but the best way to describe it is a friendly little club with a big heart.

Although the Quilmes game didn't warrant any coverage, the rest of 2011's Clausura was fascinating. The title was decided between Lanús and league leaders Vélez Sársfield on the penultimate fecha. Vélez's fixture at doomed Huracán was staged four hours before Lanús' match, and was played behind closed doors following disturbances at Estadio Tomás Adolfo Duco a few weeks earlier. Vélez left it late to confirm their win, scoring a second goal in injury time. The attention turned to Lanús, who on the back of four consecutive victories hosted Bichos. In front of a packed house it was the visitors who scored the evening's solitary goal as Nicolás Blandi slid in Emilio Hernandez's calm cut back.

Vélez were awarded the trophy with a week to spare, which meant that for the final round everyone focused on the relegation situation. It was the teams in fifth and eighth place who were battling to avoid a tricky playoff against Cordoba's Belgrano. Olimpo played out of their skins to be able to go head to head with River Plate on the season's closing Saturday. They took an unassailable early lead away at Quilmes, Martín Rolle capping a productive tournament with an eighth minute goal. This meant that nothing other than a win would be enough for River Plate, in their home tie against a Lanús side smarting from losing the championship last time out. The visitors scored on the half hour mark, only for Erik Lamela to scrap an equaliser just after the restart. River pushed forward but were caught on the break as Leandro Diaz cut inside to score a sensational winner.

Four days later Argentina's most successful football club were in Cordoba for the first leg of their humiliating relegation playoff. Adalberto Román's silly hand ball in the area saw Belgrano go ahead from the spot. When they doubled their advantage from a corner, Los Borrachos del Tablon stamped their authority on proceedings. The barra broke through a mesh fence and entered the field of play to remonstrate with members of their own team about the performance. Taking an advertising hording with them, they managed to disrupt River's best attack of the second half, bringing the contest to a halt for 20 minutes whilst police restored order. Having watched the footage on YouTube I'd again like to vent my exasperation: the visiting barra had a metal table in their possession and were using it to smash the barriers between themselves and their failing idols. Precisely how does one sneak a piece of furniture into a high profile football match?

The return leg at El Monumental on a chilly, wintery Sunday afternoon was always going to be a passionate affair. Los Millonarios gave themselves hope of avoiding the drop when Hugo Pavone scored early. Belgrano hit back after an hour, Guillermo Farre capitalising on some schoolboy defending. The decisive moment came in the 75th minute when River were awarded a penalty. Pavone squandered the chance to be a hero by blasting the kick straight into goalkeeper Juan Olave's arms. This was the last incident of note from a tie which was ended prematurely due to the volume of missiles being thrown onto the turf. Riot police resorted to firing water cannons into the upper tiers, to prevent Los Borrachos del Tablón tearing their own stadium apart.

Whilst River's players cried in the middle of the pitch encircled by stewards for their own safety, the angry barra were forced out of the ground. They went on a destructive rampage around Buenos Aires, clashing violently with the authorities. Many supporters remained inside El Monumental for hours after the final whistle as the streets surrounding the venue turned into a warzone. The AFA's reaction was to propose a complicated new league structure which would make it even more unlikely for a big organisation to be relegated. This ridiculous idea was scrapped shortly after it was conceived. Consequently River looked forward to a year of travelling to places like Jujuy and Tucumán.

Game 64

Colón v Boca Juniors - (TNKC - CIM) - 0 v 1
Sunday 27th March 2011 – 18:15
Estadio Brigadier General Estanislao López, Santa Fe

I left BA the next morning and stayed in the city of Santa Fe for a few days prior to crossing the border. Obviously my destination was selected based on the availability of football. I couldn't envisage a better way to conclude my time in Argentina than watching Boca lose again, in front of a partisan provincial crowd.   Similar to the San Lorenzo game when I'd seen them for the first time, there was one moment of brilliance which punctuated an otherwise dour contest. Fittingly it was engineered by Juan Román Riquelme, whose thunderous free kick from an acute angle caught everybody by surprise, not least Colón's keeper.

Santa Fe's central plaza had a sleepy Sunday feel to it on match day; although there was a palpable sense of anticipation the closer I got to the venue. I was grateful that I bought my ticket in advance as two hours before kick-off the fixture was declared a sell-out. I'd expected there to be an electric atmosphere inside Estadio Estanislao López and wasn't disappointed. There wasn't a vacant seat or space in the house and the noise generated was incredibly loud for the duration. I took this last opportunity to mingle with the barra brava, in the home end's populous lower tier. It was an archetypally chaotic mix of semi-naked torsos tirelessly bouncing in time to the tribal drum beats, whilst flicking one arm into the air and singing. The terrace was so jam-packed I didn't try to gain any kind of vantage point. My attempts to view events at pitch-level were thwarted by an array of banners tied to tall metal fences, and five rows of people in front of me also trying to sneak a glimpse of the action. After a while I got frustrated and looked for something interesting to do.

Wandering around the area in front of the stands I realised that I wasn't the only one ignoring the football. There were pockets of lads hanging about, chatting, smoking joints and exchanging banter, with seemingly no interest in proceedings on the field. By the time I'd walked past the menacing Los de Siempre barra section for a second time, I was beginning to attract some inquisitive looks. At one stage I turned to the crowd when I recognised a song and saw a huddle of teenagers under a large flag snorting powder off their hands. Even though I glanced in their direction for a second, one of the group caught my eye and made a threatening gesture towards me. Unable to see the event I'd paid for and feeling a little uncomfortable, I left the stadium ten minutes prior to the interval. In comparison to the mayhem inside, the silence outside was deafening as I made my way along the eerily deserted streets. I ended up strolling four kilometres back to my hotel reflecting on another footballing experience.

I still couldn't comprehend who the barra brava were. They told me their football team was the most important thing in their lives and match day was the highlight of their week. Yet many of them didn't actually watch the games, they were too busy engaging in other, often illegal activities. I'd spent 17 months amongst them, from my first encounters in Estadio Azteca to the virulent multitudes in Santa Fe. Although the ferocity had varied from country to country the behaviour patterns were virtually identical wherever I had been. Aside from the two incidents in Colombia I'd managed to avoid any clashes with this universally feared mob. Personally I've never found hooliganism to be appealing, but have to confess that without the barra I'd have written an even more boring account of football in the Americas. They were ever-present and illuminated each contest I witnessed. I'd been to some intimidating places, but couldn't accept that throughout Latin America, in every nation I visited, they were the all-controlling, malicious presence they appeared to be in Argentina.

The barra brava were most prominent in Buenos Aires, after all this was the place they originated from. Their Italian influence certainly lent a feeling of Mafia to the groups and the way they bribed, threatened and colluded with the authorities. The organised criminal element sounded like a farfetched footballing version of The Godfather, but even a cursory glance at the recent history of Italy's Serie A showed corruption was commonplace in one of Europe's top leagues.

My problem drawing conclusions: I wasn't an undercover journalist and I didn't have the ability or desire to infiltrate these gangs. I was a backpacker who was passionate about football and enjoyed attending matches. But in the brief time I spent in BA there were sufficient suspicious incidents to make me believe their barra were a secret society operating outside the scope of the law. Ramón Aramayo's death, Nacional fans being deported, Boca's ticketing arrangements and the general lethargy the police showed towards confronting anyone all contributed to convincing me there was something to these conspiracy theories. In addition I'd like to point out that I've chosen not to report on such subjects as the drug Paco, the barra intimidating players at training sessions or the clubs allowing weapons and other items to be planted in the stands prior to kick-off. But then again how could these porteño barra be serious hooligans when they kissed each other on the cheek every time they met?

2010's World Cup convinced me that there was substance to the horror stories. Since 1986, after Maradona financed a group of barra's trip to Mexico, there was a strong fanatical Argentine following at the tournaments. The exception was in 2002 when there was an economic crisis. South Africa's authorities had employed intelligence officers specifically to prevent violent supporters like the barra brava from entering their nation. To circumnavigate this issue the barra formed a Nongovernment Organisation whose official mandate was to help impoverished children and build schools. They used the NGO as a disguise to assist known criminals entering South Africa. A handful of thugs were deported and others were refused entry at border control, but it was estimated that up to 500 made it to their destination.

Hooligans going to an international football competition isn't exactly a shocking story. In this case the pertinent question was how these groups funded their trip. President Christina Kirchner denied any links with the scandal, although it was a government aide who set up the phoney NGO. Approximately 40 affiliated barra brava members flew to South Africa on the same flight as Maradona and La Selección. The total cost of the trip for the main group was thought to be in excess of $2 million. It has been widely speculated the government had financial ties with the barra and subsidised their travel. Fuel was added to this fire when pro-Kirchner banners were on display at each of Argentina's fixtures. A variety of people I spoke to in BA were of the opinion that the President traded excursions to the World Cup for assistance in gaining and sustaining power.

So what does all this mean for the future of our beloved sport? It has been proven that corruption is endemic, reaching FIFA's highest levels. Bribery, match fixing and fraud appears to be relatively commonplace in the body that governs the world's most popular game. How else can you explain Qatar being awarded 2022's World Cup? But then, considering almost every country on the planet participates, is it any surprise? Take Latin America; the majority of the nations had a young democracy still trying to find its feet after years of social inequality and military dictatorships. Why would their football leagues be any different to the societies in which they resided for the past century? In a way we should be grateful that FIFA isn't more corrupt, especially bearing in mind the diverse member states they deal with. I like to think that as we arguably 'invented' modern football the British should have the greatest influence over the way it develops. But that is just not realistic. We now have no more ownership of the sport's intellectual property rights than we do our own language. It's gone global and there is nothing we can do about it.

BRAZIL

Population – 191 million
Size – 8.5 million km^2
Time Zone – GMT $^-$3
Currency - Real
FIFA World Ranking – #4 (January 2011)
Best World Cup Finish – Winners (1958, 1962, 1970, 1994, 2002)
Biggest Teams – Palmeiras, Santos, São Paulo, Flamengo, Corinthians, Vasco de Gama, Fluminese, Internacional

You might have heard of:
Pelé, Zico, Jairzinho, Bebeto, Romário, Rivaldo, Cafu, Roberto Carlos, Dunga, Lúcio, Cláudio Taffarel, Ronaldo, Ronaldinho, Robinho, Neymar

Essential Portuguese:
Paulista – A person from São Paulo
Carioca – A person from Rio de Janeiro

Game 65

Internacional v Wilstermann - (Copa Libertadores) - 3 v 0
Wednesday 30th March 2011 – 21:50
Estádio José Pinheiro Borba, Porto Alegre.

No football trip to Latin America would be complete without visiting the spiritual home of the game. Brazil evokes images of some the world's most talented players and teams, both past and present. As there was less than two weeks left on my travels I was aware that I couldn't even scratch the surface of this continental-sized nation. I was keen to see as much as possible, starting with Copa Libertadores holders, Internacional. The club from Porto Alegre had beaten Chivas of Mexico over an enthralling 180 minutes the previous August. With the likes of Oscar, Leandro Damião and D'Allessandro on show I was hoping to finish my adventure on a footballing high. I had my eye on this particular fixture for some time as on paper it seemed like a ridiculously uneven contest, pitting the continental champions against a Bolivian second division side.

An overnight bus had taken me from Santa Fe to the Argentine/Brazilian border. At the first light of dawn I satisfied formalities, after which a decaying taxi with an ancient driver took me to a town called Uruguaya. A couple of days prior to my arrival the famous Carnaval celebrations had reached their climax. The deserted streets looked strangely eerie at sunrise, as debris was strewn around and spectator stands still blocked access to the main thoroughfare. By the time I'd got halfway to Porto Alegre I was feeling a bit uneasy about Brazil. Everyone spoke a strange language and everything was ridiculously expensive.

Before my arrival I'd been told how similar Portuguese was to Spanish. Having read some online articles without too much difficulty, I was confident that I could negotiate the final days of my tour without any problems. Unfortunately the southern dialect sounded more Germanic than Latin, I couldn't comprehend a word of it. Although nobody spoke English the weird thing was that everybody understood my version of Spanish. This created a lot of confusing one-sided conversations where I'd ask a question and was then completely baffled by the response. What I could grasp was how much everything cost. Long-distance travelling in Argentina wasn't cheap in the slightest, nor was accommodation, but daily expenses in Buenos Aires (in my case

269

public transport, football, cerveza and occasionally some food) had been reasonable. Brazil was one of the flourishing world economies in 2011 and prices reflected their financial boom.

This would explain why I burst into laughter at Inter's ticket office when they told me the cheapest seats cost over $35, the most expensive of the 65 games by some distance. I wasn't too bothered really, the return to England was looming and there was an amazing atmosphere around the ground, with jumping bars housing friendly locals getting drunk and enjoying themselves. It's not often I've appreciated drinking Skol (believe me Brazil's version was not that much better than the one sold in the UK) but with a Samba band playing in a big bar by the entrance and people laughing, joking, singing and dancing, the party spirit was infectious. It was kind of like outside an English venue, except more civilised and with far better looking women. I stood for an hour with a big grin on my face shuffling awkwardly to the beats, gazing up and down the row of bustling bars full of happy fans. I tried to recall a match where there had been such an incredible atmosphere outside a stadium. Perhaps the fact that I arrived late to many fixtures didn't help. Also the necessary restrictions imposed by the police to contain the porteño barra had worn me down a little. Consequently Brazil was genuine breath of fresh air.

Within minutes of entering Estádio José Pinheiro it became abundantly clear that this was a far superior setup to any other club I'd visited in the Americas. On the way in I was given a free programme which looked quite informative. The bathrooms boasted working sinks, toilet paper and were tiled, while the popular areas were covered from the elements. Picking a position which seemed like it had the best view (I wasn't interested in the pitch - you should have seen the blonde-haired girl in front of me) I endeavoured to concentrate on the field of play.

The teams came out carrying a Japanese flag as a mark of respect for the devastation caused by the Tōhoku Earthquake earlier that month. Each national anthem was drowned out by raucous singing from the most enthusiastic followers. Traditionally not as ferocious as the barra brava, Brazil's torcidas organizadas were essentially fanatics. Familiar sights in the torcida section included: thin banners running from top to bottom of the stand, well organised singing, and bouncing shirtless youths. There was a noticeable difference between the Inter supporters and those from other major clubs I'd visited throughout Latin America. It was like they were dancing to a different beat.

In a way they quite literally were. Although the band wasn't as

270

prominent, it was loud and the thumping bass drum had been replaced by more subtle percussion instruments, such as shakers and ganzas. These provided a hip-shaking tempo which was used as a base for the singing and dancing. It began after the anthems with a funky version of 'When the saints go marching in'. The lyrics were replaced by 'do-do' and there was a soulful rhythm which made it impossible to remain standing still. Just before half time the band paused momentarily, there was some call and response shouting and everyone turned 90 degrees to their left. The music started, they danced/shuffled four steps, clapped above their heads, spun 180 degrees and repeated the same movements in the other direction. It was a football version of line dancing very similar to the one I'd seen in Panama.

Police were observing events in the terraces while lined-up around the pitch's periphery. In each of the four corners were nominated uniformed spotters stood on short plastic stools, peering at the crowd through binoculars. They occasionally relayed information to their colleagues via walkie-talkie, but it all appeared to be a bit of a farce as there wasn't one officer to be seen amongst the spectators. What the purpose of their voyeurism was I will never comprehend. Maybe they wanted a closer look at my favourite song of the evening. It was instigated by a build-up of 'ahhhhhh's' as one by one the torcedores removed their shirts and held them front forward in the air above their heads. An unrecognisable chant commenced which involved much arm-shaking. Then, without any warning, the stand exploded into a mass of idiots whirling their shirts whilst bumping into as many people as possible.

Captivated by these strange new fan rituals, as well as the blonde girl's gravity defying physique, the first half kind of passed me by. Cochabamba's Jorge Wilstermann somehow started the brightest but couldn't fashion a real goal scoring opportunity. Having won Bolivia's Clausura in 2010 to qualify automatically for the Libertadores group stages, a rather spectacular fall from grace had seen them relegated in the year's second tournament. Despite the encouraging early signs the visitors predictably fell behind before the break. Future Chelsea star, Oscar, profited from a lucky deflection to give the home side a deserved lead.

The game was fundamentally over as it approached the hour mark. Andrés D'Allessandro was rewarded for his dominating performance when he was given a criminal amount of time and space in the box to fire into the side-netting. Formerly at Wolfsburg, Real Betis and Portsmouth, the little Argentine was playing a classic trequartista

271

role. He generated numerous openings through his positional awareness, intelligent running and effective passing. The proverbial mountain to climb got even higher after Wilstermann defender Lucas Fernández petulantly lashed out at the playmaker and received a straight red card. The hosts wrapped things up shortly afterwards with an easy third. Although there was a massive gap in terms of ability between the two teams, what impressed me about the Brazilians was how direct they were. Gone was Argentina's over passing and playing the ball wide with no end product, replaced by ruthless incision and clinical movement.

Funnily enough I wasn't the only Englishman at Estádio José Pinheiro that evening. Ozzy Osbourne was performing at an indoor arena adjacent to the stadium. The next day the brummie rocker's concert was featured as a local news story. For some reason he took to the stage draped in a Gremio flag – Porto Alegre's other large club who were Inter's bitterest rival – inciting ugly scenes inside the venue. Typical.

Game 66

Portugusea v Noroeste - (Campeonato Paulista) - 0 v 2
Saturday 2nd April 2011 – 16:00
Estádio Dr. Oswaldo Teixeira Duarte, São Paulo

São Paulo was the penultimate stop on my long and winding road. The southern hemisphere's largest city contained over 19 million inhabitants, and more importantly, over 15,000 bars. It was too vast for me to cover in a weekend so I decided to try and see as many essential highlights as possible. Naturally this involved two matches and visiting a football museum.

On Friday afternoon I headed to Museu de Futebol, located underneath the stands of Corinthians' Estádio do Pacaembu. This glitzy exhibition made a cursory attempt at being impartial, but in reality was just a multimillion dollar presentation of how Brazil was the best in the world at football. That's not to say it was a tedious experience. There were lots of interactive games and shows, including an innovative cheering section experience. I spent an amusing hour wandering around, being told off for taking photos, kicking imaginary balls at virtual goalkeepers whilst laughing about how anyone could be so self-congratulatory, no matter what they'd achieved. Returning to my hostel to get ready for a big night out, I was unaware of the significance of the empty ground I'd had my latest Zulu Army snap in. Estádio do Pacaembu was the venue in which 2011's Libertadores was won.

I set out the next day still a little inebriated from a messy foray into São Paulo's nightlife. During the Metro ride across the huge urban area I realised that I'd been so drunk I couldn't remember leaving the accommodation, let alone returning. It was a simple ten minute strut from Tiete station, as grey skies closed in, emitting the odd drop of rain. I mistakenly entered a Christian convention in an indoor complex next to the estádio and was gratefully directed to a ticket office, where I parted with $18. As I was attending a fairly low-key tie I'd not really paid attention to the contents of my bag. Soon I was holding up a queue of people while arguing with the police in Spanish.

On this occasion my flag wasn't the cause of the problem, but a yellow exercise book in which I'd been jotting notes at selected fixtures. Paper products were not allowed into Estádio Dr. Oswaldo Teixeira Duarte as they constituted a dangerous weapon. Apparently I could set my book on fire and throw it at the players. I showed them the writing inside and tried to explain I wasn't going to burn my work to throw at teams I had absolutely no interest in. Whilst contesting my futile point, a grey-haired man on the other side of the entrance was stating in good English that my best bet was to leave the offensive item at a nearby café. Undeterred, I climbed a set of stairs to the upper entrance; at which stage different officers outlined the same draconian rules. Halfway through our fire safety debate the same middle-aged guy appeared on the other side of the gates and repeated his advice about storing my notebook at a café. Reluctantly I parted with my priceless possession, returned to the turnstiles, bravely made sarcastic comments to the police in English and was permitted entry, where the gentleman was still waiting for me.

Strolling out into the arena we discussed ridiculous regulations at football matches. He indicated I'd have no problems entering the home of any of the big clubs with such an item. In his opinion Brazilians weren't fond of Portuguese expats living in their country, and were overtly strict with them as a result. He also explained Portuguesa was formed in 1920 when five teams representing São Paulo's Portuguese communities merged. When I questioned what role he had at the club he laughed and said he was a normal season ticket holder. Originally he'd only provided advice as his family were stuck behind me at the entrance while I was quarrelling with the officials.

My new amigo kindly spent the rest of the afternoon with me describing the current state Brazil's Selección, their domestic leagues and relationship with Portugal. Through Portuguesa expatriates were trying to keep their cultural flame burning, which was evident in the quantity of Portuguese national shirts being worn by fans. Many of these had a number seven printed on the back, accompanied by the name of the world's most petulant player. I took great pleasure in singing at each passing spectator: 'There's only one Ronaldo' thinking I was being highly ironic. As hardly anyone understood English I was just highlighting how much of a loser I am.

Meanwhile, as persistent showers dampened the mood, the hosts had conceded during my protracted arguments with the police. A small Noroeste contingent were making noise at the opposite end of the stadium, and there was a large pocket of Portuguesa torcedores next to them. As the squads returned after half time the police had to drive the locals into the upper reaches of the terrace, as the vitriol directed at their own players threatened to turn violent. At the end of a miserable second period, where grey skies blending in nicely with the dull concrete background, the visitors scored a second goal to claim all three points. The crowd's discontentment switched from the players to the director's box. Significant sections of the mob turned their back on the pitch, chanting abuse at Portuguesa President Manuel da Lupa.

I'd heard accounts of how Brazilian fans were amongst the most negative in the world. That afternoon in São Paulo it was very evident where this attitude originated from, as Portuguese expats screamed obscenities at the people running their football organisation. Whilst this uncomfortable scene was unfolding I noticed all the banners around the venue were hung upside-down. My embarrassed friend stated that this was the torcida's way of protesting about their relegation from Série A the previous season.

It seemed strange that a relatively small association would have followers with such unrealistic expectations. There was an eight year old child stood next to me, wearing a transparent rain mac with a Portugal Selección shirt underneath. He was throwing his arms out and glaring towards the director's box, screaming passionately how they were to blame for the demise of his club. The irate youngster was copying his father and uncle stood on either side of him. I was shocked and a little upset by the experience. No matter what I thought of the barra brava I'd always been impressed with the way they supported their team, particularly in times of adversity. I cheered myself up on the way back to the Metro with a loud rendition of Keep Right On, whilst desperately trying to remember which Colombian sister from my hostel I'd been kissing the previous night.

Game 67

Santos v Palmeiras - (Campeonato Paulista) - 0 v 1
Sunday 3rd April 2011 – 16:00
Estádio Urbano Caldeira, Santos

By Sunday the weather hadn't improved. Overcast conditions obscured spectacular views on a winding road down from São Paulo to the coast. Santos were best known for a famous former player named Edison Arantes de Nascimento. When I visited the heir to Pelé's throne was one Silva Santos Junior, otherwise known as Neymar. He was the big attraction in an important match at the top of Paulista División A between two of the largest regional sides.

As with a game of such prominence, ticket availability was scarce. Information on the internet indicated that it was a sell-out. Upon arrival it was evident there were no cash sales, although a high-tech outlet built into the main stand was distributing something. Whilst waiting in the queue I struck up a conversation with a German couple stood behind me. We established that it was only possible to purchase tickets through a credit card facility. After parting with a staggering $70 for the cheapest seat on offer, I was obliged to scan my card at the turnstiles, which printed a receipt and permitted me to enter Estádio Urbano Caldeira. I'd like to point out that the ground was half full, leading to the question: why were there no cash sales on the door?

I was pleased to find my extortionately priced seat was covered from the rain, as a slow, grey, misty drizzle enveloped surroundings. When Palmeiras' squad came out to warm up there were Santos fans at pitch-level, banging on the clear Perspex fencing, shouting obscenities with a passion that suggested the players had done something unspeakable to their family. Even visiting coach Luis Felipe Scolari was subject to a torrent of abuse, despite having led Brazil's Selección to their last World Cup title. Affectionately known as Big Phil during his time as Chelsea boss, he was serving a second term in charge of Palmeiras after an unsuccessful, albeit brief stint in west London. Approaching his thirtieth year as a football manager Scolari had spells in obscure places such as Saudi Arabia and Kuwait, whilst also managing his own nation and Portugal.

There could be no doubt as to who was the star of the show on that miserable afternoon. Within minutes Neymar had left two defenders for dead and made a midfielder fall over twice with his

276

dazzling array of step overs. As with many talented young footballers his arrogance was there for all to see. He was booked on seven minutes for a petulant reaction to a fair tackle. Although he was a class above the other players I couldn't help but think his place in the team was counterproductive. All too often he'd be given the ball in an attacking position and instead of pushing forward looking for a breakthrough he'd wait for a couple of opponents to challenge him so he had the opportunity to show off his ample range of tricks and skills. The time he spent showboating allowed Palmeiras to regroup and defend. It was amusing watching the youngster embarrass some respected senior players, but the end product was sadly lacking.

A dancing parrot and killer whale (the club's mascots) and some ridiculously gorgeous women in tight-fitting outfits waving Coca Cola flags entertained us at the interval. Estádio Urbano Caldeira was a lot smaller than I'd imagined, seating in one end was only 15 rows high. The main stand was fairly standard, but the multi-tiered end and side were very individual. Large banners represented both organisation's fanatical supporters, Torcida Jovem do Santos and Palmeiras' Mancha Verde.

Santos perked up after the break and former Manchester City midfielder Elano found the net. During the celebrations five officials (a referee, two assistants and two behind either goal line) concluded that he was offside. This decision caused Santos' torcida to embark on a slightly more elaborate version of the shirt-waving song I'd seen at Inter. Everyone removed their jerseys simultaneously and held them skywards, whilst half crouched and the rest stood upright. They took it in turns to bob up and down - a little bit like you see people doing at The Last Night of the Proms. The shirt-spinning, chest-bumping, manic crescendo was the same as in Porto Alegre, with the participants clearly having no regard for their personal safety.

With 11 minutes remaining the contest's solitary goal arrived. Former Dynamo Kiev legend, Kleber, latched onto an incisive through ball and chipped the keeper with delightful finesse. I was pleased for the veteran forward who'd battled away all match; showing Santos' young star that you need a good work ethic as well as skill to succeed. The goal prompted the home fans to stream towards the exits, hurling abuse at their team, who made desperate and ultimately futile attempts to salvage something. As I was leaving a group of torcedores were gathering to chant protests at the club's hierarchy. Outside the ground a similar event was taking place. Disconcerted Brazilians were stood by an executive entrance, directing insults at anyone leaving the venue wearing formal clothing.

Palmeiras may have won that Sunday, but it was Santos who claimed the Campeonato. Brazil's league system was a bit flawed, but in a country of 190 million football fanatics logistics were always going to be tricky. Soccerway listed every nation's domestic competitions: England's 16, Italy's 11, Spain's nine, Iran's three and Brazil's 45 (forty five). The Brazilian structure involved independent state leagues running in the first half of the year and national ones contested in the second half. After a 19 game Campeonato Paulista season the top eight sides partook in a finals tournament.

Predictably the region's four largest clubs (Santos, Corinthians, Palmeiras and São Paulo) all qualified for the semis, where Santos and Corinthians came out on top. Santos triumphed 2 v 1 in the playoff, Neymar's 86th minute second leg goal proving decisive. Many leading commentators were opposed to the state football divisions. There were copious uneven contests pitting Flamengo and their 40 million supporters against a supermarket. I'm sure it was important for the lesser sides to vie with their glamorous neighbours, although this added to the competitive fixtures the big boys had to play.

No doubt the less challenging domestic calendar early in the year allowed those participating in Copa Libertadores to concentrate their efforts on the international tournament. In 2011 five Brazilian clubs progressed from the group to the knockout section, though only Santos made it to the quarter-finals. Beating América (Mexico), Once Caldas and Cerro Porteño they made it to the final, where they met Peñarol. Goalless from the first leg in Montevideo, the second tie was held at Estádio do Pacaembu. Neymar broke the deadlock after half time finishing powerfully following a flowing move. Defender Danilo da Silva (another U-20 player on show in Arequipa) scored a winner from just inside the area with 20 minutes left. Peñarol pulled one back through a lucky own goal, but Santos should have scored more. They ran out deserved winners of Copa Libertadores for the first time since Pelé lifted the trophy in 1963. For the second season in a row there were ugly scenes at the end of Latin America's showpiece final. A mass brawl broke out, during which Neymar was filmed aggressively stamping on a fallen Peñarol player.

The National
Friday 8th April 2011 – 23:00
Circo Voador, Lapa, Rio de Janeiro

And that was it, my footballing expedition ended at the home of that year's continental champions. I hoped to attend at least one game in Rio, but it didn't happen. On Saturday I set out for Vasco da Gama but a combination of reduced tube services, torrential rain, fatigue and almost being mugged, meant I didn't get anywhere near Estádio São Januário. In honesty with a dreaded return to England less than 24 hours away, I was happy to concede my assignment was complete after 67 memorable events.

My trip finished kind of how it started, watching amazing music with an attractive young native. I'd stayed in touch with one of the Brazilian girls from Bolivia's Uyuni tour and she offered to show me round her home city. As a final extravagance I'd booked us into a plush-looking hotel I found on the internet, only to discover upon arrival that we'd been allocated some kind of sex suite. With an open plan bathroom and an indulgent mirror system, it was possible to lie on the immense bed and see a Jacuzzi through a large glass window, as well as a toilet, shower and sauna. It was a very rock and roll conclusion to proceedings, but I have to admit to being quite embarrassed by the situation. I didn't want my companion to think I specifically checked us into this accommodation so I could spy on her having a poo (although it was an added bonus!) Fortunately she was pretty relaxed about it all, and this story had a happy ending. In November 2014 Miss Rio became Mrs Freeman.

The National played a flawless set, which combined with being starved of good live music for so long, I classify as one of the greatest gigs I've ever been to. Before I was enjoying hearing about fake empires, a British journalist based in Rio, Tim Vickery, was kind enough to give me a few hours of his time. It was a brilliantly informative conversation about life and football in South America, and reassuring to discuss my unique experiences with an Englishman who understood where I'd been and what I'd seen. I don't blame him for wanting to live amongst the cariocas, he resided in an iconic and stunning city. I spent my last week of freedom sunning myself with the bronzed and beautiful on Ipanema's golden sands, and could certainly appreciate the benefits of an urban beachside lifestyle. Sat here typing this on a wintery afternoon in Coventry, I'm not in any way jealous.

Three flights home passed without incident, although I needed three mini bottles of wine to be able to negotiate the final leg. Tanned, stinking, unshaven and wiping the odd tear from my eye, I must have been a strange sight for the sharply-dressed business people on British Airway's evening commuter service from Frankfurt to London City. When a flight attendant offered me a drink, I asked for a beer and red wine. She produced a bottle Argentine Malbec and could immediately see from the look on my face that one wouldn't be enough. She slipped me another two on her way back round.

In just under 18 months I'd visited 18 countries, had three jobs, learnt a new language and been to 67 football matches in 15 nations.

Epilogue

Club Brugge v Blues – (Europa League, Group H) – 1 v 2
Thursday 20th October 2011 – 19:00
Jan Breydelstadion, Brugge, Belgium

'Braaaaaaazil, it's just like watching Brazil' - 5,500 of us were singing at the team in yellow and white. Even though only six months had passed, it felt like it had been a long, long road to get there.

My first match back in England was our Premier League death march, also known as Fulham at home. Watching Seb Larsson crying his eyes out whilst our players did a lap of 'honour' wasn't the most pleasant thing I've ever witnessed. Nor was the following Sunday. I met up with my recently engaged ex-girlfriend, saw my club get relegated, and the next day went to work in an office for the first time in 20 months. An inevitable summer exodus followed, throughout which I was too busy with my head buried in a laptop, typing this book, to be able to enjoy an occasional day of good weather. Birmingham City owner Carson Yeung was arrested and detained in Hong Kong, Alex McLeish defected to the dark side, and pretty much an entire squad of decent players who'd helped us win our first trophy for 50 years moved on to greener pastures, such as Sunderland and Blackpool. Blues were in meltdown. There were even questions as to whether we would be eligible to participate in the Europa League.

But then our new manager Chris Hughton came to the rescue. He juggled limited resources and didn't have a proper idea of what he was working with until we were six fixtures into the season. Coventry provided me with much appreciated bragging rights; Millwall arrived and left with a whimper, although away from home we looked weak. Somehow we outplayed Portugal's Nacional in the Europa League qualifying round; booking our place in the group stage after three magnificent goals and a cracking atmosphere at St. Andrews. The runners up of the previous year's competition landed three weeks later to give us a reality check. In the meantime the number of Championship games in hand started to rack up. Our squad was gelling and players like Jean Beausejour, Chris Burke and on-loan teenage striker Chris Wood were performing to their potential. We won in Slovenia and Nottingham (goodbye Mr Mclaren) before squeezing past Leicester at home. All of which setup an event that will go down in Blues folklore.

Exactly seven days prior to kick-off a message was posted on the Blues website that 300 tickets would go on general sale the following morning. I was standing in St. Andrews' Kop car park at eight o'clock that evening, approximately halfway along a queue of Bluenoses wrapped up against the elements. At 23:00 I was relieved by my dad and brother, who'd driven up from Kent to wait the remaining 13 hours to be served. After a 20 hour round-trip they had four precious tickets in their possession.

Brugge were current Belgian champions and had won both their opening Group H ties, including a victory at Braga (who'd made us look like amateurs in our first game). The odds were stacked heavily against us but we didn't care. It was the most accessible of our three away fixtures, and an estimated 9,000 Blues faithful who crossed the channel were in the mood to party. We were convinced this was the only opportunity in our lifetime to watch Birmingham City play away in a proper European tournament.

'If I grew up on a farm and was retarded, Brugge might impress me. But I didn't, so it doesn't.' My brother and I chuckled at Colin Farrell quotes scrawled over the Belfry walls, as we paused for breath halfway up its 366 steps. We'd vowed to do at least one touristy thing during our stay, so at lunchtime on match day we were climbing the tower which dominated Brugge's main Markt square. Shortly after continuing our ascent a lad with a thick brummie accent travelling in the opposite direction stopped us. He handed me a plastic bag and asked if when I got to the top I'd mind retrieving his flag for him. I was sure he was joking, but upon arrival at the summit I could see he was serious. A huge BCFC St. George's cross was hanging from the outside of the tower, flapping in the wind, on display to the whole city. Stood next to it was a surly Belgian security guard, who uttered some unsavoury words. I was going to protest my innocence but realised the empty bag in my hand incriminated me.

Blues fans had completely taken over Brugge, the square was covered in banners of all shapes and sizes. On our way through the city it seemed that around every corner was another bar bustling with blue and white bodies, singing, drinking and making merry. I'd been concerned about the impact of so many Midlanders descending on such a quaint location, and hadn't been alone in my trepidation; apparently Brugge's police and business owners had feared the worst. I'm pleased to report that by and large we didn't cause any major problems, and our general behaviour was publicly commended by the authorities.

As kick-off approached the crowds started wandering away

from the square to the ground. Most opted for complimentary coaches, but the owner of the house we were renting had instructed us the quickest and most scenic route was on foot. Ignoring various policemen's attempts to send us on a massive detour, we followed locals streaming towards Jan Breydelstadion. My cousin, wearing his Blues shirt, wasn't too enthusiastic about our course when we passed a couple of nondescript-looking bars, overrun with legions of fairly menacing home supporters. Whilst crossing a park a group of four Belgians invited us to join them for a few pre-match beverages. They were really friendly, keen to practice English and discuss Britain's football leagues. I was impressed by their knowledge of our domestic game and how excited they were about competing against an English club for the first time in over a decade. They all said the same thing: they were hoping for an impressive vocal performance from the visiting fans.

I like to think that they weren't disappointed. There was a carnival mood inside the south stand, which was dampened slightly in the third minute when Joseph Akpala tapped in for the hosts. The atmosphere was reignited 20 minutes later when the whole Blues end impeccably participated in a minute's applause, to commemorate the tragic death of Brugge and Belgian national striker François Sterchele. Shortly after David Murphy ghosted into the box to score an unexpected equaliser from Wade Elliott's cross, further enhancing the noise from the Blue boys. At half time I was grateful UEFA's no alcohol policy at Europa League fixtures didn't apply in Belgium, as we refuelled ourselves for the second period.

Both sides had good chances prior to the dramatic finale. Paulo Ibanez suffered a lengthy injury in the closing moments, prompting the fourth official to signal ten minutes of added time. Brugge had a guilt edged opportunity to clinch victory with minutes left, but couldn't find the clinical touch. And then it happened. That moment of pure joy football can give you, where time stops for a brief second and nothing in the world matters.

The clock had reached 98:57 when a long ball forward found Marlon King on the touchline. Instead of trying to see out the dying seconds, he beat his man, sending a cross into the box towards fellow substitute Chris Wood. I didn't see the ball hit the net, all I can recollect is clinging onto my dad for dear life as a wave of ecstatic Blues fans swept down the stand. It was as dramatic a goal as I can remember us scoring, and all the more sweet considering the setting and circumstances. We stayed in Jan Breydelstadion for almost an hour after the final whistle, celebrating, singing and cheering Nathan Redmond and Jean Beausejour as they warmed down. Pockets of curious Belgians waited behind, observing us as if we were an exhibit at a zoo.

Somehow I managed to lose everyone in the chaos of returning to the centre and ended up back in a strangely calm Markt Square alone. The area had been thoroughly cleaned and bore no signs of the pandemonium that had taken place hours earlier. I sat staring at the Belfry, illuminated against the night sky, thinking Colin Farrell was wrong; Brugge is a city of fairy tales. I couldn't get my head round what had gone on, not just in Belgium, but in the two years to the day since I boarded an aeroplane bound for Chicago. It reminded me:

As you go through life, it's a long, long road,
there'll be joys and sorrows too.
As we journey on, we will sing this song,
for the boys in royal blue.

We're often partisan, la, la, la.
We will journey on, la, la, la.
Keep right on to the end of the road.
Keep right on to the end.

Though the way be long, let your heart beat strong.
Keep right on to the end.
Though you're tired and weary, still journey on,
'til you come to your happy abode.

Where all the love, you've been dreaming of,
will be there.
WHERE?
At the end of the road – Birmingham! Birmingham!

Thanks

My mother and father – for bringing me into this world, and allowing me to watch them on Skype in La Paz, bickering whilst decorating their Christmas tree

The Survivors of the Road – Backpack, Laptop and iPod

Paddy and Lenny – 'The only fuckers who came to see me!' (Copyright – R.Shepherd)

The fact I saw 67 games – the number of a very special house

My muse – ever present throughout the trip

All the random foreigners who helped me along the way

Scott and Martín - for putting up with an annoying Gringo

Printworks, Coventry

Colin McGinley and Lucas Sampaio for designing the covers

@DarrenSpherical – For writing a great article and pointing out some of my many schoolboy errors (www.hispanospherical.com)

El Hombre Grande, Dios – I'm not a religious person, but there were times on that trip when there was a greater power at work. Namely: The perfect start and end to the adventure, stumbling upon and being able to work on my Mexican beach, the number of times I unknowingly came across brilliant matches, game 14, surviving the two Colombian incidents, El Amigo hostel in Sucre, the Paraguay border crossing, Bichos, and Chris Wood in the 100th minute. Gracias

13866792R00159

Printed in Great Britain
by Amazon.co.uk, Ltd.,
Marston Gate.